PRAISE FOR PERSEVERA

"Reggie Ford has written a br... ....om
pain to peace. But more than j................................ ......ating story of one young man's
battles with the generational traumas associated with racism and poverty in
America, *PTSD* is a primer on just how deeply embedded those traumas are
in our society and the factors that perpetuate them. Reggie writes with equal
honesty and introspection when recounting his family's encounters with addiction, abuse, teen pregnancy, gun violence and homelessness as he does
when exposing prejudice, tokenism, and white privilege. At one level, this is
an important book about persevering through dysfunction. At another, it is
a well-sourced call to understand and solve the larger mental health, criminal
justice, educational, and wealth inequalities facing the country."

— ANDREW MARANISS, *NEW YORK TIMES*
BESTSELLING AUTHOR OF *STRONG INSIDE*

"Reggie Ford redefines the definition of PTSD, reminding readers that the life
journey of a black man in America remains a challenge, no matter the levels of
success achieved. In this autobiography, Reggie bares his soul about growing up
disadvantaged and disenfranchised, sustaining psychological blow after psychological blow, yet never letting go of the love and hope that continue to fill his
heart. His journey takes us through the mind, spirit, and life of a young black
man coming of age in America. The lessons he shares are frank and unfiltered;
and will serve as valuable guideposts for others who may experience a similar life
adventure and are seeking true inspiration."

— DUSTIN S. KLEIN, BEST-SELLING AUTHOR, AWARD-WINNING JOURNALIST,
AND CHIEF CONTENT OFFICER OF SMART BUSINESS

"Timely and timeless, this awe-inspiring book is a must-read as we grapple with
race and trauma in America. I am in admiration of Reggie's vulnerable portrait
of his battles and his empathetic storytelling. *PTSD* will be a permanent fixture
on reading lists for those concerned with the vitality of vulnerable communities."

— CAYLIN LOUIS MOORE, AUTHOR OF *A DREAM TOO BIG: THE STORY
OF AN IMPROBABLE JOURNEY FROM COMPTON TO OXFORD*

PERSEVERANCE THROUGH SEVERE DYSFUNCTION

PERSEVERANCE THROUGH SEVERE DYSFUNCTION

BREAKING THE CURSE OF INTERGENERATIONAL TRAUMA AS A BLACK MAN IN AMERICA

REGGIE D. FORD

Copyright © 2021 by Reginald Ford.

Published in the United States by Ella Wenthom Books, an imprint of Ella Wenthom LLC.

Hardcover ISBN: 978-1-7365963-0-2
Ebook ISBN: 978-1-7365963-1-9
Paperback ISBN: 978-1-7365963-2-6
Audiobook ISBN: 978-1-7365963-3-3

Library of Congress Cataloging-in-Publication Data is available.

Printed in the United States of America

10 9 8 7 6 5 4 3 2 1

To those who suffer in silence with hidden scars that the world may never see.
Know that you are not alone.
Always remember that you are loved.

CONTENTS

INTRODUCTION: PTSD

I found myself in a fetal position, crying my eyes out as my wife tried to console me. Having had only a few hours of sleep in nearly a month, I was physically, mentally, and emotionally exhausted. The million thoughts running through my mind were muddled, and the few words I spoke were incomprehensible. The world around me had been shaken up vigorously, which resulted in an explosion of emotion that erupted on that cold hardwood floor.

I felt abandoned. The people who had been a part of my life from day one were no longer there. The sensation that I was feeling had previously led me to cry out for the comfort of my mama, but in that moment, she was the last person who could ease my pain. Thoughts about my dad had grown so deranged that my defense mechanism was to pretend that he no longer existed. Although my parents were alive and only a few miles away, they were dead to me.

I was consumed by grief. Granny was actually dead, and I felt that I had been cheated by her untimely demise and the events leading up to it. For my entire life, during chaotic times, she had been the one person to whom I could turn. But she was no longer around to tell me that everything was going to be fine.

Depression and anxiety took on new meanings for me. Leading up to this outburst, I had spent days at a time lying in a dark room, numb and distant. Sometimes I had emotional swings—moments of feeling horrible, then feeling great, followed by feeling horrible again. Other times, there were no feelings at all. When I tried to sleep, my brain was bombarded simultaneously by every thought and emotion that I had the capacity to hold. It created a sensory overload that prevented anything resembling rest or productivity from entering. I couldn't find within me the ability to turn my affliction into fuel for perseverance as I had done countless other times in my life. I lost the optimistic belief that tomorrow was going to be better than today. I was merely existing.

I knew where I was physically, but in a lucid moment, I thought to myself, How in the world did I end up here?

————

To introduce myself, I am Reggie D. Ford, a kid from the hood, a first-generation college graduate, a successful entrepreneur, and a Black man in America, and I live with PTSD, post-traumatic stress disorder. PTSD is a mental health condition that is triggered by experiencing or witnessing a horrific event. Symptoms may include flashbacks, nightmares, and severe anxiety, as well as uncontrollable thoughts about the event. Those symptoms sometimes don't present themselves until years after the traumatic event, so it is often underdiagnosed or misdiagnosed, which leads to mistreatment. In a quest to better understand myself, I had to be real with myself about the trauma I had faced in my life and how it had affected me. Admitting that there was something wrong was the first step in the process of bettering myself. Pinpointing the trauma was just another step in living a healthier life. I also had to find ways to treat it.

A common misconception is that PTSD is a condition that only military veterans experience. I have never served our country in that manner, yet I have experienced extreme trauma throughout my life, and that trauma haunts me. I'm a firm believer that we all experience trauma in our lives and that trauma is relative. Experiences that may be traumatic for me may be just another day in the life for someone else and vice versa. But it still doesn't diminish that trauma for either party.

For some people who have seemingly "perfect" lives, the moment that perfection is upended from a dose of imperfection could be traumatic. Take for instance a child from a solid family who has everything she's ever wanted and needed in every aspect of life. But one day, her parents tell her that they are getting a divorce and she would have to divide her time between two households. The perfect life she had grown accustomed to comes crashing down, triggering a traumatic event. In contrast, imagine a child who grows up as an orphan but has one sibling to confide in. That's life as he knows it, so not having parents doesn't register as traumatic. But one day, his only sibling is killed in a shooting, and just like that, he is no longer a stranger to trauma.

Although both of these situations are vastly different, they highlight the relativity of trauma. Some events are universally accepted as more traumatic; however, no person should feel belittled or made to think that their unique trauma is insignificant. Oftentimes when we talk about putting things into perspective, we tend to do just that. "Oh, my problems aren't as bad as someone else's, so I shouldn't be upset or complaining." While perspective is good to have for extending grace and empathy, it shouldn't result in normalizing what isn't normal.

There are many types of trauma. The US Department of Veterans Affairs (USDVA) highlights combat stressors that expose servicemembers to potential trauma. These include seeing dead bodies, being shot at or being attacked, receiving rocket fire, or knowing someone who has been killed or seriously injured.[1]

When it comes to the general population, trauma occurs in response to violence and abuse, including sexual assault, as well as disasters and terrorism.

While my belief that we all experience trauma may sound exaggerated, it is estimated that about 90 percent of the population has experienced some type of traumatic event in their lives.[2] Servicemembers in the military make up less than 0.5 percent of the US population, which would suggest that most trauma is experienced by ordinary civilians who have not experienced any sort of military combat.[3]

Exposure to trauma, however, does not always develop into PTSD. Almost all people who go through trauma have some symptoms of PTSD a short time afterward, but most people are not diagnosed with the condition. According to the USDVA, about 7 or 8 percent of the population will have PTSD at some point in their lives.[4] Regarding gender, about 10 percent of women will develop PTSD, compared to approximately 4 percent of men.[5] The disparity is generally attributed to the amount of sexual abuse that women endure in comparison to men. For veterans, the rates of PTSD are somewhere between 11 percent and 30 percent, depending on when and where they served.[5]

To expand upon my statement that PTSD is under- or misdiagnosed, a 2008 study showed that for patients with PTSD, the diagnosis

---

1   National Center for PTSD. "VA.gov: Veterans Affairs." *Home*, US Department of Veterans Affairs, 15 Aug 2013, www.ptsd.va.gov/.

2   Kilpatrick, Dean G., et al. "National Estimates of Exposure to Traumatic Events and PTSD Prevalence UsingDSM-IVandDSM-5Criteria." *Journal of Traumatic Stress*, vol. 26, no. 5, 22 Oct 2013, pp. 537–547. doi:10.1002/jts.21848.

3   Parker, Kim, et al. "6 Facts about the US Military's Changing Demographics." *Pew Research Center*, Pew Research Center, 30 May 2020, www.pewresearch.org/fact-tank/2017/04/13/6-facts-about-the-u-s-military-and-its-changing-demographics/.

4   National Center for PTSD.

5   Ibid.

was initially missed approximately 90 percent of the time by clinicians.[6] Insufficiencies in clinical examinations combined with the reluctance or inability of patients to discuss their symptoms (for a myriad of reasons) are cited for these misdiagnoses.

Consequently, I wish for everyone to know what PTSD looks like. For me, it's jumping out of bed, awakened by actual pains from nightmares. It's mood swings that lead to violent and destructive behaviors. It's trust issues and detachment from the world and feelings of hopelessness. It's having severe insomnia for weeks or months at a time. It's trouble concentrating because of an obsessive focus on something unrelated to the current circumstances. It's hearing sounds of gunshots and break-ins when, in reality, it's just creaks in the floor or the wind blowing. It's a feeling of emotional numbness at inappropriate times.

While these are some of the symptoms that I face, they can be different for everyone. A quick online search for "PTSD symptoms" will guide you toward a more comprehensive list. If you find that you have some of the symptoms, take it seriously. Be honest with yourself, your loved ones, and your medical professionals to figure out if you do in fact live with this or any type of mental health condition.

One of my hopes for this world is that all mental health illnesses get proper treatment. Oftentimes we experience trauma that everyone around us also experiences, so we normalize it. It's a mentality that says, "That's just the way things are," but as I've grown and encountered people from many walks of life, I've realized that the things I used to consider normal are actually extraordinary. Much of the trauma I've faced in life I argue is a result of unaddressed and untreated mental health illnesses in my social circle, especially those in my family who came before me. I refer to this as inherited or intergenerational trauma. Many times, the trauma we face is out of our control. It is what is done

---

6   Zyl, M Van, et al. "Post Traumatic Stress Disorder: Undiagnosed Cases in a Tertiary Inpatient Setting." *African Journal of Psychiatry*, vol. 11, no. 2, 2008. doi:10.4314/ajpsy.v11i2.30263.

to us by others. And while that may be the case, it is our own responsibility to respond appropriately to address that trauma in healthy ways.

Often overlooked, especially in the Black community, is how prevalent mental health conditions are. According to the Substance Abuse and Mental Health Services Administration (SAMHSA), white people are nearly twice as likely as Black people to use mental health services.[7] There are also few Black mental health professionals, so when Black people build up the courage to utilize services, it is difficult to find someone who can culturally understand their issues, which is discouraging. When Black people do present mental health concerns, they are frequently underdiagnosed, which further perpetuates mistreatment.

There is such a stigma around mental health illness because it's believed that it shows weakness. It is my thought that this mentality is a defense mechanism to help Black people endure the harshest of treatments, particularly in times when there is a lack of access to proper medical attention. If you can't get fixed, pretend you are not broken. With the passage of time and growing access to much-needed and fair medical treatment, I'll go on record to say that having the courage to acknowledge and address a mental health illness is actually one of the strongest things a person can do.

As for my own experience, I've sought multiple treatments for my mental distress. I've tried prescribed medication, which didn't seem like the right option for me because of the adverse effects it had. I've tried to self-medicate, which wasn't a healthy option and also didn't serve me well. I've tried massage and acupuncture to physically feel something, in hopes that it would help with my mental and emotional states. And I've tried sensory-deprivation tanks to feel nothing at all for the exact same reasons.

---

7   Substance Abuse and Mental Health Services Administration. "Results from the 2018 National Survey on Drug Use and Health: Detailed tables." Rockville, MD: Center for Behavioral Health Statistics and Quality, Substance Abuse and Mental Health Services Administration. Retrieved from https://www.samhsa.gov/data/.

Ultimately, what's worked best for me has been exercise, meditation through yoga, journaling, and counseling. Many scientific studies have demonstrated the positive benefits of exercising in addressing a number of mental health conditions, including depression and anxiety. While meditating or doing yoga, I can attempt to quiet my mind and try to focus on my inner self and my connectedness with the universe around me. Journaling is actually how this book was started. During the most trying times of my life, I would write as a way to decompress. Some of those journal entries have been transcribed in this book. Lastly, counseling has been probably the most beneficial for me. I now go to a professional therapist, but I have been practicing this form of therapy for years by simply talking about vulnerable aspects of my life with the people I love and trust the most. Therapy has helped me uncover some of the deepest, darkest demons inside of me, which has resulted in feelings of liberation. It's like taking the shackles off my ankles to run freely.

I mention all of these things to show that it takes experimenting with healthy outlets to figure out what works for you. We're all unique, and we must find unique remedies for whatever we go through in life. And like anything else in life, do so in moderation. If I were to obsessively talk to my therapist or do yoga a hundred times a week, this might indicate that I have another mental health condition to address. This is often one of the issues with self-medicating. The addictive qualities of drugs and alcohol can take over and turn a search for mental numbness into severe health-harming behaviors.

Throughout my life, I've had people who are near and dear to my heart who I feel have and are currently living with severe mental health conditions that affect how they have responded to the world around them, including me. In turn, I have inherited the different forms of untreated trauma that they have carried with them for years. Of the many conditions at play, depression reigns supreme. When life doesn't live up to your expectations—you have experienced extreme loss or you can't seem to ever get ahead—it makes sense to be depressed. In the age of social media, we are constantly bombarded with superficial highlight reels of everyone else's lives, which results in us feeling worse about our own in comparison. Depression may be amplified now, more than ever before, for that reason.

The key to addressing your mental health illnesses is to be real with yourself. Phony outward displays and posturing are often cover-ups for internal insecurities. The realest thing you can do is look at yourself in the mirror and be honest with how you feel. It's hard to do it, and it may not feel natural, but if addressed properly, it can be one of the best feelings in the world.

Imagine you are holding a glass of water in your hand straight out in front of you. If you hold it for a minute, it is not a difficult challenge. If you hold it for an hour, your arm will start to burn. If you hold it for a day, your arm will feel numb and maybe become paralyzed. The weight of the glass doesn't change, but the longer you hold it, the heavier it feels. The mental health stressors that we experience in life are similar to the glass. The longer you hold on to them, the more they hurt you. If you hold on to them long enough, you may feel paralyzed and incapable of doing even the most mundane tasks. It is vital to tend to your mental health so you can begin to let things go. At some point, you have to put the glass down.

This book is about my life experiences, the many traumas I've faced, and how I've overcome them. I offer commentary on how those experiences have shaped me into the man I am today. I introduce different family members and friends who have played a role in my development. While all the stories in this book are true, some names and identifying details have been changed to protect the privacy of the people involved. I also provide insight to the motivating factors that have not only guided me to write this book but have also allowed me to persevere through life and address the issues that have plagued me for years. Consistent with my personality, I've also included bits of advice that I wish I had gotten earlier in life.

The philosopher Socrates once stated, "The only true wisdom is in knowing you know nothing." This statement has always resonated with me because I have always been curious to learn as much as I can. The more I've learned, the more I realize I don't know anything in relation to the amount of information and knowledge available in the universe. I have opinions, advice, and proclamations, but I do not attest that all of them are fact. As a perfect imperfection, I realize I have flaws. This book is not intended to be a personal attack on anyone or anything mentioned, nor does it serve as the ultimate solutions manual to any situation. I do not have all the answers.

However, I do have hopes for the readers of this book. To those who cannot relate to my story, may it be a window into a world in which countless people are living. I hope that it helps you better understand the struggles and mindsets of people who have endured the harsh realities of life—realities that you may never have to face. Allow it to open your eyes and your hearts so that you may empathize on a whole new level. For the many people who can relate, I hope my story provides you comfort in knowing that you are not alone. Let this book inspire you to break the curses that have plagued you and your family for centuries. I wish for peace and prosperity in all your endeavors. But above all, I wish for healing.

CHAPTER ONE

LESSONS FROM MY MAMA

Throughout my life, my mama taught me many valuable lessons, both directly and indirectly. Her strong personality and her will to fight against the overwhelming odds were characteristics that helped shape me in a positive manner. However, I also used some of her life's mistakes and flawed ways of looking at the world as opportunities from which to grow and learn.

When I was a child, I often repeated words that I didn't know the meanings of. When I was eight years old, I was outside with my cousins playing a game—probably hide-and-seek or red light, green light. Terrell, one of my "big cousins," pulled up in a nice car and stepped out. I put quotation marks around *big cousins* only to signify that where I'm from, in the inner city of Nashville, Tennessee, we often referred to friends of the family or people whose relationships to the family were unknown as our cousins.

Terrell was always the sharpest dresser and always had the nicest shoes, shiniest jewelry, and prettiest girls. But on that occasion, something was different. My younger cousins and I were dumbfounded to see that when he got out of the car, his clothes were tattered, and his hair and beard were ungroomed. His whole appearance was just *off*.

"Ay, Terrell, why you look so raggedy?" I yelled out, trying to get a laugh from the younger kids. "You look like a junkie!" I continued, making fun of him despite seeing that my words had clearly offended him. My cousins and I were laughing, so for me this wasn't a big deal. We continued to play our game, and I quickly forgot about the encounter.

"What's a junkie?" my mama asked me as we walked into the house that night.

"I don't know."

My mama wasn't buying it, so she pressed me for an answer. "Then why did you call Terrell a junkie? You obviously have some idea of what a junkie is, so what is it?"

"It's somebody on that stuff who live under a bridge and don't take showers," I said with all the confidence in the world, as if that were Webster's definition of the word. I had no real idea what "that stuff" was, but I had heard it before in similar context.

"A junkie is someone who is addicted to drugs, and you don't need to be callin' nobody that if you don't know what you talkin' 'bout." My mama went on to tell me that what I had called Terrell had upset him. There was no mention of not using a derogatory word like *junkie* to describe the serious case of drug addiction, but I knew what she meant. She explained to me that Terrell was not, in fact, addicted to drugs. Instead, he was performing a social experiment. His brother, Quentin, was actually a drug addict. At one point in time, Quentin had been just as clean as Terrell. He had fresh shoes, nice clothes, and everybody wanted to be associated with him. But when he became addicted to drugs, he started to neglect his appearance and lived an unhealthy lifestyle.

Terrell decided that he was going to go for months without cutting his hair, shaving, or changing his clothes as often, to see how the world treated Quentin. Even adults who knew him well made comments about his appearance and began to spread rumors that he too had fallen victim to drugs. Terrell hoped to challenge those who would judge others based on appearances alone, to get them to look past their perceptions. He loved his brother so much that he was willing to be ridiculed by the public to bring awareness to the type of life his brother was enduring.

His experiment taught me one of the greatest lessons of my life: never judge a book by its cover. I must treat the custodian with the same respect I give to the CEO. Had Terrell never taken initiative to challenge society's assumptions, and had my mama never confronted me about the situation, I would have continued to look at people and judge them based on appearances. That day, I learned that what matters is what's in someone's heart.

———

My mama had me at the tender age of fourteen. I get inspired whenever I think about the courage she must have had to bring a baby into this world when she was just a baby herself. There are many reasons for teen pregnancy: lack of education and knowledge regarding sex, no access to contraception, drugs or alcohol, peer pressure, sexual abuse, lack of family support or attention, low socioeconomic status—the list goes on. I don't know the exact reason that resulted in my mama's pregnancy, but I do know that multiple factors from the list above existed at the time of my birth.

Drug use was prevalent at the house and in our neighborhood. Some of my earliest memories involved my family asking me to pee in empty pill bottles on a routine basis. My clean pee was used by someone in our house or sold to someone else to pass a drug test (either to obtain a job or deceive a doctor or probation officer). This practice was common in the hood; people knew they shouldn't be doing drugs, but the addiction or the desire for relief was so great that they chose to risk their livelihoods or freedom to get high. My mama never touched drugs and would always stress to me the importance of never experimenting with them either. She had experienced the impact that drugs had had on her parents, Big Mama and Popeye, as well as other family members, and she knew that it was not a route she wanted me to go down. However, she did smoke cigarettes, a habit I found disgusting. I always questioned why she would even smoke, but like other people's addictions, the temporary buzz served as a release. Being poor as we were, dealing with the dangers of the neighborhood, and experiencing violence and death all around us, any escape from reality was welcomed.

I never knew much about my mama's upbringing, because she never talked about it with me. It wasn't until recently that she disclosed to me that Popeye wanted nothing to do with her as a baby. It's likely Popeye didn't want to accept that he, at the age of thirty-two, had had a baby with Big Mama, who was only fifteen at the time. Whatever the reason, it wasn't a happily-ever-after type of situation. With my mama as a baby in a car seat outside of his house, Big Mama pleaded with him to take on his responsibilities as a father. Popeye's response was something out of a movie. He took it upon himself to fire gunshots at Big Mama to run her off. Feuds like that were how my mama was introduced into the world. Fortunately, she was young enough to have no recollection of that event, but the effects of those early traumas lingered within her and Big Mama.

Popeye eventually came around to accepting my mama and Big Mama as his family—or at least one of his families. He had a reputation of being a "rolling stone," a term that referred to a man who doesn't tend to settle in one place or with one person. Growing up, I would always hear references to at least one other woman with whom he had had children in between my mama, who was the oldest, and my uncle Thomas, who was his youngest and was only two years older than me. That would often lead to domestic disputes between Big Mama and Popeye, but she loved him, and I got the sense that he loved her too. We all lived together—Popeye, Big Mama, Thomas, my mama, and me—in a duplex in East Nashville, or as we referred to it, "out East."

———

Big Mama was a large woman who was not to be messed with. When I was young, I remember hearing a story about how intimidating Big Mama was. We lived in a rough neighborhood. While walking back to our house after cashing a check, she was held up at gunpoint in an attempted robbery. But Big Mama, being the powerful force that she was, wrestled the gun away from the would-be robber and turned the gun on him after beating him up. The man was so frightened and defeated that he pleaded with Big Mama to call the police on him. I presume he would have rather dealt with their punishment than to continue to feel the wrath of Big Mama.

Big Mama's life prior to my birth is more of a mystery to me than anything, but I knew she had some tough experiences that made her even tougher. I do know that there was a history of drug abuse, which could have been a result as well as a cause of some of her life experiences. Like so many other people I've encountered in my life who deal with drug addiction problems, it affected her mental capacity. To the naked eye, or if you were outside looking in, she appeared to be perfectly fine, but there were things that only those closest to her would recognize were wrong.

Still, she was such a fun person to be around. She spoke loudly and could make you laugh at any moment. Many people described her as the life of the party because at family functions, she was always the one with her portable radio playing the classics from back in the day. Her energy was very contagious, and whenever you were around her, you knew you were going to have a good time.

I can only go by what other people have told me, but apparently there were times when Big Mama wanted to and actually did physically harm me as a baby. She was such a threat that my mama got to a point where she refused to leave me alone with her and would call on my dad's parents, Granny and Pops, to look after me in her absence. After hearing some of the stories, I couldn't help but think, *What kind of person would want to harm a baby, their own grandchild at that?* As I grow older, I reflect on those times, and I am able to reconcile some of her actions. Before I came along, she was living in poverty, struggling to get by and make ends meet, and living with an abusive partner and two children—one of whom, Thomas, was a toddler with special needs, and the other, my mama, a teenager who was dealing with her own traumatic life. Within that context, I realize that it would have been hard for Big Mama to accept that a new baby, me, had recently entered their lives, adding yet another mouth to feed when they could barely feed everyone in the first place. Add drugs and physical and mental health conditions to the equation, and her actions are more than explained.

As a twenty-nine-year-old, Big Mama became a grandmother. While there may have been some trauma and drama during my early years, I remember loving times with her. She, along with my mama, instilled in me some of the positive characteristics that I possess, such as resiliency and perseverance. Watching them endure the pain of their daily lives with so much grace gave me a great example of how to handle myself when things didn't go the way I had planned. One of the greatest things that Big Mama taught me was how to go into the kitchen and make something out of nothing. There would be times when I would look around the kitchen and be so upset because there was little to nothing to eat, but after several minutes in the exact same kitchen, she would come out with a full meal to feed everyone in the house.

Over the years, my relationship with Big Mama evolved, which led to more lessons. I started making and saving money around twelve years old, and my family knew this. From that point on, I became a source of funds for many people in my family, especially Big Mama. For years, my relationship with her turned into something that resembled the relationship between a bank and a customer rather than a grandmother and her grandson. Our interactions would start off similar to how things used to be, such as catching up with each other over a few laughs, but they would eventually end with her asking to borrow money. That put a lot of strain on our relationship because it no longer seemed genuine. It felt like a transaction. And the first thing I heard if I was unwilling or unable to provide her with any money was, "Oh, you actin' funny today," in an attempt to guilt me into fulfilling her request.

Although there was that tension between us, she taught me so much through those transactions. To her credit, she always paid me back … with interest. And the interest was her idea because, honestly, I would've lent her the money and expected face value back, or nothing at all in some cases. But she understood that this wasn't fair and that there was a cost to borrowing money that wasn't hers. If she wanted to borrow fifty dollars, she would agree to pay me sixty dollars on the same day the next week. In my head, I knew I wouldn't have a need for the fifty dollars in the meantime, so it was a no-brainer for me. I was happy to make 20 percent on my money in a week. That's hard to beat. In addition to her lessons on interest, she also taught me some negotiation tactics. In the beginning, if she wanted to borrow that same fifty dollars, she would offer to pay back fifty-five dollars, and I would agree to it with no questions asked. After a while, she told me that I couldn't be soft about what I wanted and to fight back for more interest, even when dealing with her. Although our relationship had become less than ideal, she still loved me enough to make sure that I knew how to take care of myself.

In my adult years, she showed me again just how much she cared for me. On a visit to see her one day, I noticed that she had a bunch of two-dollar bills posted on her wall. I told her how I liked to collect bills and coins, so she told me without batting an eye that I could take them. For my birthday many months later, she got me a gift of collector's-item golden dollars. I was touched. Though I'm typically not a fan of giving or receiving gifts just for the sake of it, when the gifts are truly thoughtful, it means so much to me, and I could tell that she had listened to me that day and taken a mental note to show a kind gesture. It has been one of the best gifts I've ever received.

In contrast, I don't remember much about Popeye because he passed away shortly after my third birthday. A memory I have of him during his lifetime was seeing him walk through the door after returning from work in his US Army fatigue uniform. When he came in, Thomas and I screamed his name at the top of our lungs as we jumped into his arms for a hug. I'd have liked to think this happened every day, but honestly, it might've only happened once. Maybe I've clung to the memory because of how it made me feel. In that moment, I got the sense that we were one big, happy family full of love, despite whatever else might've been going on.

My only other memory of him occurred at his funeral, the first funeral I had ever attended. Because of his service in the army, he was recognized with a twenty-one-gun salute. Those gunshots terrified me more than anything. I didn't understand what was going on. It was also the first time I remember seeing my mama cry. Between the guns and my mama weeping so hard, I couldn't help but burst into tears. Death was a concept I didn't understand, but I associated it with my mama being sad. It never dawned on me until I was much older that my mama was only seventeen at the time of the funeral. Losing her dad at that age had a major impact on her, but in consistent fashion, she rarely showed the pain outwardly. That was one of the first moments when I began to associate her with strength. Instead of appearing defeated by one of life's toughest blows, she took it on the chin and continued to press on. It was just one of the traits I adopted from her.

———

One of the most humbling moments from my childhood occurred on our trips to the grocery store. Unlike most families who were able to pile all the children in the car and head down the road, my mama and I would have to wait for a cab to pull up to take us to our destination. In some cities, this is an acceptable way of getting around, but in Nashville in the mid-nineties, it wasn't the normal mode of transportation. Most people owned at least one car or had family members who lived close enough to drive them. The cab driver would pull up and ask us where we were headed. To our response, "To the grocery sto'," we would often get puzzled looks.

When we got to the grocery store, I knew what our mission was. We weren't shopping for groceries for a week or two; we'd be shopping for groceries for a whole month. When it's such a hassle to get to and from the store, we had to be as efficient as possible and make the most of our time there. We'd go up and down each and every aisle as if we were on *Supermarket Sweep*. We would literally grab something off of every aisle, mostly frozen food and nonperishables. We would eventually have to push around a second cart because we had so much stuff packed in the first.

The total for our trip was usually north of three hundred dollars. Without government assistance programs like welfare, food stamps, WIC (a supplemental nutrition program for women, infants, and children), Medicaid, and Social Security, I don't know how we would have been able to survive. Those programs kept us afloat but also scarred me. I hated that we were poor. It seemed that in the midst of other poor families, we had it worse.

Seeing the looks on people's faces as we pushed around our two grocery carts was embarrassing, but the real embarrassment came at checkout. I was sure to put all the WIC-qualified items on the conveyer belt first, followed by the items we could purchase using food stamps. If we had picked up any items that required cash, those had to get scanned last so that our payment process would work. It gave me so much anxiety because I absorbed the frustration from every angle. I knew the cashier was annoyed that we were taking so much time sorting through our carts. The people behind us were perturbed because they had to wait for what seemed to me like an hour. And Mama would let me have it if I accidentally mixed up a WIC item for a food stamp item—or worse, a cash item, "wastin' money."

After checkout, we had to call the cab driver to pick us up. Sometimes we would work it out with the same cab driver who had dropped us off to swing back around when we were finished, but other times, we had to wait for a new one. During my elementary and middle school years, I felt immense pressure sitting outside of the grocery store with tons of food and no ride, while other children from school walked by, making rude comments and laughing.

When I would refuse to make the trip or try not to be seen by hiding my face, my mama would tell me not to worry about what other people thought of me, because they weren't perfect themselves. She used her words to reinforce my self-confidence while also letting me know that if someone made fun of me for something I couldn't control, they weren't people I wanted to associate myself with anyway. These experiences have taught me to remain humble and to realize that no matter where life takes me, I could very well still be the embarrassed little child outside of the grocery store. That humility allows me to see everything in life as a blessing, even the bad. I learned to be grateful for it all. When you come from nothing, you appreciate everything.

For years, I referred to myself as neither an optimist nor a pessimist, but instead a realist. That way of thinking meant I took the specifics from each situation and applied an attitude to it based on the details. *Is the glass half full or half empty? Well, it depends on your intent. Are you pouring water into the glass or pouring water out?* During my most naive years, my realism was positive, leading to more optimistic conclusions. As life took its toll on me, I realized that my realism started to shift toward a more cynical and negative view. *Is the glass half full or half empty? Who cares; the glass will break one day anyway.* To combat my pessimistic mind, I challenged myself to see the positive in everything in life because I knew there was always some good even in the most unfavorable situations.

———

My mama tried her best to shield me from the hardships we faced. Whether it was poverty, crime, or violence, my mama would make sure that if she was around, my exposure to those realities was limited. When we watched television shows or movies that weren't appropriate for children, my mama would cover my eyes and ears during the scenes she didn't want me to experience. Oftentimes the scenes involved a violent killing or someone shooting up drugs, and other times there were sex scenes, which made her go into full protector mode. As the music from the soundtrack built up to hint that sparks were flying between two characters, my mama would look at me and place her hand over my eyes. That just made me more curious. I tried my hardest to peek through the cracks between her fingers to catch a glimpse of whatever it was that was so taboo. Usually, all I would catch were the moans from the woman in the scene, but sometimes I would see a woman's body parts.

I always thought that my mama's biggest fear with my exposure to sex on screen was that it would cause me to have sex at an early age and result in a teen pregnancy like it had for her and Big Mama. With her best attempts, there were just some things that my mama couldn't protect me from experiencing. As my mama became a young adult, she and I moved out from living with Big Mama and Thomas to an apartment complex called Terrace Park in the Donelson neighborhood. We didn't move directly into the apartments after leaving Big Mama's house, though.

The inconvenient thing about public housing is that sometimes you're forced to move out of one place before the next place is prepared to accept you. That was the case nearly every time we moved. During many of these transitions, we were essentially homeless. My mama had too much pride to ever classify our situation that way, and until recently, I felt the same. But for weeks or months at a time, we wouldn't have a permanent address or a place to call our home.

During that particular transition from Big Mama's to Terrace Park, we stayed with my cousin and her three children who lived out east too. I don't remember much about our stay there, but I can recall that the neighborhood was where I had my first sexual encounter. I was only four years old and the girl was just a few years older, but she seemed to have way more experience than her age would suggest. Some children are forced to grow up quicker than others, and she was a prime example of that. She forced herself on me. She was persistent—almost aggressive but not threatening. We didn't have intercourse, but there was touching, kissing, and humping. Looking back, I can't help but wonder what that girl had experienced that made her so interested in taking it there with me. Perhaps she had suffered from sexual abuse and was crying out for help. I also think about how that experience shaped me. While other children were learning their ABCs or how to tie their shoes, I was learning how to kiss and where to touch girls.

Recalling that experience made me think about my mama and Big Mama. They were so young when they had children, and I wonder if they had gone through anything like I had at that age, or even younger. Maybe my mama was scarred from her own experience, and that's why she was so protective of me. I also wondered if it was something that only my family had dealt with or if teen pregnancies were common in other households and if they had any correlation with sexual abuse at an early age.

I found that the peak for teen pregnancies occurred in 1990, just a year before I was born.[8] In that year, the teen pregnancy rate for Black women was 223.8 per 1,000 pregnancies, compared to the teen pregnancy rate of 116.9 per 1,000 for women of all races in the United States.[9] After digging deeper, I realized there was a strong correlation between child sexual abuse and teen pregnancies. And during the time of my birth, child sexual abuse rates were also at an all-time high of around 150,000 cases per year.[10]

---

8   Maddow-Zimet, I, Kost K, and Finn S. "Pregnancies, Births and Abortions in the United States, 1973–2016: National and State Trends by Age." New York: Guttmacher Institute, 2020, https://www.guttmacher.org/report/pregnancies-births-abortions-in-united-states-1973-2016.

9   Ibid.

10 Jones, Lisa, and David Finkelhor. "The Decline in Child Sexual Abuse Cases." *PsycEXTRA Dataset*, Jan 2001. doi:10.1037/e478782006-001.

On the heels of the crack cocaine epidemic, my theory is that drug abuse played a huge role in leading to those numbers, especially knowing the disproportionate effects the epidemic had on impoverished Black communities. If my mama had been one of those statistics, it would have easily explained her protective measures around me regarding both drugs and sex.

Instead of directly addressing the issue for what it may have been, I kept it to myself. That's what I had learned to do: take it on the chin and press on. I didn't show any signs that a sexual encounter at that age had any effect on me, but it had a lasting impact. From then on, I was extremely curious about sex. And despite my own fear of becoming a teen parent and following in the footsteps of my family members, my curiosity led me to losing my virginity at thirteen years old, the same age my mama was when I was conceived.

———

Terrace Park was a huge complex that housed thousands of people, many of whom were on Section 8 (a government-subsidized program that allows private landlords to lease houses and apartments to low-income renters), including us. I don't know what we paid in rent; it could've very well been one dollar. Although most of the people who lived there were poor just like us, I felt ashamed. For what seemed like the entire duration of our stay at Terrace Park, we didn't have a couch. Instead, we had a Kicker box, a subwoofer with two giant fifteen-inch holes in the back as our "couch." For a kid who was new to the neighborhood, I suffered so much embarrassment whenever friends would come over to our apartment.

I was five years old and about to start kindergarten. I wasn't nervous about school, because my mama had spent so much time preparing me for everything I would need to know in the classroom. I was, however, anxious about meeting new people. Luckily, it wasn't long before I made friends at school and in Terrace Park. Most of my friends were older than me. I still refer to them as "the third graders." I looked up to them very much; in my eyes, they seemed like adults.

The third graders taught me a lot—good and bad. They showed me how to shoot a basketball and would tell me that Santa wasn't real in the same moment, stealing all the innocence I had still been holding on to. My first fistfight (if you can even call it that) happened in front of the third graders. A boy my age came out of his apartment with a large toy microphone and started chasing me with it, trying to beat me over the head. I took off running as fast as I could, but that was frowned upon by the third graders.

"Stop runnin', Reggie! Don't be scared! Fight him," one of them yelled out to me. I didn't want to let them down, and I definitely didn't want to get the reputation that I was afraid of anybody. My mama had taught me to never pick a fight, but if somebody started a fight with me, I had better finish it. When that thought crossed my mind, I stopped running, turned around, and punched the boy right in the gut. He bent over in agony, and when the third graders lifted his head up, he was crying.

"Reggie won that one!" somebody exclaimed, which made a few people chuckle. I felt proud that I hadn't let them down. I wasn't going to be picked on for being scared of anybody again.

After that day, the third graders had a new respect for me. I was often called out to fight younger kids who had rubbed them the wrong way for one reason or another. They called it "handling their light work," a reference to drug dealing that I eventually learned. I enjoyed it—I was relentless, and I knew that as long as I kept swinging, I'd connect, and it'd be over. I rarely got hit, but when I did, it lit me up and made me want to hurt the kid even more.

Seeking approval from them didn't stop at fighting. Whatever they wanted me to do, I did. On the school bus, they wanted me to sit next to a girl and kiss her—pucker up. Tell a joke about a kid because of what he was wearing—get 'em.

One day when we were waiting for the bus to take us to school, some boys came from the back of an apartment building and called a few of us over to help them out. When I got to the back of the apartment, I realized they had found the family's spare key and were raiding their kitchen.

"Go in and grab all the snacks. They up in the cabinet and in that closet. I'll stay out here and watch," one of the third graders ordered. We ransacked the place. After taking all the snacks and filling our backpacks with them, I got a terrible feeling about it all. It was different from fighting because I was going behind somebody's back and violating their home. What made it worse was that I knew whose house it was; in fact, they were sitting at the bus stop, clueless to what was happening. I can only imagine the feeling they all had when they returned home that day.

I vowed that from then on that I wasn't going to break into anybody's house again. That time, it was only chips and snack cakes. Next time, it could've been money, electronics, guns, or jewelry. I didn't want to have that on my conscience. But that didn't stop me from breaking into abandoned apartments in my teenage years. Groups of kids with nothing better to do to escape the heat of summer would squat in abandoned buildings just to hang out. Sometimes the hangouts turned into hookups or, even worse, crime scenes. Several times when we had nothing to eat or were sick of filling out surveys to get free Whoppers from Burger King, we would use those abandoned apartments to order pizza. When the pizza-delivery person showed up, we would jump them and rob them for the pizza and their cash, and sometimes other teenagers would even steal their cars as we laughed and fled to a safe place to fill our bellies. I now realize how horrible that was. Nowhere in that pizza-delivery person's job description did it mention the threat of being beaten, robbed, and carjacked. After one too many incidents like that, restaurants stopped delivering to our neighborhood.

I could hear my mama's voice in my head telling me that I knew better than to behave like that. If she had ever known about any of those situations, she would've beaten me. That's why I made an effort never to get into trouble at school, because she'd find out and be even more upset that she would be forced to find a ride to pick me up. Between 7:45 a.m. and 3:45 p.m., I was an angel. But one day, she found out about the kinds of things that my "friends" and I were up to.

The third graders and I had planned on going to the Dollar General store to buy a few things, so I tagged along, even though I didn't have any money. When we got there, I saw a pack of mechanical pencils for ninety-nine cents that I desperately wanted. I asked a few guys if they could get them for me. No one had enough money to get whatever they wanted, let alone get something for me too. So, they told me to stuff them in my socks and walk out of the store. I did, and it worked. No alarms went off, and the store clerk had no idea that I had shoplifted.

That night, I went to finish my homework with my shiny, new mechanical pencils. My mama would always make sure I was on top of my work, making me redo it if it was too sloppy or having me repeat exercises for things that I got wrong. When I took my work to her after I was done, she picked up the pencil to erase a mistake I had made.

"Where this pencil come from?" she asked, knowing she had never bought it for me.

"I got it at the dolla' sto' earlier."

"With who money?" she interrogated.

"Um … nobody's," I responded, feeling guiltier now than I had ever felt in my six years of existence.

"So, you stole it?"

I nodded my head and started to cry because I knew she was disappointed in me—but more importantly, I knew she was about to beat my ass. And she did. It was one of those whoopings where every syllable was accompanied with another swing of the belt: "Don't (pop) you (pop) e- (pop) ver (pop) steal (pop) ..." Sometimes I felt like she was making up longer words just to keep it going. I cried so hard as she told me that she wasn't raising a thief. Finally, she barked at me to stop crying because we were going to return the pencils.

When we stepped outside, she spotted the third graders and yelled to them that they ought to be ashamed of themselves for stealing. I'm not sure that anyone else stole anything, but she assumed we had all done it. We walked through the wooded area behind our apartment complex to the shopping center where the Dollar General was, as my buddies and I had done earlier that day. She told the store clerk what I had done and returned the opened pack of mechanical pencils and apologized as she yanked me by my arm out of the store. The third graders were furious at me when we walked by them for the second time.

"Why didn't you just say I got them for you, stupid?" one boy whispered to me as I walked by. Before that moment, I hadn't been in a position where I'd needed to deceive my mama, so it hadn't occurred to me that all of that pain could've been avoided had I just told her that another person had bought them. I'm glad I didn't lie, though, because I wouldn't have been taught such a major lesson: never take what isn't yours. If you want something, you get it the honest way.

She also taught me another important lesson that day.

"You ain't gotta go 'round doin' what everybody else doin' just because. Be a leader and not a follower. You better than that," she lectured. It was just what I needed to hear. From then on, I didn't let the third graders—or anyone, for that matter—talk me into doing something I didn't want to do.

———

My parents were never together during my childhood. My dad and my mama never clicked as a couple, so I was used to not having him around. I wouldn't find out until much later that he was abusive to my mama, physically and emotionally, so I'm glad she was able to escape that situation. I'm sure somewhere in my subconscious are memories of him beating her or being extremely mean, but I must have been too young to now be able to recall those memories. My dad lived in Nashville too, so I would see him occasionally, but he wasn't close to being a father figure in my life at the time. After my paternal grandfather, Pops, whom I'd always seen as a positive male figure, my mama's boyfriend, Mitch, was the closest thing to a father I had at the house.

Mitch and my mama met when we lived in Terrace Park after one of my friends played matchmaker and got them together. Mitch was my buddy's older cousin who had recently moved to town from Texas. My first impression of him was positive, mainly because he came highly recommended from one of my best friends; he was also intelligent. He was one of the first people I knew who read for pleasure. Most important, he was nice to my mama, and she seemed to like him. So, he was cool with me.

A little while after they started dating, he moved in with us, and I had to adjust to having a new man in the house. It wasn't as bad as I would've imagined. He never tried to act as my dad, and my mama didn't let him discipline me, but he did teach me many things, such as the mnemonic phrase "righty-tighty, lefty-loosey" when fixing my bike. Stuff like that will always stick with me.

One of my most vivid memories of Mitch occurred on a day when he got into a fight in front of a huge crowd outside in Terrace Park. He and the other guy had had a boiling feud that escalated that day.

While riding a bike, Mitch swung and connected, which knocked the other guy down. He then got off the bike and beat the crap out of that guy. The fight happened in front of a ton of people, causing the guy who got beat up to be extremely embarrassed. He and his ego were so battered that after the fight, he threatened to shoot up our apartment. He may have threatened to do more than that, because we configured extra blockades by the front and back doors, as if we were expecting someone to bust through them. Because of the threat, I was told to stay clear of the windows. For a while, I played video games and slept on the floor to stay below them. I don't recall any retaliation, but it was an experience that scarred me because I was always on edge, and it felt like something bad could happen at any moment.

Instead of showing fright or other emotions that arose from some of these early traumatic moments, I internalized them. That's what I saw everyone around me doing, especially my mama. "Black don't crack" was not just a reference to the youthful appearance of aging Black people but also a belief that Black people were strong enough to not break down during tough times. Never did we debrief each other to check in on how it felt to endure those experiences. The expectation was that we appear unfazed, either as a coping mechanism or for survival.

CHAPTER TWO

DEFINING NORMAL

After just a couple of years of living in Terrace Park, we were on the move again. We were headed back out east to a place I will always consider home. Leaving my friends from Terrace Park was hard at first because I had made strong bonds with a few kids. The day we moved, one of my friends rode behind us on his bike as we rolled out in Mitch's blue pickup truck, all the while screaming, "Don't goooo!" as I cried out, "Noooo!" I was still screaming long after we got on the interstate, which caused my mama to turn around and yell at me, "Boy, you better shut up. He can't hear you no mo'." And that's what I did. I shut up and watched the clouds pass by with tears rolling down my face.

We moved into a duplex in the heart of South Inglewood, a subsection of East Nashville. Living in an actual neighborhood with houses was a nice change of pace from apartment living, but it wasn't always the safest place to be. My first impression of the new place was that there must be a lot of break-ins because we had burglar bars on the windows and huge security doors in the front and back. Those doors only worked to keep unwanted guests out if you actually locked them. One day, my mama, Mitch, and I were sitting in the living room watching TV with the big door open and the security door closed but not locked. All of a sudden, a man whom we had never met opened the door in a panic. He was actively evading arrest from the police and asked if we would hide him. Shocked at the request, my mama said, "Hell naw, but you can go out the back door!" He jetted out the back. We all looked at each other, perplexed at what had just happened. The feeling was unsettling. Just as suddenly as the man had appeared, so did the police. They questioned us, but we acted like we didn't know what they were talking about, and they eventually left.

That was the code. As much as we hated having a stranger barge into our house, we couldn't stand the police even more. Nine-one-one was never a number we dialed intentionally unless we were extremely desperate, and that was rare. The police seemed to bring on more issues than protection, so we chose to protect ourselves.

That day, I started looking at the neighborhood a little differently. I kept my guard up and made sure I was aware of my surroundings. I stayed safe and out of trouble, but I was always seeing or hearing things that happened very close to home. When I was nine, I was awakened by a few gunshots that sounded like they were right outside my window. I peeped out the blinds and saw a man running from behind my neighbor's house while being chased by another man who was shooting at him. I got so scared that I jumped off my bed and lay down on the floor. I didn't see if the man managed to catch up to the guy he was pursuing, and I'm glad, because I know that would've haunted me even more than it already does. I slept that entire night on the floor. Anytime I heard gunshots after that, I was generally unfazed, but I would always make my way below the windows just to be safe. A few gunshots weren't about to make me lose a game of GoldenEye 007 or Mario Kart.

———

Fifth grade was a transformative year for me. It happened to be the first time I ever played organized football, a sport that would change my life and provide me with a number of opportunities. For years I had wanted to play, but we couldn't afford the registration fees, and even if we could have, I'd probably have missed a majority of the practices because of our lack of transportation. That is, until I found out that my friends were playing football at the Center, less than a mile away from my house, for Backfield in Motion (BIM). "The Center" was what we called the neighborhood community center, South Inglewood Community Center in our case. BIM was a nonprofit organization started by a wealthy philanthropist. After volunteering to coach an inner-city team, he had recognized that the lack of resources often led to poor attendance from family members and even his own players on the team. He started BIM to help alleviate some of the barriers families faced, while also providing additional educational support with after-school tutoring. Best part, the services were offered at no cost to families, so people like me who couldn't afford to pay for league entry fees or expensive equipment could now play organized football. BIM used sports as a hook to draw in at-hope boys, and through its program, it helped to mold them into better versions of themselves.

The sports hook worked, but I had no idea about the larger impact that joining BIM would later have on me. Before I was able to join the team, however, I had to make sure it was something I wanted to commit to. I watched the team practice and saw all my friends having so much fun and noticed that the coach, a student-athlete at Vanderbilt University whom everyone referred to as Coach Johnny, seemed to be having just as much fun coaching them. After practice was over, Coach Johnny asked me a few questions to gauge my interest before giving me an application to take home to have signed by my mama. I was so excited that I filled out all the papers as soon as I got home and ran to my mama to get her signature. Without even fully explaining what was happening, I asked, "Mama, can I play football at the Center with all my friends?"

"I don't see why not."

"Okay, sign this line," I said as I pointed to the application. "And that line," I said, flipping the page to another disclosure. "Okay, now initial here." You would've thought I was a used-car salesman with how quickly I got her to fill out that paperwork. It was official. I was on my first team, the South Inglewood Tigers. Outside of my family, I had never been a part of anything larger than myself. The pride and sense of community that football provided were critical in my development over the years.

Even though I was on the team, I had to sit out the next day because there was a game, and I didn't know any of the plays. I probably could've picked them up pretty quickly from my days of playing popular video games such as Madden NFL and NFL Quarterback Club, but I wasn't given that chance. I watched the whole game from the sidelines and cheered my Tigers on as I sported my jersey. Throughout the game, a white man was handing out free Taco Bell to all community members who had come to watch the game. When the game was over, I walked up to the man with my team, expecting Taco Bell like everyone else. He told me that if I hadn't played, I should've come and gotten food with the rest of the spectators and refused to give me any. I was cold and hungry, and in my head, I had all kinds of bad words for that man. I didn't know it at the time, but that man who refused to give me any food was the CEO of BIM, Coach Joe Davis, the wealthy philanthropist and a man who would later have a huge impact on my life.

To play in games for BIM, everyone had to complete mandatory tutoring before practice. Going to tutoring was never an issue for me because I was already in the habit of completing my homework before going out to play. Only difference was that I had to do my homework with my friends and volunteers around. While easy for me, some kids chose not to play because they refused to cooperate with the tutoring mandate. That gave me the opportunity to play earlier than I probably would have otherwise.

I played cornerback and wide receiver that first year. However, at that age, there were few passing plays, so I focused mostly on defense. After getting used to hitting, I ended up being a decent player and was asked to be in the all-star game at the end of the year. I learned early on that I wasn't a good loser, because our team had lost a few games, and we didn't make it to the championship, but the all-star game was a good consolation. I was very excited because the game was being played at Vanderbilt University's football stadium. We played our all-star game the same week that Vanderbilt was set to play the University of Florida. We were introduced to many of the players from both teams, which was the coolest experience I'd had to date. Football was already opening my eyes to a whole new world. I made up my mind then and there that I wanted to play for Vanderbilt when I was old enough.

That same year, my life changed more than I would've ever expected. Up until that point, I had always felt like an only child even though, on my dad's side, I had two brothers living just a few miles away (although I only knew that one of them existed at the time). We rarely saw each other, so it was easy to feel like an only child. But that December, my mama gave birth to a beautiful little girl, Secret. My mama didn't show much of a baby bump during her pregnancy, and we had never discussed the possibility of my having a baby brother or sister, so I had no idea it was happening. Communication was not our strong suit as a family. A few days before Secret was born, I came home to a note from my mama that read, "I have a bladder infection and had to go to the hospital. Be back in a couple of days." It was strange that neither my mama nor Mitch had come home, but I didn't think too much of it. Just like it was any other day, I did my homework and got myself ready for school the next morning. When I came home from school the next day, I started getting concerned, and that's when I got the call from my mama asking me, from a few options, what I wanted my baby sister's name to be. Secret seemed fitting. That's how I found out my baby sister would be coming home a few days later.

Loneliness started to set in, so I called my paternal grandfather, Pops, to come and get me. He told me that he couldn't until much later because he only had his semitruck, but that once Granny got off work, he would come. Not satisfied with that response and knowing his willingness to do whatever he could for me, I made myself throw up and I called him right back and told him I was sick. He came right away and picked me up in his semi. Unfortunately, it got stuck on our street, and he had to spend a lot of money getting it out. I should've just waited. He brought me back home just when my mama and Mitch returned from the hospital with baby Secret. I remember first laying my eyes on her and thinking she was perfect. Seeing how small and fragile she was, all I wanted to do was protect her. I wanted to be the best big brother anybody had ever had. I often wondered if that feeling I had to watch over Secret was the same feeling my mama had when she first laid eyes on me.

———

As time went on, I noticed that my mama and Mitch started drifting apart. Sometimes he would come home, and other times it'd be days before I saw him. In his absence, I stepped up by taking care of my sister whenever I was asked. Most of my time after school was spent babysitting her and doing homework. Sometimes, as early as ten years old, I would be left alone to take care of her by myself. I didn't mind, though—she was a well-behaved baby, and the responsibility actually helped me grow up a lot quicker.

After several months of noticing the distance between my mama and Mitch, I realized something that shook my world. I was in my room playing video games when I heard someone leaving by the front door. As I looked out the window, I saw a taller, light-skinned man with braids, whom I'd never seen before. I didn't know why he was here, and I was curious. I later found out that this man was actually Secret's biological father. My mind was blown. All that time, I had thought Mitch was my sister's dad, and I was happy with that. Mitch had been good to me and my mama and even Secret in her infancy. All of a sudden, some random man was the father of my baby sister. I didn't know how to express it then, but it made me angry. Initially, I thought, *Did my mama cheat on Mitch with this dude?* As a ten-year-old, I couldn't understand the dynamics of the relationships among adults, but I tried, and every time I did, I ended up mad. Of course, I couldn't be expected to fully understand everything my mama was dealing with, just as she couldn't have known everything I was experiencing. Healthy forms of communication may have helped to bridge that gap, but for us, it just wasn't there.

That was the first time I was actually mad at my mama. Before, I would be upset if she whooped me or didn't let me get my way, but never was I truly mad at her. I also started to distrust her because, in my mind, I thought she had been unfaithful. My distrust extended to men as well. I didn't want men near my mama or Secret, because I didn't know their intentions, so I just assumed they were negative. That feeling toward men wasn't anything new. As a younger child, I had always felt uneasy around my dad whenever he would talk to multiple girlfriends right in front of me.

Being upset about what was going on at home didn't affect my performance in school. It made me want to do better, especially on the football field, which turned into a safe haven for me. When sixth grade came around, I had so much confidence going into the next season that I tried out for quarterback. My first pass was terrible. It was a tight spiral, but I had never learned the concept of leading a receiver, so I threw the ball basically where he was standing on the line of scrimmage. Coach Johnny came up to me and explained the concept, and it clicked. I was throwing the best balls down the field and eventually earned the starting role.

I played well and led the team to the championship that year. We ended up losing to our East Nashville rivals, but it was a successful season nonetheless. I made the all-star team again, and I got some revenge from the year before. My confidence skyrocketed. At the end of the season, I was awarded offensive MVP and got my first trophy for athletics. I'd received a few trophies before for academic achievements like having straight As all year, so this wasn't my first time receiving an award for my efforts, but the sports award was so much cooler to me. For years, I had seen other kids flaunt their trophies, and I had wished I could do the same. Finally, I had gotten that opportunity.

After the season was over, BIM needed a way to incentivize children to continue participating in the program and attend tutoring sessions, so they committed to giving a computer to any student who came to every session in the off-season. I had never had a computer and knew we couldn't afford one at the time, so I was dedicated to getting one through the program. I went to every tutoring session and tried to encourage my friends to do the same, since we were going to be at the Center anyway, playing basketball or hanging out. Not many people cared to continue going to tutoring, though. By the end of the year, only two students had honored the commitment and received a computer—a young Cambodian kid and me.

The computer was a huge, clunky white box of slow software programs, but I didn't care. I had earned it. Because we didn't have internet, all I did on the computer was play around in the Paint application or Minesweeper. I would occasionally get a disk with free AOL software. I'd pop one of those disks in and have internet for about thirty total hours after hearing the dial tone and a screeching noise. That noise gave me chills. As great a gift as the computer was, it wasn't close to the best thing I received during those tutoring sessions.

BIM hired certified teachers and utilized volunteers. That's how I met a student named Justin from a local private school, Montgomery Bell Academy (MBA). Justin was passionate about helping underserved populations. It didn't take long for him to realize that I was a bright student who excelled in the classroom. Once I was done with my homework, he would challenge me to see if I could complete more advanced work. Once the concept was explained, I would usually get the answer right. He was so impressed by the work I was doing and by the commitment I had in attending each tutoring session that he decided to introduce me to MBA.

I had been to MBA earlier in the year because that's where BIM held their preseason jamboree, but I didn't know much about the school other than its nice facilities. My next introduction to the school was at a football game on a Friday night that I attended with Justin. I arrived to a sea of thousands of people around the stadium for the high school football game. I had never seen anything like it. There were tons of people there—boys and girls, old and young. But there weren't many Black people. That was the most outstanding feature that I remember from the game. Before that game, I had never been in an environment where I was a racial minority. That didn't stop me from enjoying the game, though.

That night, I was given a program book with all the players and information about the team. I said to myself, "I'm going to be on the cover of this program one day." I held on to that book for a year and a half. I kept it in the cover of my binder so I could always be reminded of my goal. I was later introduced to the admissions office and given the rundown of what it would take to become a student at Montgomery Bell Academy and what they thought the opportunity would provide for me. I would have to take a standardized test and maintain good grades and behavior in my current school. But from the looks of it, I was a shoo-in. From my end, I had been pretty much sold as soon as I had gone to that first game.

I was always on top of my responsibilities when it came to schoolwork or getting tasks completed. I took that same drive when it came to knocking out the admissions requirements for MBA. My mama didn't know much about the entire process, but I made sure to read and reread all the instructions, so as not to miss any deadlines or requirements. Honestly, many times, all I would need from my mama was a signature on a document, and I would be on my way to figuring out the next steps. I did that often. Sometimes, to get it done quicker, I wouldn't even tell my mama what she was signing. I knew what I wanted, I learned what I needed to do to get it done, and I got it done. Soon thereafter, I had been accepted into MBA to start in the eighth grade. It was probably my proudest moment to date. Before knowing about MBA, I had thought I would get into a magnet school for gifted students through the luck of the lottery, but that was never a guarantee. To know that my hard work had paid off gave me a sense of accomplishment that I had never felt before.

In the meantime, I had to go back to public school and wait until it was time to start at MBA. Sixth grade at Dalewood Middle School was probably my worst year academically, and it had nothing to do with my efforts or understanding of the material. Instead, it boiled down to my teacher, who never seemed to grade anything. She'd assign us work and not collect it—not just a few times but the entire year. She was an older teacher who loved talking about tennis and her best friend who was battling cancer, but she did little in regards to teaching. When she gave me my first ever B, I was furious because I knew it wasn't a reflection of me as a student. But mostly I was angry at the thought that it would hurt my chances of getting into MBA. It felt like the fate of my future was in somebody else's hands—somebody who didn't care enough to do a good job—somebody whose negligence could undo all my hard work.

At home, things were stressful. Big Mama and Thomas had moved in with us. There we were again with a packed household: me, my mama, Secret, Big Mama, Thomas, and sometimes Mitch. We were all in the two-bedroom duplex, living in close quarters. During that time, I was testy. My personal space was limited, and every time I looked up, somebody would be bothering me. I preferred being alone in my room, which I kept clean just the way I liked it. When I came home and saw that things were out of order, it would cause me so much stress that I would get mad, which caused repeated fights between me and Thomas. I just didn't like having a lot of people in the house. I could never calm my mind.

In addition to being crowded, the duplex we lived in was deteriorating. For months, there was a hole in the floor separating the living room from the kitchen. If I wanted to go to the kitchen to eat or cook, I had to hop over a large cavity the size of manhole in the street. At one point, we had a puppy who would occasionally get stuck under the house in the crawl space because it had gotten too close to the hole and fallen in. We eventually started covering the hole so that the dog wouldn't fall, but it was still a hassle. That little puppy ended up getting stolen from us one day. It was sad, but the truth was it was one less mouth we had to feed. No tears were ever shed for that poor little puppy.

After a while, Big Mama and Thomas moved out, and we were on the move again. My mama, Secret, and I were moving south of town to an apartment complex in Antioch called Valley Brook. When I found out we were moving, I was devastated. These were the most formative years of my life. I had grown close to my friends and felt like I had found a home out east.

The move to Antioch was a trend for many families in my neighborhood. There had been a major two-day tornado outbreak in East Nashville in 1998, during which many parts of the community were destroyed. So, there was a huge exodus to parts of the city farther away from downtown. Developers and real estate investors offered longstanding homeowners quick large sums of cash for their homes, and gentrification started to take place. Home prices and property taxes started to increase, forcing out many lower- and fixed-income families who had grown roots in the community, replacing them with well-to-do families. The trend was that the more expensive the community got, the whiter it became. Similar developments were occurring all over the city of Nashville.

———

I initially didn't know anybody at Valley Brook, and it was hard making friends. But after a while, I found out that two of my good friends from out east were also living in Valley Brook—a girl I had a huge crush on and her older brother, who looked out for me like a big brother. They helped me make friends around the community when I was still new to the neighborhood.

A few months into living there, something unexpected happened. There was a knock on the door, so I opened it. There stood a scrawny little kid with nappy braids and glasses whom I had seen around many times. I was confused as to why he was at our door.

"Is … is you lil' Reggie?" he passively asked in a drawn-out southern accent.

"Why? Who askin'?" I responded skeptically.

"You my bruhdda," he insisted. "We got the same daddy. My name Kevin." I was so confused. I didn't know what to think.

"Oh, aight bet. Good to meet you, lil' bruh," I said to him as I started to close the door. After the door shut, I yelled, "Mama! This lil' boy just said he my brother!"

She explained to me that Kevin, who was two years younger than me, was in fact my brother. She added that my dad hadn't claimed him as his child for years, so he didn't want to tell me about him. I was dumbfounded. I thought to myself, *At twelve years old, I'm just finding out about a brother I've had for ten years?* I didn't how to take it. I wasn't ready to just accept this young boy as my brother. I didn't know anything about him or his family.

It took a long time, but living in the same apartment complex helped us bond. Our friend groups overlapped, and we would always play together. His mama loved the role model I was for him, so she often invited me over to spend time with him. I got to meet his other siblings, and it was almost like entering into the Twilight Zone. They knew everything about me and my dad, but I knew nothing about them. After a few years of lots of catching up over the phone and hangouts, Kevin became just as much of a sibling of mine as Secret and the youngest sibling on my dad's side, Jarrett, whom I had known since his birth and had spent time with occasionally.

The move to Valley Brook introduced me to yet another school, Croft Middle, and more anxiety to meet new people. I enjoyed my new school, but it opened my eyes to a lot of different things. I'd never been in school with so many white people. I didn't know who Kurdish people were, but the school had a large population of them. I later learned that Nashville has the largest Kurdish population outside of the Middle East. In retrospect, that adjustment prepared me for the transition to MBA, where I would become a racial minority.

Sports were atrocious at Croft. One reason was that we only had seventh graders playing on our middle school team while other schools had seventh and eighth graders. One year didn't seem like much of a difference at first, but when it was the difference between a little boy with a high-pitched voice and a young man going through puberty, the contrast on the sports field was stark. Football wasn't as enjoyable as it had been a year prior. After an entire season, we were winless.

During that season, I suffered the worst concussion in my life. My coaches labeled it as a minor concussion, but in retrospect, it was extremely severe. The game was against Apollo Middle School. One moment I was riding to the game in my friend's car, and the next I was waking up at 10 p.m. on the couch. My mama, who was informed by a friend of mine, told me that I had collided head-to-head with a player from the other team. As was the protocol at the game, I was asked a series of questions that I couldn't answer correctly, one being, "What is your mom's name?" When I could not recall the answer to that question, I began to cry and shiver like I was freezing cold in the hundred-degree heat. All of that was recounted to me, because I have no memory of it. My mama told me that we had lost and that the coaches had told her that I couldn't go to sleep until midnight. Ignorant to the effects of concussions and their long-term impact, I returned to practice a few days later. My coaches expressed how proud they were of me for coming back and not sitting out the last game like a "sissy." I realize now how toxic that comment was and how potentially life-altering my actions were, but I didn't know any better at the time, and neither did the coaches.

After football season was over, basketball season began. Other than a couple of brief AAU seasons, I hadn't played much organized basketball.

Though I had previously been too young to play basketball for my schools, it was my favorite sport and one I would continue to play into high school. Again, we were terrible but ended up winning a few games just because there were some teams out there that were worse. Although I enjoyed basketball more than football, I almost didn't play that season; getting a ride home from school after practice was more difficult, since no one else from Valley Brook had made the team. But luckily, some other families helped out. I also didn't have money to buy the team shoes, and I feared being the only person on the team who had different shoes than everybody else. I told Pops that I needed shoes to play basketball, and his response was, "You go to school, you tell 'em you po' and you can't afford 'em." When he said that, I started crying on the inside. I got the most gut-wrenching feeling in my stomach and swallowed a big gulp while trying to prevent the tears from streaming down my face. Because I didn't want to accept that I was poor and I didn't want to be the odd man out, I considered not playing basketball at all. A few days later, Pops miraculously found the money to get the shoes so I could join the team and not feel like an outcast. I was ecstatic.

That year, other than my basketball shoes, I had one pair of shoes that I wore every single day—all-black mid-top Nike 20s. One day, the girl I liked the most in my grade looked at me and said, "Ew, you wear them shoes with *everything!*" She wasn't wrong, but I hated that she had pointed it out. It was soul crushing and made me feel like the little kid sitting outside the grocery store again. But there was nothing I could do about it, so I focused on what I could control—making good grades and staying out of trouble.

————

Before we moved again to a place called the Park at Hillside to be closer to MBA, we stayed with Big Mama and Thomas. They lived in the Edgehill projects out south, and although I had lived in Section 8 housing my entire life, we had never lived in the projects until then. I had spent time in the projects, so I wasn't too unfamiliar with the surroundings, but I saw some crazy things in those few weeks we lived there.

At the time, I just wanted to get out of the house so I could spend most of my time at the basketball court. I used to walk to the court with Thomas, who was a lot bigger than I was, but with his intellectual disability, he acted much younger. Part of the reason why I would walk with him was so he could look intimidating in case anybody had ideas of jumping or robbing us. The other reason was so I could introduce him to people.

I was a battler on that court. I was five-foot-five and could nearly dunk, and the older guys loved it whenever I would attempt to. They liked how I played, especially after I blocked a layup of a guy who was about six-foot-four, which made them respect me a little bit more. I used that as the moment to introduce them to Thomas. I wanted everyone to know who he was, so they would look out for him and wouldn't try to bully him. Thomas loved wandering off and walking around by himself. He often talked to himself and would even yell at times, and I didn't want anybody to take it the wrong way or think that he was causing drama. I had to get them to see that he had the sweetest heart in the world and wouldn't hurt a fly.

On those walks to and from the court, we would see all kinds of things. People doing or selling drugs, having sex in semidiscreet places, engaging in fights that resulted in weapons being pulled—you name it. Most of the time, we pretended like we hadn't seen anything and just went on our way. It was the safest thing to do. After seeing all that we had seen, I felt like I needed something to protect myself, so I started keeping weapons on me. I had pocketknives, screwdrivers, and brass knuckles, but those wouldn't have stood a chance against a gun. I wanted to get a gun of my own, but I didn't know how to get my hands on one. And I knew my mama would kill me if she ever knew I had one. She hated guns.

After we moved into our apartment, I had a friend who had come across a gun and was selling it. I had to have it. I ended up paying for the black-and-silver pistol. I rarely ever showed anybody the gun. Most kids who came across a gun were quick to brag and would take it everywhere, but I didn't want to have any accidents, so I made sure to keep it in a safe place. I had the gun for several years and only pulled it out a handful of times.

The most unforgettable time was when, at nineteen years old, I actually tried to use it to harm somebody else. The tension between me and a man who had violated the peace of mind of my entire family had escalated so much that I was driven to a point of insanity. After months of stalking him, I followed him home after work. My intent was to shoot him and drive off, hoping that I could avoid any consequences due to my well-thought-out plan. When it came time to do it, I fired and missed. All of a sudden, my life flashed before my eyes. I held the gun in my shaking hands as I cried, thinking about the consequences of my intended actions and how dumb I had been. I had been hurt badly by that person, but nothing would have justified taking his life, so I ran away from the situation. I grabbed the shells, hopped in the car, and cried the entire way home.

Having the gun gave me a false sense of power. I knew that if I were to get in an altercation with somebody, I could always use it as leverage, but that was a dangerous game to play. I wasn't ready to kill, so there was no need for me to have a gun. The next time I got the gun out was to discard it—never to be seen again.

A few years into living at the Park at Hillside, my mama had her third child, a little boy named Demorius, Demo for short. I was fifteen years old and not happy about the new addition to the family. I was frustrated with my mama because I thought it was very irresponsible of her to bring another baby in the house when we were barely getting by. I never voiced my frustration with her, but instead I took it out on Demo. In a totally opposite fashion to how I treated Secret when she was born, I was extremely distant from Demo. I didn't want to hold him or be near him. Whenever he needed a diaper change, I refused to do it. His cries irked me more than anything I had ever heard.

I was also upset with my mama because of the father of her baby. It wasn't my place to tell my mama whom to date, but I never clicked with Demo's dad. Part of my reason for not liking him was that he reminded me so much of my own dad, and I held a lot of resentment toward him. Unlike the relationship I had seen with my mama and Mitch, and even the boyfriend she had before Demo's dad, it didn't seem like they were meant for each other. They would argue a lot and even get physical. Once when my girlfriend was over, I just blared music in my room so that she wouldn't hear any of their altercations. That same night, I thought I heard them tussling, so I ran out of my room to go protect my mama, only to see her slam the door in my face. It confused the hell out of me. *Was she the abuser? Did she not want me to help her?* I just didn't know, and she wasn't one to ever discuss things like that with me.

Although I was originally upset, I eventually grew to love my baby brother. He was just too cute not to. He had so much personality and was very smart. He had a bit of a speech impediment, which made him sound even cuter. It was also cool getting to see my baby sister act as big sister with him. I knew I had to always be a good role model for both of them. My self-interests aside, I decided they would be my motivation to work harder.

———

Throughout those years that encapsulated the majority of my youth, I experienced immense trauma. During elementary and middle school, I had friends who were killed due to gun violence, and I also had a few friends who were the perpetrators in murders. I was fourteen years old when a close friend of mine, Shug, who was only fifteen, was murdered. The loss still haunts me as I replay the events leading up to his death. He was shot six times at the park, just a few yards away from where children's softball games were being played. Heartbreakingly, my middle school crush was murdered at sixteen years old, and her brother, who looked after me in Valley Brook, died several years later of a drug overdose. When I was sixteen, an elderly store clerk, Mrs. Wilson, from the neighborhood shop that I visited nearly every day in South Inglewood was killed by a fourteen-year-old child. The news of her passing devastated me, especially when I considered that a child whose mind wasn't fully developed was responsible for her murder.

The first time I had a gun pulled on me had been right outside Mrs. Wilson's store. I was ten years old. I had just gotten my regular snack pack, a bag of Flamin' Hot Cheetos and a Candy Apple Faygo to drink. As I was walking in the same direction as traffic, I leaned over and spit toward the street. I hit a man in the passenger side of a car directly in the face with a huge loogie. Twenty feet ahead of me, the car screeched to a halt. I froze, and before I could open my mouth to apologize, I saw a gun come out of the passenger-side window. I dropped my chips and drink and darted in the opposite direction. I hopped over a fence and made my way behind some houses where I hid out for about an hour until I felt the coast was clear. When I finally headed home, I walked in a totally different direction. The neighborhood was like that sometimes. Without warning, things could go from calm to chaos then back to calm. Sometimes the smartest thing to do was run. Other times, the situation might've called for a standoff.

Basketball games often turned into arguments, which turned into fights. The second time I had a gun pulled on me, I was twelve, and it started with a dispute on the court. After a few choice words with my own teammate and good friend, he decided to go and grab a gun. When he came out pointing the gun in my direction, I was far less afraid than I had been the first time because my blood was boiling with rage and adrenaline from the heated altercation that had preceded it. And while my life didn't flash before my eyes, I recall counting every breath I took while trying my hardest not to blink as my eyes filled with tears. As our other friends tried to defuse the situation, I just thought to myself, *That could've been my last breath*, over and over again. Looking into his eyes, I got the sense that he didn't want to hurt me. He was merely proving that he had access to a gun. After the crowd deescalated us, we all went home. The next time he saw me, he gave me a hug. But I felt so disrespected that I never felt the same way about our friendship again, though we remained cordial.

I never told my mama about the things I experienced because that wasn't how our relationship had developed. We didn't talk about suffering, because it didn't feel like suffering when everyone else was going through the same stuff. The only form of communication that she may have shared was music, which expressed her feelings. Music was the soundtrack of her pain, though I didn't realize it then. Mary J. Blige was on blast all the time at our house because she sang about struggles that my mama could relate to. When it came to verbalizing those struggles in her own life, my mama was incapable. Or perhaps it was just difficult describing what was considered normal everyday life in the hood.

CHAPTER THREE

ABANDONED AT BIRTH

had a complicated relationship with my father. I loved and despised him. His actions impacted the way I lived and altered so many aspects of my life. I spent my entire life striving to be better than he was, yet I had so much admiration for him. When I think of an ideal father, I think of someone who is there to build you up when you are down. I think of someone who cheers you on as your biggest fan, no matter the circumstances. I think of a protector. I think of a provider. I think of a person who loves unconditionally through good times and bad. On occasion, my dad has exemplified many of those traits, but he is far from perfect.

As a child, I rarely saw my dad, even though we lived in the same city and many times were just a few miles away from each other. My mama spent a lot of time trying to get out of the relationship with him. She didn't want me to have much of a relationship with him either on account of his abusive behavior and involvement in criminal activities. And although I rarely saw him, I have vivid childhood memories of my dad.

For weeks, I'd repeatedly call him just to ask to spend time with him or for him to keep his promise to buy me something like a video game or a pair of shoes. He loved buying me stuff. I always had new clothes and shoes, usually Tommy Hilfiger and Air Jordans. I had every pair of Jordans that came out for several years. It was like that was the only way he could show his love to me. It would take weeks or months of calls from me or my mama to get him to keep with his promises, but he would come through. But instead of joy, he would leave me feeling the same sad sentiment each time. He'd hand me whatever it was while saying, "Tell yo' mama to stop callin' me." Then he'd vanish, deflating any excitement I had had in that moment and making me feel worse than before.

When we did spend time with each other, his body would be present, but his mind was often on so many other things that he paid little attention to me. As a treat to make the moments more memorable, he'd let me sit in his lap and steer the car as he controlled the pedals whenever we drove around town. Once, at five years old with a contact high from all the weed my dad and cousin were smoking, I whipped the car up and down the street with music blasting in my ears. My dad and cousin were deep in conversation, and I could tell my dad wasn't paying too much attention to the road, or he just trusted that I wasn't going to crash the car, because he wasn't correcting the wheel as much as he usually did. My cousin chuckled as he looked at me and said, "This lil' nigga really think he can drive," to which my dad responded, "Man, I ain't touched this wheel in 'bout five minutes … he got us." Luckily, we made it to our destination, but in retrospect, despite what my dad thought, I did not have us.

And while my dad may not have paid attention to everything that was going on, my impressionable brain was focused on everything he was doing. I knew where his "stash spots" were, the places he discreetly kept drugs, weapons, or money in case of a traffic stop or raid. Even at two years old, I was an active observer. While driving us around, my dad stopped at a store to get a few things. Because he knew he'd be in and out, he left me in the car while he went in. As I've been told, when he came back out, he saw me waving around the pistol that he had placed underneath his seat. Struggling to lift it up, I tried to point it out the window. He quickly got into the car and grabbed the gun away from me. I bet he had thought he could have stealthily put the gun under there and that nothing would come of it. Of course, I could've seriously hurt or killed someone, even myself. As luck would have it, nothing bad happened.

From what little I knew about my dad, I tried to mimic many of his habits. In elementary school, I became entrepreneurial after witnessing what my dad did for a living. I was watching television in my dad's room when I saw a baggy wedged between the stereo and the small entertainment center it rested on. Curious, I tugged on the baggy until I saw small tan-colored rocks. I knew they were drugs, but that was all I knew about what I was looking at. I didn't tell anyone. I simply placed them back where I had found them and continued to watch cartoons.

Seeing how those tan-colored rocks were packed into that baggy inspired me to want to recreate a similar product to sell at school. I grabbed a ton of sandwich bags and filled the corners of them with sugar and tore them off like the baggy I had found, twisting the tops to keep them closed. While my teachers saw me as a gifted angel, I was selling baggies of sugar for twenty-five cents in the back of the classroom where we hung our coats and backpacks because I was trying to emulate my dad.

―――

My dad made sure that Christmases and birthdays were always over the top. My fifth Christmas in 1996 was no exception. As a child, I loved remote-control cars more than any other toy. That Christmas morning, I came downstairs to see a huge racetrack set up with tons of different remote-control cars on it. The track was about the size of our entire living room—as it was in my memories. I also got a mountain bike that year. That bike was built for a person much older than I was, but my parents always liked to brag about how I had been able to ride a bike without training wheels at an early age, and this was another way for them to brag even more. To tell the truth, I hated that bike. Once I was on it, I could ride it just fine, but getting on and off was such a challenge. I'd often have to just jump off, which would cause it to crash.

A few years later, I had a birthday that was just as memorable. At the time, my mama worked at NASCAR Café, a NASCAR-themed restaurant with an attached fun zone, which was where we had my eighth birthday party. I was having the time of my life with all of my friends and cousins. My dad had been drinking and was starting to get drunk as the party progressed. I didn't notice how drunk he was until he decided to join me on the arcade racing game I was playing. It was my favorite game because I could pretend like I was on a motorcycle and lean in and out of turns like I had seen so many people do in real life, including my dad. The moment he got on the bike, it became much harder to maneuver because of his added weight. It was nearly impossible for me to move against his body, and he was so drunk that he was turning the wrong way and making me crash into the side walls. He was leaning in my face, asking me if I was having fun. I wasn't. His breath reeked of liquor, and all I wanted to do was get away from him. After that game was finished, that's exactly what I did. The joy I had been feeling was sucked right out of me.

When I ran away from my dad that day, I didn't realize that it would be one of the last times I would see him for a long time. On April 9, 1999, just fifteen days after my birthday party, my dad was arrested. My mama got a call to turn on the news, and there he was. Face plastered on the screen for multiple charges including possession with intent to sell, possession of a deadly weapon, aggravated assault, evading arrest, and attempted homicide on a police officer. All of those charges had occurred while he was on probation for similar crimes he had committed earlier that year and years prior, but he'd never faced an attempted murder charge before. I had grown used to my dad going in and out of jail, but as I watched the news that night, I knew it was going to be different. If I tried, I'd still be counting the number of tears I shed that night.

It didn't take me long to realize that his bid was much different than the previous ones. He wasn't going to be home on the weekend or a few months later. I don't know how much time he was sentenced to, but it didn't seem like I would ever see him again based on what everyone was telling me.

"Yo' daddy going away forever after this one."

"Yeah, they gone send yo' daddy down the road."

"He fucked up when he messed with that police officer."

"Better get used to seeing him through glass."

Those words angered and saddened me more than anything. Even though my dad wasn't the best, I still loved and admired him. I craved his attention, and now there was no way I was going to get it.

Things changed for me after my dad was arrested. The shoes and the clothes stopped. My mama would try to make sure I had nice clothes and shoes, but it was a struggle for her. My dad's parents, Granny and Pops, who had always picked up the slack in place of my dad, stepped up even more. Still, I went from rocking all the new Js to getting clothes off the rack at Walmart. I was sad because I knew my friends would make fun of me, but it was my new reality, so I had to deal with it.

My mind shifted so much after I realized that he was going to be gone for a long time. Going back to school was hard because people had seen the news report and were asking me about what had happened and, even worse, were telling me what had happened. Someone said they heard he had killed a cop, others said he had been caught with packs of dope. The rumors were spreading like wildfire. I wouldn't find out the specifics until several years later. But after those first couple of days, I got angry. I didn't want to talk about my dad and his mistakes. I just wanted to prove everybody wrong when they said I was just like him. I didn't even like people saying I looked like him. I wanted to be better than him in every way possible.

———

For the remaining years of elementary and middle school, I'd start the week off in a terrible mood. I could never explain the feeling when I was a child, nor could I pinpoint why I felt that way, but every Monday and Tuesday, I'd be in school feeling a strong hatred toward everybody. As I reflect, I honestly believe that I had a mood-altering chemical imbalance that was triggered by something in my environment. I didn't want to talk to anybody, and I was constantly on edge, waiting for someone to say or do something that would get me even angrier. I started fighting as a way to release my aggression, but I'd always wait until after school. At school, all I wanted to do was get my work done and not be bothered by anyone. I felt like nobody understood what I was going through, even though I wasn't the only person who had an incarcerated father.

Days when our teacher didn't show up and we didn't have a substitute were the best. We'd get our work in a folder and be sent to another classroom to sit in the back and complete our assignments. Before lunch, I'd be done with all my work for the day, and I could just sit there and sulk. That's all I wanted to do. At the time, I didn't realize that my feelings and thoughts about the world around me were a result of anything other than disliking other people. I would occasionally feel sad about not being able to see my dad, but I couldn't put it into words that articulated my true emotions.

For nearly seven years, I told people that the last time I cried was the night my dad was arrested when I was eight. It was a defense mechanism to mask the hurt that I was actually feeling inside. I fell victim to trying to present myself as this overly masculine guy who didn't show any feelings, a toxic trait, when actually my emotions were eating away at me. Truth is, I cried all the time. Instead of talking to my mama or my friends about what I was feeling, I'd wait until I was in the shower. In there, nobody could hear me cry, and if they saw me after, I could disguise my tears with water from the shower.

I always loved playing basketball outside in the rain, and I didn't realize why for many years. It wasn't easier. Trying to dribble a basketball over a puddle is virtually impossible. But unlike everybody else who would run in the house whenever it began to pour down outside, I'd just be grabbing my ball and putting up shots. I would always think to myself that I was going to make it big during those sessions. *Everybody else sittin' on they ass while I'm gettin' this work in* is what I would mutter in my head. I also thought that people driving by would notice me and say, "That kid is gonna be somebody." I'd work on drills, running up and down the court trying to exhaust myself. I used to wonder if I was putting in more work than Kobe Bryant or Michael Jordan, thinking that maybe people would be chanting my name like theirs one day. The whole time, tears were pouring down my face.

My pain wasn't an exclusive result of my dad's situation, but that was a huge factor. If you've ever experienced having a loved one in prison, you know how much it consumes you. It takes energy wondering if they are being treated humanely by the guards. I would wonder if my dad was being jumped, shanked, or raped in jail, because I knew those acts were common. I never asked him about it, but it was a constant concern of mine.

Of all those things, I assumed he had gotten jumped at least once because he became a Crip. When I found that out, I automatically started to associate myself with the gang. I never thought about joining, but my wardrobe gradually became all blue, I started addressing my friends as "cuz," and I took offense to anyone in opposition. When approached by gang members in my neighborhood who were Gangster Disciples (GDs) or Bloods, there was never a question to my loyalty. "Nah, I'm cool, cuz," was my usual response when people wanted me to be down with them. Thankfully, it never ended with them taking offense or with me taking a beatdown. Most of the time, they were people who had a lot of respect for me, so it wasn't an issue.

My loyalty to the Crips carried on well through college. I didn't learn about historically Black fraternities until going to college, but when I did, I viewed them in a similar light as gangs. They preached a brotherhood that lasted a lifetime, had pride in wearing their colors, and bad-mouthed the other frats to the point of disrespect. I went to a few interest meetings but knew I had a family who didn't flaunt Greek letters, so I passed on all of them. This was a direct result of how much I loved my dad. I thought that anyone who was affiliated with a rival of his gang would be a threat to him, so I didn't want to be associated with them. I saw myself as a lone wolf most of the time anyway.

Visiting my dad in prison was a tough experience. I would usually go with Granny and Pops, but occasionally I would go with one of my dad's girlfriends. While the ride there was full of excitement to finally see him, that feeling quickly faded as we approached. We would pull up to the prison, and I would see the barbed wire along the fences and think about how bad the living situation must have been there. Going in and hearing the buzzer sound as they opened and closed the doors will always stick with me. I had to first be searched and walk through a metal detector, then I had to wait for the corrections officer to buzz me through the first gate. I'd wait for that gate to close before getting buzzed through the second gate. I would walk down the hall and repeat that process. Naive and not considering that all those measures were more so for the prisoners on the other side, I used to think to myself, *Damn, I'm only ten!* Even though I was a visitor, that whole process made me feel like I was a criminal being put in jail, another prisoner.

Initially, the visits were conducted through a glass partition with a phone or speaking vent. After a while, my dad and I knew which seats to go to because the sound quality was better at some compared to the others. I'd be the first one to sit down in the third or fourth chair on the right. He'd come out, and we'd start the usual small talk.

He'd ask, "How you doin' in school?"

"Good. Still got all As," I would respond.

Then he would rapid-fire shoot me a few more questions. "That good! You seen yo' brother?"

"Nope."

"You get my letter?"

"Yeah, I got it." In his letters, he would always tell me how he was working to get out of there so he could be back home with me. After a few minutes, he'd get up and go to another seat to talk to whoever had brought me there. When visitation time was up, he'd get in line with all the other prisoners and walk to the door that led them back to their cells. As he had instructed me, I put my fist up to the glass window and he put his up there too, mirroring mine as if to say we were united through that departing gesture. That was our routine every time.

In an attempt to reduce his prison sentence, my dad got married while incarcerated. Granny and Pops put up a pretty penny for him to tie the knot since he had no way of paying for it. It was so strange to hear he was getting married. It wasn't like he had been in a consistent relationship with his soon-to-be wife. Honestly, I knew her growing up as a child, but I had always thought she was a member of the family, not a potential stepmother. She would occasionally take me on visits to see my dad too. I didn't have a problem with her at all because I had already known her. She was always nice and was cool in my book, although it did irritate me whenever she would call me "son." I felt like she had good intentions, so I never told her how I felt.

Shortly after they got married, while my dad was still in prison, they got a divorce. Knowing my dad, I knew that it wouldn't have lasted long anyway. I had known most of the girlfriends he had had even while he was married, but the last straw with his new wife was actually a result of her having a baby with another person. Since it wasn't his baby, just like that, they parted ways. My grandparents were pissed off to hear that they had wasted money to marry them, and now they had to contribute even more so that they could get divorced.

Granny and Pops put up with a lot from my dad. He had started getting in trouble with the law at a young age, and my grandparents had always bailed him out. Pops always reminded me that my dad hadn't worked five full years in his entire life and how disappointed that made him. Once, my dad even got Pops involved with some of his dealings in the street. Many years ago, my dad had gotten into it with someone over some money owed. That led the other guy to my grandparents' house, where my dad was living at the time, but that day, only Pops was home. The guy showed up with a group of friends and explained to Pops that my dad had instructed them to wait at the house until my dad retuned. Recognizing them, Pops let them in. However, their story was a lie, and they tied Pops to a chair and held him hostage at gunpoint as leverage to get what they wanted from my dad. Fortunately, they didn't hurt Pops much and were eventually satisfied enough to let him go and leave. My dad brought so much drama to their lives, yet they were always there for him whenever he needed them.

After a few years in prison, my dad was able to have contact visits. I was finally able to sit down at a table with him and hug him. We would usually have a meal from the vending machines that were in the visitation area. Sometimes we took pictures in front of the fake tropical backdrop. I always hated taking those pictures. There was nothing about the experience I wanted to remember, and having a picture was a constant reminder of it.

After those visits, I started resenting my dad more than I admired him. I would leave feeling so empty inside, and that void lingered for years. I knew that this experience was nothing I would ever want to put the people I loved through. I knew I didn't have to be locked up in a cage and surrounded by barbed wire and told what to do. Occasionally, he'd go months without calling because the prison was on lockdown or he was in the hole or he just didn't have money on his books. In my young mind, I knew that was no way to live.

The times he would call became a burden more than anything. My mama wouldn't have dared allow me to accept a collect call from him, but if he had money on his books, he could prepay and call a select group of numbers.

"This call will be recorded and monitored. I have a prepaid call from 'It's ya' daddy, booooyyyyyy,' an inmate at a Tennessee state correctional facility. To accept this call, press nine and hold."

We'd get on the call, and it was the same spiel as our visits: how was school, what sports was I playing, why I haven't seen my brother Jarrett (the only one I knew about at the time), and false promise after false promise. I hated when he asked me if I had seen my brother, as if I had much control over that. When I was three years old, my dad had his third son, Jarrett, and for about fourteen years, I had probably only seen him five times that I remember. It wasn't that we didn't get along—I actually loved that I had a little brother—but it just wasn't as easy for us to hang out as my dad imagined. Neither of us could drive, which meant we were dependent on our mamas to takes us to each other's house. My mama didn't always have a car, so that was out of the question most of the time. The few times we did hang out were either over at Pops and Granny's house or at Jarrett's house. One of the few memories I have of Jarrett before our dad went to prison was of the three of us taking "family pictures" at the mall. We all matched in our black-and-white-and-red outfits with our new Jordan Jumpmans. Other than that time, I can't remember when my dad facilitated a hangout. Every time he asked if we had seen each other, I would roll my eyes as I responded no.

Growing up, I had always felt like an only child, even though I knew Jarrett existed. One day at our Pops and Granny's house, before our dad went to prison, I finally got the sense of what it would be like to actually live with my younger sibling. My dad had a fish tank in his room that was full of piranhas. He'd sometimes let us feed them tiny goldfish. We thought it was so cool to see those fish strike and tear the goldfish apart. When Jarrett and I were left alone one day and got bored of watching TV and chasing each other around outside, we started to explore. We headed to the fish tank and saw a piece of dead goldfish floating at the top and dared each other to stick our fingers in to touch it before the piranhas could bite us. We both did it success-fully, but that game wasn't fun enough to continue for long. I then asked Jarrett, "You wanna see somethin' else?" He of course agreed, so I lifted up the mattress to the bed to reveal a pump-action shotgun and a pornographic magazine. His eyes opened wider than the Grand Canyon. We proceeded to flip through the magazine and just touch the shotgun. We didn't pick the gun up or anything, but feeling the cold metal gave us a rush that neither of us had ever felt before. Our hearts were beating fast, and our hormones were raging from seeing the naked women in the magazine. It was exhilarating for our prepubescent minds. By that time, Granny had heard us snickering and decided to come into the room. From her vantage point, all she could see was two boys on their knees with their hands in between the mattress and the box spring. She didn't have a clue what we were doing.

She asked, "What y'all in here doin'?" like she had caught us in the act of something bad.

"It was him!" Those were the first words that came out of Jarrett's mouth as he ripped his hands out from under the bed and pointed at me. I gave him a death stare, but I kept my composure.

"It was him what? What he do?"

"I stuck my hand in the fish tank and touched one of them dead fish," I responded as if that was the worst thing I had done that day. Although misleading, it wasn't a lie.

She told us to be careful messing around with those fish but didn't press the issue further. When she left the room, my heart was pounding even more, and I was furious that he had just ratted me out so easily.

I looked at Jarrett and said, "Ay, you gotta go home." He probably cried after that, but I didn't care. I didn't want to be associated with a little brother who was going to snitch on me like that.

The bond between us grew stronger throughout the years. We often talked about the different experiences we had had while our dad was in prison, and we both remember the phone calls. After I'd press nine and wait, my dad would get on the phone saying the same things. Within five minutes of talking to me, he'd always ask me to dial another number for him, sometimes several numbers, so that he could talk to people who weren't on his approved call list. Without fail, I would do so. I don't remember all the phone numbers I've personally had in my life, but I do remember some of these numbers because they are ingrained in my long-term memory. "Foe-eight-five-oh-nine-foe-oh" almost has a poetic ring to it. I probably dialed that number over a hundred times throughout the years. On the other end of that call was one of his girlfriends. She'd pick up, and my dad would tell me that it was okay for me to put the phone down. He'd call out my name a few times to check and see if I was still on the line, and sometimes I stayed on to see what they were talking about, but most of the time I was so pissed off that I just put the phone down and went on about my day. And like that, my phone call with my dad was over.

———

Growing up without a father in the home was always difficult, especially when I saw other people interact with their dads. During my adolescence, there were always occasions where fathers were invited to see what was happening at school. Seeing my friends and classmates with their dads left me with a void. Regardless of how my friends criticized their dads' parenting styles, the fact that they were there was priceless to me. I had imagined that a complete family structure would magically remove the complications that arose in other aspects of life. The image of a "normal" family tree, one with no broken or extraneous branches, had always signified a symbol of peace to me.

Even before my dad was incarcerated, I had never understood why he didn't want to spend time with me or my brothers. I had realized that not having a relationship with my mama made it more difficult, but that had never stopped Pops and Granny from making time for me. When I found out that Pops wasn't my dad's biological father, I often wondered if that had something to do with my dad's distance.

If he was crying out for his biological father's love and attention to no avail, maybe the only way he knew how to respond was by repeating what he knew.

Absentee fathers have always been prevalent in my community. Between 1960 and 2019, the number of children living in single-mother families in the US went from 8 percent to 21.4 percent.[11] For Black children during that same time period, the percentages went from 20 percent to 46 percent.[12] According to research, children from single-mother households tend to do less well in school; have more emotional and behavioral problems; have worse physical health; are more likely to use drugs, tobacco, and alcohol; and are more likely to become delinquent. Teenage boys in single-mother households are also more likely to become teen fathers. In the long run, adults who have grown up in single-mother households attain lower levels of education, earn less, are more likely to be incarcerated, are more likely to have out-of-wedlock births, and are more likely to be divorced.

My dad had fallen victim to nearly all of those statistics. Although my dad had Pops around for most of his life, being abandoned by his biological father may have prevented him from truly bonding with Pops or viewing him as a father early in his life. That was also the case with how I viewed Mitch during the few years he was with my mama. While I can reflect and try to understand the motivations behind my dad's behaviors, the pain that he caused me can't be undone. While I escaped falling victim to many of those statistics, the emotional, mental, and behavioral issues did arise. As a child, I was not able recognize them for what they were or directly pinpoint the root cause of them. More than anything, the pain and abandonment was usually converted into a motivation to do better.

---

11 US Census Bureau, "Current Population Survey," March and Annual Social and Economic Supplements. Source of 1960 data: US Bureau of the Census, "1960 Census of Population, PC(2)-4B, Persons by Family Characteristics," Tables 1 and 19.

12 Maddow-Zimet, I, Kost K, and Finn S.

CHAPTER FOUR

FILLING A VOID

In 2006, after serving more than seven years, my dad was released from the Turney Center Industrial Complex, a state prison in Only, Tennessee, just an hour west of Nashville. It was such a momentous occasion. I was fifteen years old, and it was the first time we would see each other outside of the penitentiary gates since my eighth birthday. A lot had changed. The night he was released, some of his best friends got together to throw a party for him at a hotel suite. They picked up me, Jarrett, Kevin, and a couple of girls. My brothers and I played video games, but we observed everything else that was going on. It came to a point where every adult in the party was drunk and high. My dad came up to me and my brothers and kept telling us how happy he was to see us and that he was never going to leave us again, hugging and kissing on us belligerently, which reminded me of being at NASCAR Café all over again.

Suddenly, he looked at me and said, "You think you big and strong?" That was his way of challenging me. He wanted to wrestle. He was a wrestler in middle school and used to brag about how good he was. At that point, I was excited. I wanted to show him that I had been working out and that I was a much bigger kid than he remembered when he had first gone to prison.

It was a pivotal moment for me. For so long, I had this image of how big and strapping and strong my dad was, but when we wrestled, I was able to pick him up and throw him down on the bed. I know he was drunk at the time, but he had been working out in the penitentiary. He had stamina and everything, but it didn't matter. I knew at that point, at fifteen years old, that I was bigger and just as strong as my dad. That finally took away the image I had had of him for so long.

While he was locked up, we had always talked about playing basketball, so one day he came to the court with me for a game of one-on-one to see who was the better player. He had bragged about how he would school other people on the yard, so I wanted to see what kind of game he was working with. Again, I quickly realized that I was much more explosive and quicker than he was. I blew past him for easy layups. I saw that he was a subpar shooter, too. The only real advantage he had on me was his weight, and even that wasn't enough. I ran down a loose ball that he was after and slashed past him to take possession. In the process, I made him trip over himself and scrape his knee. That was around the end of our hooping session. I thought to myself, *He gon' need a little practice 'cause this ain't prison ball.* After he had hyped himself up so much, I had had these grand expectations of him, which once again he didn't live up to. It reminded me of a scene from the movie *Space Jam* where Charles Barkley gets his shot blocked by a five-foot teenage girl after losing his skills. After she blocks him, she says, "You're not Charles Barkley; you're just another wannabe who looks like him." Though it had been fun to spend that time with my dad, that's how I felt about him at the end of the day.

The longer he was out of prison, the more it all felt like a sham. Everything that he had written and promised to us over the years about being there for us didn't come true. He came to sporting events, but other than that, it seemed like he didn't care.

Nine months after being released, he wound up back in prison again. I was a junior in high school at MBA when I received a call one morning while getting ready to leave for school. "You know I'm back locked up, right?" My dad delivered the news that made me drop the phone and start crying. I didn't know the specifics of why he was back in prison or what was going on, but I knew one thing—he had lied. He had said that he would never leave again, and he had failed to keep that promise. The uncontrollable feelings that had plagued me during elementary and middle school reemerged.

That day, I put on a facade to get through school. I walked into breakfast with a huge bottle of Gatorade and told my buddies at the table not to touch it as I went to grab my food. When I came back, I saw that my best friend, De'Anté Hughes, had helped himself to a cup full of Gatorade. Without thinking, I took my anger and aggression out on him. I threw food at his face. He threw some back, and I threw more. Then I stood up and proceeded to choke him. He grabbed me and wrestled me down to the floor. In the midst of it all, I came to, and suddenly I realized that he was not the person I was angry at—it was my dad. At that moment, I let go. Our friends managed to pull us off each other. I tried to apologize, but he wasn't hearing it at the time; he grabbed his bag and stormed off.

Later in the day, I talked to some of my coaches, advisors, and friends at MBA to let them know what had happened that morning. Even though I was in such a privileged environment, the troubles from my past were still lingering around me and affecting my behavior. My best friend eventually forgave me; if there was anyone in the world who understood me and the issues I was facing with balancing the troubles of home life with the perfect setting that was our high school, it was him.

I found out later why my dad went back to prison. He was attempting to get back into the same lifestyle that had landed him in prison in the first place. Pops and Granny told me that they had been paying the car note for my dad to help him get back on his feet. At some point, he requested money from them to fix the car, and they obliged. But instead of fixing his car like he had said, his real plan was to buy drugs with it. He drove down to Atlanta and back with the money they had given him, and on his way back, about an hour outside of Nashville, he got pulled over. He was charged with multiple offenses, including aggravated assault, evading arrest, and possession with intent to sell. After hearing that story, I thought to myself how selfish he was to have taken his parents' money and used it to buy drugs and to have lied to them about it. He had children who were depending on him to be there, but he was too self-centered to realize that. It just didn't make sense to me, and it made me angry again.

For the better part of the year, my dad was in prison. I was upset because, that year, we had a talented football team. If he didn't support anything else in my life, he supported my athletic career and would come to every game. During his time in prison, we went on a historic run in Tennessee high school football history. We were ranked in the top twenty-five nationally and boasted an undefeated record of 13–0 with a state championship title under our belts. I wish he had been there to witness that.

When my dad went back to prison, I know it hurt me and my brothers, but it also hurt Granny. She had sacrificed so much for him. She had helped him get a car to go back and forth to work. She had helped him get an apartment. She had helped him pay child support. She did so much for him, and he threw that away for a couple of dollars of drug money. After he went back in, she vowed not to talk to him. While he was in prison the second time and for a full year after he got out, she did not want anything to do with him. She didn't answer his phone calls or let him visit her. I became the intermediary between them.

My dad needed his mom in his life, and he would try his best to coax her into thinking that things were going to be different, that he was going to be better. She did not believe it. All her life, she had done such a great job of working hard and treating people right, only to have a son she resented because he was the complete opposite of what she had expected of him. She told me countless times that I was the baby she had never had; she wanted me to know that she wished she were my actual mama.

When my dad got out of prison the second time, he started dating and living with Jarrett's mama. One day, Kevin, Jarrett, and I got together to come up with a plan. When my dad returned home, we decided we were going to show him the pain he had caused us while he had been away in prison. He had hurt us emotionally and mentally, and so we wanted to hurt him physically. Our intent wasn't to beat him to a pulp, but we wanted to send a message that we were fed up with his actions. When the time came, we managed to lure him out into the yard on the pretense that there was something weird in the grass. Being fresh out of the pen, his skepticism and attention to detail were high, and he knew we were up to something, but he followed us anyway. We dropped him on the ground and started throwing body punches—left, right, left, right, left, right. Though we were kind of playing and laughing, in that moment, I got mad and started throwing heavier punches to do some real damage. We eventually let him up and told him to never leave us again or he would get it worse. It was the only way we knew how to communicate to our dad how we had felt because of his absence over the years.

While he was still dating Jarrett's mama, something else happened. He called me while my brothers and I were all together in my car, so I put him on speakerphone. When I asked him what he was doing, he responded that he was hanging out with a girl. Jarrett had a look of pain and disgust on his face. In his mind, he had thought that things were going to be better and that our dad and his mama were going to be together in true fairy-tale fashion, but that just wasn't the case. Our dad was the same old guy who used to drive me around to different girls' houses when I was a baby.

When I hung up the phone, Jarrett said, "Y'all daddy ain't shit." That was common for us to do whenever we felt upset with our dad— we would refer to him as *your* daddy to the other brothers. In those moments, we wanted to completely disassociate ourselves from him. I felt Jarrett's pain and thought that it wasn't fair for our dad to put us in such a predicament to feel the types of things we were feeling. These experiences had a huge impact on the way we lived our lives and the way we treated women. It also impacted the way we trusted people, an ongoing battle for me and my brothers.

———

When my brothers and I didn't have the words to express how we were feeling, we relied on music to speak for us. Writing and listening to sad songs became a form of therapy for me. Whenever I was mad or upset, I would jot down lyrics to take my mind off whatever had aggravated me. When I was eighteen years old, something took over me one night. At three in the morning, with a lot on my mind and heart, I got up and went to my closet after writing down a couple of lyrics that turned into the hook for a song:

At times life seems real hard, but you gotta be harder.
Don't give excuses, they don't go far, just give me my father.

In that song, I laid out all the frustrations that my brothers and I had with our dad. A lot of it touched on his absence, his caring about our academics and sports but not ever being there to support us in those endeavors, his treatment of women, and his belief that another child being born would make his life that much better. Each verse ended with the lines:

I don't want you to feel sad or think that I'm speakin' out because I'm mad.
I'm just thinkin' about the times I could have had, had I had my dad.

After I recorded the song, I played it for him, my mama, my brothers, and their mamas. There was a resounding consensus of emotion. Everyone who listened to the song broke into tears. It was so true. It was so real. It was so painful. It had so much context, and it was also applicable to a lot of other people's lives regarding how they felt about their men who chose the streets over their children and families.

It resonated so much with people because it described the impact of something that is normalized in the Black community and in the lives of their children—absentee fathers. For me and my brothers, we were becoming men without any guidance. I take that back. We were becoming men with improper guidance.

All my emotions culminated in a song full of pain and passion. After I shared that song, things got a little better between me and my dad. As the years went on, we grew closer and hung out more. We shared some intimate moments. We became good friends, and at times, I would say we were best friends. It was the relationship I'd always wanted with my father. Although he continued to do things that I didn't necessarily agree with, I accepted him for who he was. Without that grace, I don't think we would've ever been close. I had to look past some awful things: his treatment of women, his irresponsibility in caring for the dogs he "bred," his recreational drug use, and his choices to continue living a criminal lifestyle.

I knew my dad was highly intelligent—he demonstrated this often—but he focused his efforts on illegal acts. I always wished that he would just clean himself up and live a life that would bring everyone around him less stress, but I didn't allow his lifestyle to keep us from bonding. To have a relationship with my father, I had to forgive him for his past. I used his life experiences as life lessons of what not to do. That was the method I took, and it led to a good relationship with my dad for the time being.

I even had to forgive him for going to prison for our relationship to grow. One of the best things you can do for your own mental state is to forgive. Forgive yourself for the things in your past that you can no longer change. Learn from your mistakes and strive for continued improvement. Forgive the perpetrators who violated your peace and joy. By holding on to resentment and anger, we are only hurting ourselves further, which turns us cold and bitter. Forgiveness takes time, but it liberates you from the shackles that someone else has over your mind. By learning to forgive, you open yourself up to loving. And when you are able to love, you will be able to live freely.

———

Although my dad's nickname was Snake, I felt like it should've been Cat because there were countless times when he cheated death as if he had nine lives. There was a story from when I was a baby of a time when it was thought that he had died. My mama was outside holding me on the porch at Pops and Granny's house where my dad lived at the time. My dad was preoccupied with working on his car. Out of nowhere, a guy came up from behind the house with a gun and aggressively but stealthily told my mama to shut up and take that baby, me, into the house. A few moments went by, and she heard multiple gunshots. My mama just knew my dad had been killed, or at the very least, shot. Instead, as we looked out the window, we saw my dad chasing the man down the street, shooting at him. Over the course of my life, I've had recurring dreams of the image that my mama described in that story. I often see it so vividly. For my dad to have been working on a car with his head down and focusing on whatever he was fixing, it's nothing but miraculous that he escaped death that day.

My dad loved to drink and indulge in recreational drug use. What made it even worse was that he would do all of that while driving or riding motorcycles. It was crazy to think how he had survived all the accidents he had had on the road while living so recklessly. We would drive through town, and he would point out poles or trees that he had sideswiped in the years past from his wild driving. This happened on multiple occasions and resulted in many broken bones and a few surgeries, but he survived them all.

The story from the night he was arrested after my eighth birthday party introduced me to another one of his near-death experiences. It wasn't until one of his parole hearings many years later that the details were revealed to me. Apparently, he had gotten pulled over on the interstate, and the police officer, instead of pulling up behind him, pulled up in front of him for whatever reason. He then proceeded to walk toward my dad's car. According to the police officer, he saw what he thought was a gun, which was actually just a cell phone, so he drew his own gun. He then jumped on the hood of the car and fired a few shots that went through the passenger seat. At that moment, my dad sped off, and the officer fell off the car hood and suffered a concussion. My dad's kneejerk reaction to preserve his life resulted in the attempted homicide strike against him. My dad hightailed it but was eventually apprehended sometime later. I was so surprised to hear that story in the parole hearing. Until that day, I had no idea what had transpired that night. That was the lifestyle my dad was living. He could have been killed by a police officer. He could have been dead on the side of the road, but instead he managed to beat death again.

Something else happened at that parole hearing that I'll never forget. When they recounted the story of what had happened that night, we all got the sense that they were going to deny his parole. Jarrett's mama pleaded to the judge that my dad had children and that he needed to be home to take care of them. She continued with a compelling argument. The judge heard her out and responded as if she had heard that argument a million times. "Ma'am, we do not allow children to affect our decision in these matters, because if he had been taking care of his children instead of breaking the law, he wouldn't be in this situation in the first place." I remember her comment as clear as day, and I thought it was very true. It reminded me that it was his decisions that had taken him away from us. It wasn't the police's fault. It wasn't the judge's fault. My dad was to blame.

As I got older and learned more about true American history, I began to understand, too, that although my dad had made those decisions himself, society had also created the perfect storm that put him in the position to make those choices in the first place. I was forced to think deeper about the prison system. One thing that has always saddened me is that, growing up, many people in my community could name more state and federal penitentiaries than colleges or universities. Why was that the case? As highlighted so poignantly in *The New Jim Crow* by Michelle Alexander, beginning with the Thirteenth Amendment, which abolished slavery in the United States except as punishment for a crime, laws were passed that unfairly targeted Black men in the criminal justice system. One in three Black men spend time in prison, while only one in seventeen white men meet the same fate.[13]

In 1970, around the time my dad was born, the prison population was 357,292.[14] But around the same time, the incarceration rate for Black men skyrocketed and became much higher compared to other races. There was a war on crime, a time when mental health illnesses like drug addiction were criminalized because Black people were fighting a battle with the highly addictive crack cocaine. There was a war on drugs, where crack cocaine was treated as more illegal than cocaine because crack was mainly found in Black communities. Even drugs that would later be legalized in many parts of the country, namely weed, landed many Black men in prison for unreasonable amounts of time, sometimes for life. Those political agendas were euphemisms for a war on Black people. In fact, 75 percent of people in state prison for drug conviction are people of color, although Blacks and whites use drugs at roughly the same rates.[15] There are currently 2.3 million people in the nation's prisons and jails.[16] In 2016, Black men were 6.5 percent of the population but made up 40.2 percent of the prison population.[17] The odds were stacked against my dad and people just like him, including many other absentee fathers.

In addition to that, when poverty, crime, and drugs are all you see and all you know, what else would you do? Selling drugs, robbing people, and committing other crimes were all a means to an end. It was a way of getting money when there were so few opportunities available in the community. It was a perpetuating cycle that led to fatherless homes. Fatherless homes of children who were bound to commit the same crimes

---

13 Bonczar, Thomas P. "Prevalence of Imprisonment in the US Population, 1974-2001." *Bureau of Justice Statistics (BJS)*, 2003, www.bjs.gov/index.cfm?ty=pbdetail.

14 DuVernay, Ava, and Jason Moran. *13TH*. USA, 2016.

15 Ibid.

16 Sawyer, Wendy, and Peter Wagner. "Mass Incarceration: The Whole Pie 2020." Prison Policy Initiative, 24 Mar 2020, www.prisonpolicy.org/reports/pie2020.html.

17 DuVernay, Ava, and Jason Moran.

and become absentee fathers as well. Those were all things that I took into consideration when justifying the actions of my dad, but it was also the same thought process that made me want to put an end to the cycle.

———

When I was a child, I remember thinking about whether or not I would cry if my dad died. My answer back then was that I wouldn't because I didn't have any kind of relationship with him to care enough to express that kind of emotion. Sometimes I would say that I wouldn't even bother going to his funeral. It was that bad. I held that sentiment for nearly a decade. It wasn't until we got closer that those feelings started to evolve. My hypothetical "what if" was tested one day when I was twenty-one years old. I got a call that my dad had been in a bad accident. He had been rear-ended by an eighteen-wheeler on the interstate. The story from his perspective was that he was on the verge of running out of gas, so he pulled over to the shoulder and filled his gas tank with a gas can that he had in the back of his truck. As he got back into the car to turn on the ignition, the truck slammed into him.

I didn't know how serious it was until I got to the hospital and saw him in the bed hooked up to tubes and monitors. He had bandages all over his body and face. I was told that he had broken bones near his eye and in his spine, as well as a few more injuries. When I looked at him in the bed, I thought there was a chance that he wouldn't make it out alive. I cried at that possibility. I wasn't prepared to lose him after building something that I had wanted for so long in my life—a good relationship with my dad.

More accurate versions of that story were revealed later through talks with my dad and at the court hearing when he sued the trucking company. Based on what I gathered, the story went something like this: my dad, along with two girls who happened to be strippers, drove down to Alabama for a party. The girls performed and my dad testified to having had something to drink and smoking weed. On the way back, the story pretty much aligned with what I had been told before. My dad had me and Kevin testify about how the injuries had affected his life. It wasn't until after we testified that we found out about the drinking and smoking, or at least his admitting to it in court. I think it goes without saying that he didn't win the case.

He eventually recovered from that accident, and just like a Final Destination film, he had escaped death again. However, that accident might've become the root cause for a more recent scare. After the surgeries to repair his injuries, he was prescribed strong opioids and other types of medication. In line with the national opioid crisis, he became addicted. Since that accident in 2012, I doubt there has been a day when he hasn't taken at least a couple of pills. He eventually moved to Huntsville, which is an hour and a half hours south of Nashville. To feed his addiction, he'd go to a pill mill in Clarksville, an hour north of Nashville. Sometimes those visits at the unethical clinics would take eight hours or longer because the prescribing "doctor" would book so many patients in a day that nothing ran efficiently. It's disgusting when you think about how places like this contribute to the national epidemic of opioid addictions. On one of my dad's trips to Clarksville, he overdosed while driving. He was somehow rushed to a hospital and was provided medical treatment in time to save his life.

———

We started to bond even closer after I graduated from high school. That period overlapped with the time when Pops started to have severe heart problems. His heart wasn't functioning properly, and he was set to have the open-heart triple-bypass surgery previously mentioned. My dad and I went to the hospital together and saw him hooked up to so many machines that he basically looked like he was already dead in the hospital bed.

Before knowing what the outcome would be, we just held each other while we cried and told Pops that it wasn't his time yet. It was the first time that I felt close to my dad. Feeling his pain at the possibility of losing his stepdad made me reflect on how it would feel for me to lose my dad. It was something that I knew I wasn't ready for.

My dad and I shared a lot of intimate details about our lives with each other, as well as crazy experiences and stories that I don't think I will ever mention to other people. Some things are just better left unsaid. Other things have a statute of limitations associated with them. It had taken the better part of twenty-two years, but during this time in my early twenties, I felt I had finally gotten to a place where I loved the relationship that I had with my dad.

The one strain that we had in our relationship was my disapproval of his criminal lifestyle. I knew that as hard as it was for him to maintain a living as a felon, some of the things he was involved in would ultimately result in his incarceration again. Just two years after feeling that our relationship had blossomed, he called me while crying because he had made another mistake. Before he could finish explaining what had happened, I already had a feeling that my intuition was right.

"I'm so sorry, Reggie. I done fucked up." He told me he had been arrested and that the crime might send him back to prison.

"I don't want to go back to jail. Man, I *can't* go back," he said as he sniffled. I had no idea what was going on. I told him to calm down and that I was on my way to see him. When I got to his house, he was sitting outside in his car with tears running down his face. He was holding a gun. I asked him what was wrong, and he proceeded to tell me the story about how he had gotten caught selling drugs again, but this time to a confidential informant (CI). The bullets in the gun were intended for the CI.

I reasoned with him with a clear mind and let him know that his intended actions were only going to make his situation worse. I told him that catching a body wasn't going to help him escape prison; it would only add to his sentencing. With his criminal history, there was a possibility that he would never see the light of day. I wondered why he hadn't thought of all the consequences in the first place before attempting to sell drugs again, but I guess the reward was worth the risk. We sat in the car, crying with each other for a long time and talking about how this wasn't what he needed to do. Even though I knew he didn't want to hear it, I tried to convince him that he should just face his consequences and that nobody's life had to be taken in the process. We eventually calmed down. I went my way. He went his. Ultimately, all his charges were dropped. I wanted him to use that as a wake-up call to finally turn his life around. If prison was the last place in the world he wanted to go, I thought, *Then don't do anything that would lead to a prison sentence.* It seemed simple enough to me, but I also didn't have the pressures of a convicted felon. I still hoped it got through to him though.

That was the relationship that my dad and I had cultivated. Whenever anything went wrong, we talked to each other about it. When things went well, we celebrated it. Through the ups and downs, we were there for each other. I felt like we had finally made up for the many years when we had had no relationship at all. My behavior and thoughts had become healthier than they had been in my younger years when he was absent. And while I couldn't change the past and forget about the damage that had been caused, I could respond positively to the growth we had made. A void that had once been there no longer existed. Emotionally, it felt like we had soothed a long-standing wound with aloe and a bandage. But as good as it felt to resolve those issues, that wound was later pried open.

CHAPTER FIVE

AREA OF REFUGE

A special type of love exists between grandparents and grandchildren. My relationship with Pops and Granny was starkly different from that between me and Big Mama. Because my father was in the streets, he didn't do much in the realm of raising me, but his parents picked up the slack. Initially, they were skeptical as to whether I was truly their grandchild, mainly because the story they had been fed by my father was that I didn't belong to him—the same stories, rather lies, he told about my brothers Kevin and Jarrett too. A saying I used to hear growing up goes, "Mama's baby, daddy's … maybe," meaning that without a paternity test, you never know if the man said to be a child's dad is actually the father.

Despite all that, once I was placed in their arms for the first time, they instantly fell in love with me, and I fell in love with them. They were true godsends for me during the times when there was a lot of drama at our house with my mama or with Big Mama and Popeye. To escape the stresses at home, I would visit them and, whether it would be for a few hours or a few weeks, I would enjoy every moment of it. It was a different living situation than what I experienced at home. There wasn't any screaming back and forth. There was no drama. Although they may have threatened to spank me if I was out of line, they never did.

During the many years when I would go over to their house, I never attempted to go outside and meet the kids in their neighborhood, because everything I wanted was within the walls of their home. Most of the time, I was curled up at the foot of the couch with Pops, watching old Western movies or horror films. If I got tired of that, I would go into the room with Granny and watch whatever soap opera or talk show she was into at the time. If I ever did go outside, it would be with one of them. A lot of times, it was just me and Granny because Pops drove trucks all around the country and would often be out of town. However, whenever he was in town, I was his shadow. Pops was much more social than Granny, and we would go on trips to other family members' houses where he would usually play cards and talk trash to anyone and everyone he could. I would be stuck to his hip until I saw a cousin my age; then I would finally run off to play with them.

Granny and I had our own outing ritual. Nearly every weekend, we would hop into the car, take back roads to the nearest Walmart or flea market, get a few things, and head back down the main road so we could stop at KFC. We took the back roads mainly to look at all the nice houses in the neighborhoods we would pass, a routine that started when I was young, because those houses had the best Christmas lights. Although we did some of the most mundane things, I loved our time spent together.

As I got older, my memory started to get fuzzy on past events, and Granny would always remind me of how when I was a young child, I would tell her that I never forgot anything. She would follow that up by asking me if I remembered stories that I had no recollection of because they had happened so long ago. She loved reminding me of the times when my parents would leave me with her and Pops for a night or a weekend, and how they would explicitly instruct her not to give me a pacifier because they thought I had outgrown it. I was still a baby, but the expectations were that I was supposed to act much older than I was. In fact, they had thrown all of my pacifiers away, but what they didn't know was that Granny always kept several backups in her nightstand, and just as soon as they would pull away, I would head to the nightstand and pop a pacifier in my mouth and curl up in bed with her. Upon their return, I would hear the music blaring from my dad's car, and I would jump up and toss the pacifier behind the bed and act like I was asleep when they walked in so I could stay with her another night. That sequence of events epitomized the relationship I had with my grandparents. The loud music was a metaphor for the chaos that I would be returning to by getting back in the car and driving off with my parents. To avoid that, I would pretend to sleep so I could enjoy more moments of peace. The definition of *pacify*, "to bring peace to," was literally what the moments with my grandparents did for me. Despite the instability of my daily life, time spent with them was nothing but peaceful.

When Granny finally had to take me home, she would give me a consolation. She told me that if I ever cried, I could call her and she would come right over to pick me back up. And according to her, my response every time would be, "I cry last night," as a way to skip the whole waiting period. She had the biggest soft spot for me, but she also had to go to work the next day before I could be back with her the next evening.

Starting when she was seventeen years old, Granny worked for an insurance company her entire life, and she enjoyed every minute of it. When I got older, I realized how much she liked it there. There would be times when I would pull up to her house and she wouldn't be home because she was voluntarily working overtime. She didn't do it for the money; she was doing it because she simply enjoyed it. On the other hand, Pops spent his entire career as a driver of eighteen-wheelers, moving families all over the country. His job was a lot less predictable, and sometimes he would be on the road for weeks or months at a time. But just like Granny, he loved what he did.

Of the men who have had great positive impacts on my life, the first person who comes to mind is Pops. I watched how hard he worked, and I saw his never-ending commitment to his family. He showed me that the world didn't have to be a dark and cold place where everyone fended for themself in a cutthroat type of way. Instead, he taught me through his actions that you could be extremely generous and selfless and still enjoy all that life has to offer. He taught me many things and inspired me to follow my dreams. I could tell that he believed in me simply by the way he would talk to me and the things he would say. "You gone go to college, get married, and buy you a house" was a refrain from my childhood that only Pops uttered. No one around me was speaking those type of words to me because it just wasn't a part of the reality they had experienced. Other than buying a house with Granny, Pops hadn't experienced these other things either. The way he would phrase things instilled confidence without putting too much pressure on me. It made want to go make him proud. He would say things like, "Do the best you can—that's all you can do—and watch it pay off."

Strangely enough, Pops was my first drinking buddy. When I was nine years old, he let me take sips of his beer, Miller High Life. He was doing it to teach me how it tasted so that I wouldn't like it, but I ended up enjoying it. His plan had backfired, but I knew not to drink anything without his permission. The first time I got drunk, I was ten years old. During Christmas break, I'd had two beers while on the phone with my dad, who was in prison at the time. I kept repeating, "Everything feel like a dream." Everyone thought it was hilarious because I was so young, but I can only imagine how upset they would've been had my alcohol intake in my early years become detrimental to my life. I've always been cognizant of my alcohol intake because my dad's biological father, Archie, died at the age of forty-four from liver disease as a result of an addiction to alcohol. I also saw addictive tendencies in my father, and I knew that I had to be cautious with it. I stayed committed to not allowing alcohol to affect my life in a negative way, and I didn't have a drink after my ten-year-old drunkenness until I was twenty-one.

———

Following my seventh-grade school year, I was ready to start making money. After seeing the cable man installing services for someone in my building, I got curious. He used a key to open a lockbox for the cable hookups. After he left, I inspected the lockbox and discovered it was actually broken and didn't require a key at all. I found the coax cable that corresponded with our apartment and screwed it in. Like magic, we had cable. I simply slid the cover back on the lockbox and went inside to enjoy the shows I had missed out on.

My entrepreneurial juices started to flow. Being bored, needing money, and seeing an opportunity, I decided to break the boxes on all the apartment units. A crime, nonetheless, but I was young, dumb, and broke. One of my friends joined my endeavor, and we decided that we'd go door to door and tell people that we would get their cable turned on for just twenty dollars, and at the end of the month, we would charge a ten-dollar service fee to keep it on. Our plan was to beat the cable company to the boxes at the end of the month and unscrew all the cables that we had hooked up so that they wouldn't be on to us. Once they were gone, we would go back and screw them in. Of course, some people already had cable, some people told us off, but there were enough families who wanted cheaper cable—and we were the solution. Before we knew it, we had clientele.

That business endeavor didn't last too long. We failed to account for the fact that the cable company didn't always come out on the same day every month. When people wanted to begin or end their service, the company would schedule a technician to the job. A little over a month went by before they were hip to our scheme and struck back. All the boxes that we had broken into were suddenly replaced with reinforced lockboxes that were welded together much better than the previous ones. We couldn't break them to save our lives. Shortly thereafter, our business was over. People who saw us around wondered why their cable had been turned off, and we had to tell them that the jig was up. Everybody understood; plus, they had already gotten the benefit of a month and a half of reduced cable, and they weren't too mad. I can't say the same about the cable company, though. But I considered it payback for all the times they disconnected our service while I was watching a Disney Channel movie.

The motivations that led me to that business are the same ones for young Black men who begin selling drugs. With little exposure to the multitude of jobs available, lack of opportunities to pursue the proper training and education to obtain those jobs, and discrimination in hiring practices, many young Black men are forced to do what they see and know. I happened to see and know the process of hooking up cable units. At that time, had I possessed the same desperation for money and witnessed a drug deal, chances are my business model would've been different. To combat negative behavior, we require exposure and opportunity to good things. Too often, in neighborhoods like mine, young men are only exposed to being an entertainer, an athlete, or a drug dealer. Opportunity is presented through sports leagues and schools to pursue a career in sports, and older drug dealers provide opportunities for younger ones when they recognize a need and interest. If the same were to be done in other career fields, outcomes in these communities would be vastly different.

Prior to my mediocre stint in the cable business, I sold T-shirts, candy, and fireworks, utilizing my inherent knowledge of economic concepts, such as supply and demand, to be successful. The summer after my seventh-grade year, I worked with Pops traveling the country and moving families to their new homes. Pops had agreed to pay me fifty dollars per move, and I was more than satisfied with that. This happened during the last summer before I was to go off to MBA, so I felt some regret in not being able to spend the summer with my friends, but my time with Pops proved to be much more valuable.

We made our way up the East Coast, taking pictures and stopping in random cities I had never heard of. The trip took us as far northeast as Watertown, New York, a small town 328 miles northwest of New York City and about forty-five minutes from the Canadian border. Our first job was in Suffolk, Virginia. I wasn't, and still am not, a morning person, and that job started bright and early. When I got out of the truck that next morning (we had bunk beds in the back of the truck where we would sleep most nights), Pops had already hired some help and gotten started on the job without me. As I walked up to the house to meet the owners, rubbing sleep out of my eyes, they told me to get to the bus stop if I didn't want to be late to school. In Nashville, we had gotten out of school nearly a month before the kids in Virginia, so the owner had thought I was a random neighborhood child curious about their move. Pops told them that I was his little helper and that I would be moving them. They quickly put me to work. As I passed

Pops rolling out some boxes on a little red dolly, he told me that he was only going to pay me forty dollars for the day because I had woken up late and hadn't gotten a full day's work in. I was hot, but he was right. Our agreement had been fifty dollars for a full move. It taught me not to sleep when there was work to be done and money to be made. I literally couldn't afford to miss out on another payday, so I used that as motivation; no matter how tired I was, every morning we had to work.

Trying to impress Pops, I went hard. I would pack four or five boxes of books on a dolly and pull them on the truck myself. If he needed help with something like a dresser or washer-and-dryer unit, I was there in a skip. He even taught me a trick to carrying large items like that on my back by using long straps as leverage. I had "that young man's energy," he would always tell me. Pops frequently told me that I was a much better worker than my dad had been at my age. When he was younger and would go on trips with Pops, my dad was often caught lying down in the air-conditioning, sometimes even sleeping on the job. "Yo' daddy used to kick boxes. If they didn't move, he wouldn't even try to pick them up," Pops used to tell me. I was proud knowing that I had outworked my dad. It made me think that if I kept it up, my outcome in life would be vastly different from his.

We made a pit stop back in Nashville before heading west. When Pops told me about a bridge in Louisiana that stretched over twenty miles, I couldn't believe it and looked forward to crossing it. I could tell when we were nearing Louisiana because the air got extremely humid. I usually rode with my head out of the window because Pops was a chain-smoker. He would go through a carton filled with two hundred cigarettes in a week like he was trying to beat the world record for most Tareytons smoked. I couldn't stand the smell of the smoke. Well, other than the first light of a cigarette, which smelled different from the rest. I found myself anticipating his next cigarette just to smell that first puff. There was something in the chemistry that made you want to try them with an enchanting first inhale. Thank goodness I never did. After getting my whiff of the first puff, I would go back to hanging my head out of the window. At the time, I had long hair that was braided, so all the smoke lingered on me. I smelled like an old trucker, but I didn't mind. I was just glad to be on the road doing what Pops loved to do so much.

When we were nearing the bridge, Pops made sure I was awake. I wiped the sweat off my face after being drenched by the humid summer air and just marveled at being over the water for so long. So many questions were going through my mind, but two stood out: "What happens if your car breaks down?" and "Can the police pull you over on this bridge?" My mama and I had never had a reliable car growing up, and we often broke down everywhere. When I was ten years old, she got her first car, a teal Chevy Beretta Indy pace car that was used in NASCAR races. I don't know how she stumbled across that car. The other question about the police stemmed from the distrust and hatred I had of law enforcement at the time. In the hood, we were taught that the police were bad. The police weren't there to protect and serve but rather to harass and intimidate.

The summer was coming to a close, and I had to get back to get ready for school. I made about $2,000 that summer but ended with about $1,800 after food, souvenirs, and some shopping. What would I do with my $1,800? I liked how all that money felt in my hands, so my first inclination was to just save it. But I was reminded quickly that I needed to spend some of it on new clothes and supplies for school. I was fine with that because that meant I'd still have about $1,500, a lot more money to save than I'd ever had in my life. At least that's what I thought to myself, but it seemed everybody else had a different plan for me and my money.

I finally returned home and was welcomed by my mama. She asked me how the trip had gone, and I gave her some high points, but I left out the bit about the money. Days went by, and I was feeling the pressure of telling my mama and Big Mama how much money I had made. In the back of my head, I knew that as soon as they found out, they would ask me for a loan or ask me to buy something for them. It was one of the main reasons why, when I was younger, I would hide money in the air vents, soles of my shoes, and broken window frames—basically anyplace where I knew people wouldn't find it. It was my nature to hide it if I wanted to keep it for myself. I did it by necessity.

I eventually cracked and told them how much money I had. Big Mama asked to borrow some, but my mama told me that I should buy a car. I was too young to get a hardship license, so I didn't think that I needed one. She finally revealed her hand and asked me to buy *her* a car. At the time, we didn't have a car at all. The Chevy pace car was long gone—it had caught fire while my mama was on the interstate a few years before and burned to the ground on the side of the road. We had been without a car for a while and living in a new part of town where we could get a quick ride to the grocery store, so it wasn't a high priority.

I was upset that my mama had asked me to spend my hard-earned money on a car, so the next weekend I went to my grandparents' house, I told Pops. He told me that if she needed a car, I should get her one.

"That's yo' mama," he reminded me, as if I had all of a sudden forgotten what my relationship was with her.

I fought back, "But why should I get her a car with the money I worked hard for? She could've worked and made her own money and got herself a car." My mama had jobs on and off but never maintained employment for an extended period. Being a child with no bills or mouths to feed myself, the fact that there were few opportunities of employment for her never dawned on me.

He still wasn't on my side. "She raised you, and feed you, and do everything for you. Least you could do is get her a car. You'll make the money back. Plus, how you expect to get back and forth from school?"

That was the dagger. How was I going to get to and from my new school? MBA was a private school, and they didn't have a busing system like all the public schools in town. I knew this when I had applied and figured that I'd just catch the city bus every day until I figured something else out. I knew I'd be embarrassed hopping off the city bus every day while everybody else pulled up in their BMWs and Mercedes-Benzes, but that was something I was going to have to face.

I eventually conceded and bought a car for my mama after Pops agreed to reimburse me for half the cost. It was a 1988 box-shaped Buick that we got from one of my cousins' boyfriends for eight hundred dollars. As you could imagine, it wasn't the nicest whip, but it was something that could get us from A to B. It was a former dope boy's car, so it came with a nice radio and loud subwoofers. I couldn't tell you what size the subs were because the key didn't work to unlock the trunk. In fact, it didn't even on the doors to the car, so they stayed unlocked. It wasn't long before the nice radio was stolen.

That was my first time truly experiencing the Black Tax, the economic burden that Black people face to support their parents or other family members. The Black Tax leaves the donor with less money to save or invest, thus keeping a would-be successful, productive individual in the cycle of poverty—the reason that leads to the Black Tax to begin with. At least I would have a ride to school.

Many people have criticized the shallow definition of the Black Tax, as it could be applied to any racial group. Instead, a more systemic issue is raised. Shawn Rochester, author of *The Black Tax: The Cost of Being Black in America*, examines how the Black Tax, which he defines as the financial cost placed on Black Americans by people and/or institutions who have conscious and unconscious anti-Black racial biases, creates a massive financial burden on Black households that dramatically reduces their ability to leave a substantial legacy for future generations.

Rochester poses the question: How is it that after four hundred years, forty-plus million Black Americans (approximately 14 percent of the US population) still only own 2 percent of American wealth?[18] He explores the racial biases that have perpetuated those findings as they relate to many forms of discrimination in the labor market, education system, housing, financing, and even the GI Bill. He highlights that 75 percent of all Americans have an implicit preference for white people over Black people, a figure that was determined by Harvard University's Implicit Association Test.[19] Moreover, he attempts to demonstrate the economic head start that slavery, sharecropping, and convict leasing provided for white Americans by quantifying the value of the once 100-percent tax on Black labor, also referred to as slavery, making America the wealthiest country in the world. Rochester roughly estimates that the economic value of enslaved Black people in today's dollars is $22 trillion; however, the net worth of Black Americans is only $1.5 trillion.[19] He estimates that another $15 trillion dollars was extracted from Black Americans during the Jim Crow era.[19]

Whether or not those estimates are valid, a couple of things are obvious: white Americans benefited for centuries of free labor, and Black Americans were and continue to be economically discriminated against. The pervasiveness of the Black Tax extends from the most economically successful Black Americans all the way to the most economically disadvantaged.

As I saw in my own life, the Black Tax often leads to family tension. Additionally, financial concerns are one of the many causes of

---

18 Rochester, Shawn D. *The Black Tax: The Cost of Being Black in America and What You Can Do to Help Create the 6 Million Jobs and 1.4 Million Businesses That Are Missing in the Black Community.* Good Steward Publishing, 2017.

19 Ibid.

mental-health stressors like anxiety and depression. As a thirteen-year-old, I didn't realize the impact that the Black Tax would have on my mental health and the health of the relationships in my family, but it affected them both.

———

Although Pops and Granny were basically saints to me, they still had their flaws. They both smoked a bunch of cigarettes. Granny eventually stopped, but Pops was a chain-smoker who seemed to live off nicotine. Pops, in the hopes that I wouldn't follow in those footsteps, also told me about the times he had hit women and cheated on them. Granny's advice was mostly about taking care of my health because "You get old fast," as she would put it. The biggest vice that they both shared was their addiction to gambling. Throughout my childhood, "the number lady" would come knocking on the door to collect the lottery numbers and cash for the night, every night. "The number lady" was an employee of the numbers house that reported to "the big house," an underground lottery system based off the Illinois or Kentucky lotteries because there was no lottery in Tennessee at the time. I didn't know then how much money they were putting into the lottery system, but it turned out to be a ridiculous amount. There were nights when they played their numbers and the total would come out to be well over two hundred dollars, and that was a daily occurrence. Granny had a ritual that she called her "rundown," which typically took her about an hour or more. She had created a spreadsheet of every number that had fallen in the past several years and would look for patterns to determine what numbers she wanted to play that day. It was similar to modern-day computer algorithms. Pops was much simpler when it came to his numbers. He picked numbers he liked and played those each and every night.

I learned a lot about how to play numbers. When I was ten years old, they allowed me to play my own for the first time and gave me some money to do so. My first inclination was to just put the cash in my pocket, but they encouraged me to play to show me the ropes. I played a few numbers, including my birthday, 325 (March 25). That night, I sat and watched the nightly news with much more excitement than ever before. The numbers started to come up: the first number was three, and the second number was two. I started to think that I was a lucky charm. The last number came up—it was a seven. I was so close, but close didn't win me any money. What it did was make me want to play more to get that rush of potentially hitting. I was so close that I thought if I just played one more time, I would get it. After a few more times of playing, I decided that gambling wasn't for me. I didn't like to lose, and I had no control over it.

In addition to playing the lottery, Granny loved to go to bingo. She would go every weekend she could. Her dream was always for me to turn eighteen and go with her. Although I avoided gambling, I appeased her one time and got to see her in action. She was a professional. When I was there, she spent a ton of money, but she made a bunch as well. I'm not sure what the net outcome was, but she enjoyed it, so I don't think she cared too much about that. Pops wasn't into bingo; instead, he frequented casinos. He would go to a casino and mindlessly play slot machines for hours. He would play until he ran out of his last dollar and would walk away seemingly unfazed. Whether it was a couple hundred bucks or tens of thousands of dollars, he didn't mind putting it at risk in the casino, as long as he got the entertainment. The summer I traveled with him, he would inevitably stop at the nearest casino. When he got back to the truck, he would ask to hold some of the money that he had already paid me until we got to the next truck stop because he was out of cash. I was always hesitant. I figured if he had run out of all the cash that he had, why should I have the confidence that the cash I'd give him wouldn't disappear as well? He would always uphold his end of the deal, but it seemed like a terrible waste of money to me.

Granny and Pops would often comment on how tight or stingy I was with my money, but the reality was I just didn't like the feeling of being broke. I knew that if I saved my money, when it came time to get something I truly wanted, I would be able to do so. But that wasn't the mentality of everyone around me. Pops would often tell me to spend my money because "You can't take it with you." It wasn't until he had retired that this sentiment changed.

Other than those bridge loans to get Pops from the casino to the truck stop, they never asked me for anything. They provided so much support for me financially and emotionally by being a safe haven for me, and they never expected anything of me in return, other than to be there and to love them. Granny was always good for a twenty-dollar bill that she had tucked away to give to me right before I left the house—she would hand it to me after giving me a goodbye hug and kiss. Throughout my childhood, they provided things for me that I probably wouldn't have had otherwise. When I wanted a basketball goal, I woke up in the middle of the night on Christmas Eve to see Pops acting as Santa Claus with a large box with a hoop on it. When I was short on tuition for private school, Pops made sure that I was able to attend school by footing the difference so that I got the best education possible.

He was just that generous, and it didn't stop with me. He provided for a lot of people in the family. All those years, he had led me to believe that he was a struggling truck driver, but in reality, he was making a great living. In fact, there were times when he was making over $150,000 a year driving. That type of income, plus having a lot of his expenses paid for by his company, could've resulted in his ability to save a bunch of money or to accumulate many assets, but that didn't happen. Although he made a lot of money, his generosity to family members who were in need and his gambling habits left him flat broke year in and year out.

When it came time for him to retire after a life of physically demanding work, he had no money to his name other than what he was going to be getting from Social Security. It crushed me to see how hard he had worked, only to struggle in retirement. All I wanted was for him to have everything he wanted and deserved, but his financial decisions over the years had made that hard. He taught me a lesson from his mistakes: I had to take care of my own finances, and to take care of my family, I had to take care of myself first. Just like they tell you on airplanes, in the event of an emergency, make sure your oxygen mask is put on properly before helping someone else. If you aren't taken care of, you will be of no help to anyone else. I think about the generational curses that he could have changed had he had better financial literacy and better money habits. When I reflect back on my reasons for starting a career and a company in personal finance, I know that witnessing his financial outcomes played a major role.

Most people associate wealth with having a lot of money. However, like success, wealth is relative. You can be wealthy if you have an abundance of whatever it is you truly desire. It just so happens that our society forces us to desire money over many other things because of its necessity in our daily lives. Even when we associate wealth with money, wealth is not a particular dollar amount but rather a mindset. If you have a wealthy mindset, the money follows. Wealth requires consistency, hard work, and discipline. It requires having knowledge and implementing that knowledge to achieve a set goal. It is about adding value to the lives of others. Money is a byproduct of all those things, rather than the end goal.

Get-rich-quick schemes put money as the end goal; however, *rich* is fleeting while *wealth* is long-lived. Getting rich quick is like going to the gym and picking up the heaviest sets of weights, hoping to be in shape after one workout. The desired results don't present themselves that quickly, and the chances that you will get hurt by doing this are high.

When we disassociate wealth from referring only to money, we get to what ultimately matters. Family, happiness, health, vitality, and spirituality are just a few ways of measuring wealth. Wealth is closely tied to value. If you are able to obtain those things you value most, you shall be a wealthy person.

———

Right before I graduated from high school, Granny and Pops split up after being together for my entire life and even longer. Though they had never married, they were one of the only couples I had seen together consistently, and they had always been my example of true love. All of a sudden, they were parting ways, just as I was gearing up for one of the biggest transitions in my young life. Everything was turned upside down.

I tried to coax them back together by playing my own version of *The Parent Trap*, but nothing worked. There were multiple layers in their breakup that I never understood, but from talking to both of them about it, it boiled down to financial stress. It put me in a tough place because the home that had always been my safe haven would no longer be the paradise for me that it once had been. It never seemed complete after that. Fortunately, I never had to pick sides, and I could tell that they still had a cordial relationship because they would frequently communicate. I found some peace in that.

A few months after the breakup, Pops's heart failed him, and the doctors thought it would be best if he had open-heart surgery. Before he was scheduled to go into surgery, he took me aside at a family function and told me about the procedure and started to cry. It was the first time I had ever seen him cry, which made me cry too. His worry was that because of the intrusiveness of the surgery, there was a risk that he wouldn't make it out alive. He kept saying, "Whatever they say, you mine. You mine. Remember that." I knew this was a reference to the people who would say that he wasn't my biological grandfather, but blood couldn't have made us any closer. I reassured him that I was his and that he was mine too. After I went back into the house, the song "You Are Not Alone" by Michael Jackson came on, and I broke into tears. I had to leave because I didn't want anyone to see me crying. In my mind, I thought the message of the song foreshadowed what I would hear, had anything happened to Pops. Fortunately, his surgery went well, and he was soon on the road to recovery. I was very relieved.

One benefit of being born to young parents is that it gives you extra time with your grandparents. My childhood, filled with so much stress and trauma, was leveled out as a result of my grandparents, who were able to redefine "normal" in my life. Instead of having to be on high alert at every waking minute, I was provided moments of tranquility when I could drop my guard and enjoy life for what it was. My area of refuge existed in a small two-bedroom house with people who saw me as a blessing in their lives and treated me like one as well. Having two people who loved each other and who loved me unconditionally planted seeds in my mind that no matter how crazy things were in one place or aspect of life, there was always hope for something better. I am very grateful for those relationships, because without them, I do not think I would be the man I am today.

NORMALIZATION

When we are born, we do what we see and what we are taught. That is all we know. From a mental-health standpoint, those who raise us are the first influencers of how we think about and address mental-health issues. A child born to a family that is cognizant of the importance of mental health will emulate and begin to normalize the healthy behaviors of their parents. The opposite is true for a child who is born to a family that is unaware.

The trauma that I faced as a child didn't have a name. At least, I didn't have the vocabulary to give it a name at the time. Because I was surrounded by so many people with shared experiences, including my parents and grandparents, what I now call traumatic was just "the way of life." This mindset was the adaptive response to such a chaotic world. Generations before me also had a similar way of life, learned from their parents and grandparents as far back as the beginning of time. To survive and not be consumed by the fact that life was far less than ideal, we told ourselves the lie that there was no better way of addressing the mental-health issues we faced—at least for Black people.

The "Black don't crack" mentality was a coping mechanism. Instead of addressing the potential hardships or traumas that caused Black to crack, we ignored them. Instead of talking about the struggle or the pain, we internalized it as a sign of "strength." Therefore, this perceived strength became "normal." Demonstrating anything other than this strength was considered to be reserved for white people.

As I continue to evolve in my mental health journey, "normal" for me, as a Black man, has taken on a whole new meaning. Internalizing pain is no longer normal. Verbalizing my pain is normal. Resorting to violence is no longer normal. Expressing how I feel is normal. Holding in tears is no longer normal. Releasing tears of sorrow and joy is normal. Demonstrating strength at all times is no longer normal. Exhibiting vulnerability at times is normal. Redefining normal is a natural course of growth. To achieve mental liberation, the first step should be to understand what thoughts and behaviors you have normalized.

My childhood was marked by the normalization of many traumatic experiences that I didn't realize at the time. There can be no healing in the environment that harmed you. Through those years, I remained in the environment that required the normalization of those experiences as a means to survival. However, I continued to carry those tactics with me as I began to escape that world toward better opportunities for growth.

CHAPTER SIX

LESS BLACK

ontgomery Bell Academy (MBA) is one of the most prestigious schools in the city of Nashville. Located in the wealthiest part of town, Belle Meade, a former slave plantation, the neighborhood was worlds away from where I had grown up. Because it's a preparatory school for boys, many people joke that MBA stands for "Mama's Boys Academy." As an alum of the school, I've heard it thousands of times, and it never bothers me. When I started at MBA, I was just that—a mama's boy. I took pride in the taunt more than offense.

When I was accepted to the school, I had no idea what getting in would mean for me and my life. Until my actual enrollment, MBA was just an illusion represented by a football program that rested in my binder cover and my memories from a few visits to the campus where I had felt like a complete outsider. An excerpt from the "About MBA" web page was telling of the type of place I would be entering:

Welcome to Montgomery Bell Academy! We are the only all-boys school in Middle Tennessee, founded in 1867, *and proud of our roots and foundations dating back to the 1780s. MBA's long history is intricately woven into a vision and mission of developing "Gentlemen, Scholars, Athletes" and keeping current in our world. We relish the spirit of boys and work hard to ensure that **a boy's effort and excellence and character define him—not his last name or zip code.***

The school, full of history and tradition, was started just after the end of the Civil War by Montgomery Bell, a successful manufacturing entrepreneur whose nickname was "Iron Master of Middle Tennessee." The term *master* was fitting as he had owned many enslaved people before becoming an abolitionist and emancipating over 150 of them, sending many to Liberia. Bell started the school for the "education of children not less than ten or more than fourteen years old who are not able to support and educate themselves and whose parents are not able to do so." As time evolved, so did the socioeconomic status of the average student. When I enrolled, I felt that I was one of the few students who actually lived at the socioeconomic level that the school had been designed for nearly 150 years earlier. "Gentleman, Scholar, Athlete" was the school's ideal and something I got used to hearing all the time. A successful student was well-rounded, respectful, and held themselves to a higher standard in all aspects of life.

The school had beautiful buildings with green courtyards surrounding them. The athletic facilities rivaled that of many colleges, and the areas dedicated to the arts and sciences were one of a kind. The school mandated a dress code of a collared shirt, khakis, and nice shoes, but on occasion, students were required to wear blue blazers and ties.

Upholding a good appearance was and still is a major priority at MBA. A few years prior to my starting, when I was introduced to the admissions office, I was told that I would have to cut my hair because I had braids—and also that my earring was not allowed. At the time, I thought it was a minor sacrifice on my part to attend a better school, and I was more than willing to adjust without putting up a fight. In hindsight, I resent that I hadn't been allowed to bring things that were culturally appropriate for me to my new *white* school. As a representation of the "diversity and inclusion" of the school, I wished I had stood up for the inclusion of my ideas, culture, and overall uniqueness, rather than just my mere presence as a Black body. But as a child, I was too young, too naive, too powerless, and honestly too ignorant to express how disrespectful it was to make me change my identity to assimilate to make those around me feel comfortable.

If it hadn't dawned on me before, I quickly realized that I was in a completely different world. Instead of a principal, there was a headmaster, a term that I still carry qualms about due to its connection to enslavement. Instead of detention, there was demerit hall that was served on Saturdays. Rather than being forced to eat the same subpar lunches week in and week out, there was a buffet of delicious food prepared by a chef. There were fewer than thirty students in a classroom—more like twelve. Nobody fought. Everybody seemed to be smart in their own right. The vocabulary was advanced. The clothes and shoes were different. Haircuts, to me, looked like something out of a British film.

The phrase "We all know someone who …," referring to the mutual connections that everyone seemed to have, made me feel like I didn't know anybody at all. For example, I had never met anybody who "had driven a golf cart into a pool." I didn't know anybody who played golf, let alone owned a golf cart. The *someone* my peers would describe was usually unlike anyone I had ever known. There was also an honor code and pledge that was required on every assignment: "On my honor as a gentleman, I have neither given nor received aid on this work." That one blew my mind. *You mean to tell me I can't get help from nobody on my homework?* I thought. That wasn't the case, but that's what it felt like for me as a newcomer.

When I found out I was going to MBA, I got a list of books that I was required to read during the summer before starting the next school year. To be honest, it was a shock to me. Previous summers had typically been a time of no schoolwork, but MBA wasn't like the other schools I had attended. On top of reading, I had to answer several questions in essay form to demonstrate my understanding of the material. I hadn't read a full book cover-to-cover in my life, and all of a sudden, I was expected to read four in one summer *and* write about them. It was all overwhelming.

Luckily, I had been on the road with Pops that summer, which gave me plenty of free time for the reading portion. When it came to the essays, I followed the instructions given to me: "Please answer each question to the best of your ability in size 12 Times New Roman font, double-spaced." It struck me as strange that the teachers preferred everything to be double-spaced, but I figured they had a good reason for it. I had never had to type any assignment for school because not everyone had access to a computer where I came from. I had to use Granny's computer to complete the assignments, since the computer I had received from BIM had already failed.

I started to write my essays, and I double-spaced everything—literally. "I _ _ thought _ _ the _ _ protagonist _ _ was _ . . ." I did that for eight total pages, covering all four books. When it came time to spell-check, I chose not to, because there were red squiggly lines on my entire paper, alerting me to the fact that there were extra spaces in between each of my words. I thought, *Oh, that's why they wanted me to double-space it—so they could be sure that I'd actually proofread my writing instead of letting the computer do all the work.* I was wrong.

When I finally got around to turning those assignments in, I realized quickly that my paper looked a lot different than everybody else's. "Why are there lines between all your sentences?" I asked one of my classmates. He told me that his paper was just double-spaced. I shook my head in disbelief. There I had been, spending so much time writing those essays and ensuring that there were two spaces in between every single word while trying to get my paper to be the correct length, when in reality all I had had to do was write one page and press the shortcut, CTRL + 2. I can't do anything but laugh at it now.

Initially, I didn't know what I was going to wear on the first day because I didn't own a single collared shirt or set of khaki pants at the time. After finding out the dress code, Granny made sure I had a few shirts and a couple of pants to get me by right before school started, but it still wasn't enough. One day, my mama came into the house with a large black trash bag and dumped out a ton of hand-me-down collared shirts to choose from. I chose about ten shirts, some that I knew I could grow into, others that fit just right. Just like that, I had a wardrobe ready for school.

My transition from public school to MBA was extremely tough and one that I felt I was enduring alone. For starters, weeks before school started, we were in the process of moving from Valley Brook to the Park at Hillside, when we stayed in the projects with Big Mama and Thomas. Because of the school's prestige, I assumed I was going to be the only homeless person waking up on a couch in the projects on my first day of eighth grade, and I was probably right. As my mama dropped me off for the first day of classes, we walked to the door, and I saw myself in the reflection. I was wearing a freshly ironed, collared red shirt. I was so proud of myself, and at that moment, I told myself, "I'm gon' make it out and do big things."

To my surprise, I was the only Black person in my grade. In fact, I was the first Black person to ever sit in class with some of my classmates.

I didn't think that was possible because I had always been in school where Black students were the majority, but still, we had a few white kids around. The feeling of being the only one was extremely isolating. I didn't have one kid I could go to and talk about the good ol' days of being in public school or make pop culture references that would be understood. I felt like I was on a deserted island. There were several Black kids in the grade above mine, but the high school was slightly separated from the junior school (middle school), so our schedules didn't line up in a way that allowed me to see them much.

Football was my first real introduction to MBA. I had gotten to meet everybody on the team in the summer, so by the time school started, I knew some familiar faces. Those first days were very awkward. After our first practice, a teammate had exhausted himself so much that he threw up on my shoes as we were huddled up listening to the coach talk. Before that practice, we had gathered in the Roberts Room outside the main gym, right before getting our equipment. The kids looked at me like I was a character out of a comic book or something. "That's my man, *Reggie*," one kid emphasized with so much pride simply because he was the first person to know my name. I was unamused by all the stares and comments. I knew they probably didn't have experiences like mine, but their ignorance to a world outside of their own was highlighted through some of the questions they asked me. One of the most memorable questions was, "Do you live near the Titans stadium?"

For many of my classmates, the only reference they had to Black communities was when they went to the Tennessee Titans football games. The Titans stadium was and still is located in downtown Nashville, or the "inner city," as it was often called. Near the stadium were sections of public housing where many Black people lived. My classmates had assumed that since I was Black, I must also live in those projects. Again, my naivete at the time didn't allow me to respond the way I probably would today. A simple "no" accompanied by a half-hearted eye roll was all they got out of me.

Growing up, I had played quarterback. When the coaches at MBA got wind of that, they asked me if I wanted to try out for quarterback for the team. When I told a couple of my teammates that I had been presented with that offer, they told me it was a long shot and made sure I knew that there had never been a Black quarterback at the varsity level at MBA, and so I probably wouldn't be able to play quarterback for anything other than one year. It was a discouraging message, especially along with the other times I had been asked to play in the championship games for soccer or lacrosse, a sport that was foreign to me, merely to guard the other team's best player. Hearing that made me think there was no way I would be the first Black quarterback at MBA, so I decided to decline the offer to continue playing running back and defensive back. Little did I know that turning down the offer to play quarterback would mean that my time playing offense at MBA would be short-lived. I think back now at what could have happened had I decided that I actually wanted to play quarterback. I could've been a part of history at the school, but hindsight is twenty-twenty.

MBA also introduced me to a whole new vocabulary and way of talking. My name was even pronounced differently. I went from being "Reggie" with the emphasis on the "eh" sound to being "Reggie" with the emphasis on the "R." I'd never heard insults like "cunt" or "douchebag," but those were common phrases among my peers. The term *half-brother*, which I had never said, was often used to describe my brother Jarrett who also attended MBA for a couple of years. Another word that I learned early on was *token* in the context of, "Hey Reggie, how does it feel to be our token Black kid?" The only time I had heard the word was at Chuck E. Cheese, referring to the coins used to play games and win prizes. I interpreted the question as meaning, "Hey

Reggie, how does it feel to be the Black kid we brought in to win the state championship?" And at the time, I was cool with that, so I responded with, "It feels good." After hearing chuckles from a group of boys, I asked someone what the actual meaning of *token* was as they were using it. Lo and behold, the word was defined as such: "denoting a member of a minority group included in an otherwise homogeneous set of people to give the appearance of diversity. "[20] After finding that out, it didn't feel as good as it once had.

One of the most offensive things ever said to me came from a kid in my grade, Jake the jokester. He thought it'd be a good idea to tell a joke. "Hey Reggie, what's the difference between a Black person and a bag of shit?" I didn't like where the joke was headed, so I gave him a death stare and told him not to even bother finishing it. He continued anyway. "The bag," insinuating that Black people were nothing more than a pile of waste. He got such a kick out of it, and a few other guys around who thought it was funny enough laughed too. I was furious. Never in my life had I personally encountered someone bold enough to behave that way to my face. I knew I couldn't beat him up because I would've gotten in trouble, labeled as the misbehaving Black student, and kicked out of school—but I did punch him. I wanted to cause so much more pain, though. Metaphorical cuts like that to my pride and mental state were repetitive to a point where I forced myself to become numb to them so that I wouldn't lash out. I've suppressed many memories from my time at MBA as a defense mechanism. In institutions where marginalized people are underrepresented, overpowered, and undervalued, blows like that occur all the time. The expected response from marginalized people is to be the bigger person or otherwise be labeled as the perpetrator. Thus, appeasement becomes our form of survival.

---

20 "token". *Oxford University Press*. Lexico.com. 20 May 2020. https://www.lexico.com/en/definition/token

On top of the ignorant comments and questions, I would often get blank stares after I spoke. Those stares were usually followed by one of the following phrases, "What the hell are you even saying?" or "Are those even words?" or "Is that English?" It used to piss me off so much to complete a full story, only to have one of those questions asked of me. I was already shy—I had a huge gap in my teeth that embarrassed me, and I was different from everybody else, so the last thing I wanted was to bring attention to myself and be forced to repeat things. I took the onus on myself to become more articulate. I didn't speak much, but when I did, I wanted people to understand what I was saying and to take me seriously.

The first few experiences I had with my classmates outside of class or football practice occurred at our high school football games, when we would watch as fans and imagine how dominant we would be when we made it to the varsity level. Those games also happened to be the first experiences I had with the girls from the neighboring sister schools Harpeth Hall and St. Cecilia Academy. Just like my experience with most of the guys in my grade, I was a novelty to those girls. Initially, I wanted nothing to do with them. Coming from the hood, the lesson we were taught was not to mess with those white girls or you'd catch a case; in other words, date a white girl and it would end in legal troubles somehow, some way. It wasn't until I encountered few attractive girls at one of the football games who really seemed to like me that I showed any interest. But I always kept the wise words in the back of my head. However, I was informed by my classmates that it didn't matter if they liked me or if I liked them because their families would never allow them to date a Black guy anyway. So I guess I was just supposed to admire from afar.

When classes officially started, I met my homeroom teacher, Mrs. Pettus, who taught English. An amazing educator, she cut me slack on my summer reading assignments that were incorrectly double-spaced because she knew the content was there. After a brief exercise of introductions, we immediately hopped into the material, which was a review of our summer reading. Everything was moving too fast for me. In public school, I usually spent the first three days making sure I was at the right school or in the right teacher's classroom. Never had I been assigned any significant work on the first day, but MBA was different. We were diagramming sentences, reading huge chunks of books, and writing papers—and that was just for my first class. By the end of the day, I had more homework than I had ever had in my entire life. But I couldn't let anyone down, including myself. I knew I had to knock it all out and do it well, even if that meant staying up until one or two o'clock in the morning.

We had an early creative writing assignment in that English class in which we were allowed to write about any topic that interested us. I decided to take a page out of my life and wrote about the kids I had grown up with. The story described their journey from playing basketball in the hood all the way to the national AAU basketball championship in Orlando, Florida. Much of the story was based on actual events, but it was embellished a bit because we had never made it close to a championship. The story concluded with a boy named D'Angelo making the game-winning shot and being carried off the court by roaring fans. When D'Angelo returned home from the tournament, he told his mama all about what he had done, and she was so proud of him and all that he had accomplished.

I received a good grade on the paper, but I also got a comment that said, "Very good; however, I think D'Angelo's mom would've been at the game if it were the national championship. That part wasn't quite realistic." In writing the story, his mama's absence had been so natural to me that it hadn't struck me as unusual. I had been so used to playing games and not having any family members around to support me that I'd just thought it was commonplace. That one comment in red letters made me think a little harder about my experiences. Everything that had been normalized in my life started to feel not so normal after all.

Despite the difficult transition, I didn't have many behavioral issues in school. The only time I got in "trouble" occurred on a spring afternoon. (I still don't think I did anything wrong, hence the quotation marks around *trouble*.) While waiting on a ride home from school, I noticed a kid stealing money from Jake the jokester's locker. Trying to play the good Samaritan, I went to Jake's locker and took the remaining bills and put them in my pocket for safekeeping. When a furious Jake got out of practice and noticed his money gone, he stormed into the waiting area, inquiring if anyone knew anything. By that time, the thief had already gotten picked up. I informed Jake of what had occurred and returned him the rest of his money. He was appreciative but angry that the thief had gotten away.

A few days later, I was headed to my first visit to the honor council to testify on what had happened that day. In front of me were about ten fellow students and a stern-looking teacher, Madame O'Connell, who had been elected to be on the council to judge the stories of everyone involved. It was the most intimidating thing I had ever had to face at MBA up to that point. It felt like I was on trial for a crime, and I hadn't done anything wrong. But that's not what the council believed. Apparently, I had also been accused of stealing money. Someone had told them that I was passing out Jake's money to other people to buy drinks. In my head, I knew that I had given one dollar to my friend to get a drink, but that dollar had come from my own money.

In a split second, I decided to lie to the honor council. I told them that I had indeed given out a dollar of his money to someone else, but other than that, I hadn't done anything wrong. My thought process in that quick moment was that they would've never believed me had I told them that I actually had money of my own, being the poor Black child in the school. I thought lying on myself would make my story seem more "realistic," to quote Mrs. Pettus. I hated that I had lied. I had degraded my own value, like so many people around me, and that ate away at me. Ultimately, I got off with a warning, and I knew honor council was a place I never wanted to return to. I had been intimidated by the system. Like the 97 percent of criminally convicted people in the real legal system, I had essentially accepted a plea bargain because of my lack of faith that justice would have been served any other way.[21]

———

I adapted well to life at MBA. I was among the top of my class academically, I played in sports at a high level all year around, I participated in the arts, and I volunteered for several causes that I was passionate about. In fact, I did so well that I was awarded one of the highest honors, "Gentleman, Scholar, Athlete of the Year," after my first year there, and I also raked in honors in Latin, a class required of all students at MBA. I also won an award that came with a five-hundred-dollar check. At the time, I thought it was a way to show pity for the "token" Black child by providing charity. I later realized that everyone who had received that award, and not all of them were poor, had been given the same check.

Although I had done well and knew that MBA would continue to provide me with an unmatched education for my future, I did not intend on returning for ninth grade. Socially, my attending MBA was one

---

21 Innocence Staff. "Report: Guilty Pleas on the Rise, Criminal Trials on the Decline." *Innocence Project*, 7 Aug. 2018, innocenceproject.org/guilty-pleas-on-the-rise-criminal-trials-on-the-decline/.

of the toughest things I'd ever had to endure. There was a rigid dichot-
omy between the two worlds in which I lived. I would be in one world
full of abundance and all that life had to offer by day, only to return to
my normal living situation by night. I was still in the hood, while my
classmates were returning to their beautiful homes and seemingly perfect
families. I had decided that I would be much happier as a person if I
wasn't being held in constant comparison to others who were on such
vastly different wavelengths than me socially. I desperately wanted to
return to public school, so that I would not have to hear the ignorant
comments and stereotypes about people who looked like me.

I hated it when people asked about my parents or why my parents
didn't show up to anything. I often tried to skip certain functions because they weren't applicable to my life. For instance, the school hosted
an annual father-and-son dinner. I never wanted to go because I didn't
have a father to go with. Instead of letting me skip the event like I
wanted, they had a coach stand in place of my dad—usually one of the
Black coaches, so it looked more natural. I hated that. I would've been
more content going home and avoiding the reminder that my dad was
in prison. The school also had a mother-and-son breakfast. My mama
never came to any of those, so I would usually go for the free food and
sit in the back with a few buddies who were without their mothers too.

Common questions that people in the MBA community would
ask were "Who are your parents?" or "What do your parents do?"
or "Where did your parents go to college?" I hated answering those
questions. I would be forced to tell them my complicated story. "You
wouldn't know my parents. They are about twenty years younger than
your parents. My dad is in prison for selling drugs and never graduated from high school, so he didn't go to college. My mama is in between finishing cosmetology school but thinking about starting barber
school. She didn't finish high school, so she didn't go to college either."

It gives me anxiety just thinking about it. I think about the last sentence in the excerpt from the "About MBA" web page: "We relish the spirit of boys and work hard to ensure that a boy's effort and excellence and character define him—not his last name or zip code," and wonder why I was ever even asked who my parents were.

While at school I was viewed as the "token" poor Black kid, in my neighborhood I was looked at as a sellout. I was often teased about going to "that white school" by friends and family. The teasing would go as far as to call me an Oreo (Black on the outside but white on the inside) or just flat-out white. It is commonplace in the Black community to say that a Black person who speaks articulately is talking like a white person. As problematic as that belief was, it seemed like the more educated I got, the more people equated me with being white. The more successful I became, the whiter I appeared to others. I thought this was so demeaning to the Black race in general because it implied that being Black meant being uneducated and unsuccessful. The complexities of that mentality drove me crazy. Why were people so self-degrading? It infuriated me so much that whenever I got a hint of someone implying that I was white, I would disassociate myself from them. I knew who I was, and I for sure wasn't white.

The strange thing about being called white by my own people was that I had never felt blacker than when I was at MBA. A dark circle appears much darker when pasted on a white background—like a fly in milk. I was the fly drowning in the milk that was my new school. I guarantee you: you don't feel less Black when every day you learn new racial slurs and stereotypes directed at you. You don't feel less Black when your history teacher emphasizes the "E-R" when saying the N-word while reading text as you feel eyes peering at you. You don't feel less Black when you are mistaken for one of the other few Black students who looks nothing like you. You don't feel less Black when your casual clothes make you look like a "thug," as described by your coaches and teachers. You don't feel less Black when you are asked to represent the Black race as the symbol of diversity for an entire institution. And you definitely don't feel less Black when every day you pass by the statue of a slave owner whose nickname was "Boy Hero of the Confederacy" on your walk to the library.

For the first time in my life, attending MBA was a constant reminder of my blackness. A reminder that wasn't a pro-Black message that made me feel proud to be who I was—in fact, it was just the opposite. Every day was a new discovery that the color of my skin was looked at, either consciously or subconsciously, as a negative strike against who I was as a person. Similar to the personal trauma that I had endured outside of school, I viewed this new racialized trauma as a normal course of life. Thus, I forced myself to assimilate to my new environment; or rather, my new environment forced me to assimilate to it. The need to compartmentalize grew as I would shift back and forth between my two alternate realities, my home life and school life. Mentally, it was exhausting. The concept of my racial identity became more real for me than at any other time before. However, even though the impact was immense, I didn't realize the trauma it caused until much later in life.

CHAPTER SEVEN

WORLDS COLLIDE

've always been phenomenal at compartmentalizing different aspects of my life. Sometimes my ability to compartmentalize is so good that I often can't recall memories outside of the circumstances that relate to my present environment. For instance, I may have a difficult time answering a simple question about what I did at work if my mind has shifted to a leisure activity that I am currently enjoying. The ability to compartmentalize was a skill I was born with but also one I was forced to foster as an adaptive measure to survive my dysfunctional life. In the different arenas in my life, it took a shifting of my mind to properly adjust to the environment. Home required a different mindset and set of tools than school did. School took a different mental focus than my neighborhood, especially when I was going to school with people who had grown up differently from me. Sports was yet another shift in my mindset. And to adapt to each, I separated them in my mind as being unrelated. While staying genuine to my true self, I would be reprogrammed each time I entered a new arena. Like the squares of a waffle, each compartment represented one of those areas. The good, the bad, and the ugly of each arena remained there and didn't spill over into the others. At least it was like that for the most part, until my worlds began to collide.

While at MBA, I experienced a roller coaster of emotions as a result of the dualities in my life. On one hand, I was meeting new people who would eventually become closer to me than family, and I was being introduced to a life of promise that was very different than what I had experienced during my upbringing. On the other hand, I was still being haunted by the traumas of my past. No matter how good I got at compartmentalizing, the two worlds would ultimately collide.

Despite the social challenges, at MBA, I received a world-class education that continues to provide endless opportunities for me. Its structure allowed me to build the skills and confidence to take on any endeavor. But most important, I met great people who were invested in my success. One of the coolest peers I had in class, Joseph Sloan, was intentional on making sure I had at least one friend from day one. He knew a few people from the previous schools I had attended from his days of playing AAU basketball with them, so he used those connections to break the ice with me. It didn't take him long to invite me over to his house and introduce me to his family.

My first impression of the Sloans was that they were too nice. I thought it was fake. Mrs. Sloan had the biggest smile and would hug me with so much passion. Mr. Sloan was much more stoic. He was large and intimidating, which made him appear scary, but once he got to talking, he lit up like a star. Joseph had a little sister, Hilary, who was just as kind. Early on, they accepted me as their second son. I felt so much love from them. I can't begin to enumerate the meals, rides home, and life lessons they provided. So, they were one of the only families that I told about my plans. Because of the social barriers I was experiencing, I intended to return to public school instead of returning to MBA for ninth grade. Joseph was the first person I told, and that conversation went like this:

Me: Hey, man, I want to thank you so much for being such a good friend, but I ain't coming back to MBA. I think I'm gonna go to Overton or Hillsboro next year.

Joseph: Dang, for real? Well, it was so good having you here for a year. Maybe we'll play each other in basketball.

Me: Yeah, I hope so!

Joseph: I'll miss you, bro.

Me: I'ma miss y'all too, man. Aight, bye.

Joseph: Bye.

Not even five minutes went by before I got a call from Mr. Sloan. The first thing he said was that Joseph was so absentminded for not trying to convince me to stay. He went on to plead with me, telling me how much I would benefit from staying and how MBA and the Sloans as a family would benefit from my presence. I could hear the pain in his voice, as if he was torn up to hear that I didn't want to return. He continued to build a case for staying and asked if he could come see me in person. I agreed.

But before he could come, the word got around, and several other people called. Some of them actually drove to my neighborhood and showed up to talk with me in my living room about what an amazing opportunity I had in front of me. One of the people who tried to convince me was Coach Davis, the man who had refused to give me free Taco Bell at my first football game. He was also a football coach at MBA. Throughout my whole process of getting into MBA, he had been present because they were taking a chance on me, and he wanted to make sure I was a good fit for the school and that the school was a good fit for me. Hearing him tell me that I should stay at MBA wasn't as convincing because I wasn't sure what to think of him at the time.

I was still feeling out his intentions. He was always strict about how I dressed or about speaking clearly when introducing myself. He claimed he was building character, but most of the time I felt like he was just being a dick.

As a way to get people to stop trying to coax me to stay, I explained to them that the tuition was way too much for us to maintain, just to give them a reason other than the fact that I hated showing up to a whole new world and playing a new role every single day. At the time, we were committed to paying about $189 a month, which was a huge discount compared to the all-in cost of approximately $25,000. Still, we couldn't afford it. My concern about tuition was quickly combatted with comments that I would not ever have to worry about paying it again if I returned. I was grateful for the fact that if I chose to return, I would receive a world-class education for free, but that didn't resolve the true issue—no one could throw money at the real problem I was facing.

The turning point occurred when Mr. Sloan eventually came to my house. He expressed so much care for me and even started crying. I was not expecting this at all, so it made me pay attention. *Why is this man crying about which school a ninth grader chooses to go to?* I thought. *Are they only interested in my athletic ability?* But I knew from that day that my education was much more important than anything I did on the field or court, at least to Mr. Sloan, if to no one else. He saw a future for me that I couldn't see for myself.

During one of the visits, someone asked me to just come out and practice with the football team, to see if that would change my mind. At that point, after Mr. Sloan's genuine expression of concern, my mind was pretty much made up. Metro Nashville Public School system had already started classes, and I still wasn't enrolled, so it was almost a given that I would be returning to MBA. If not, I would have been in violation of truancy laws at the public school. I got to practice two days before our first game and was sold that I was going to start high school at MBA. A guy on my team joked with me, "Hey, Reggie, how does it feel to miss summer workouts and practices and know you're going to be starting in a couple of days?"

I just chuckled and said, "It feels good."

The love that these families showed me was not a rarity during my time at MBA. I seemed to get love from everybody—from administrators, teachers, students, and parents. I spent so much time on campus and at my classmates' homes that it felt like I was becoming a part of their families. All the things that were once so foreign to me started to become a part of my everyday living. Even though I was still different in so many ways from the traditional student, I felt like I had finally started to find my stride.

———

A major factor that played a huge role in my transition was that I was finally able to see the other Black students more. Our classes didn't overlap often, but lunchtime was always a time to unite for a dose of normalcy. The school had admitted two other Black kids in my grade, but they seemed so different from me that we never truly clicked. At the very least, it showed me that the school recognized how isolated I was and had attempted to alleviate that feeling. It was a valiant effort. Instead, the older kids in the grade above me understood me better. Most of them were Black, but there were a few white kids who had had similar experiences to us, which made them a part of the crew. We were all cut from the same cloth. We had grown up in similar neighborhoods. Some of them had dads in prison. They knew what it was like to go through the transition. In fact, one guy, Fonzo, had actually grown up in Terrace Park with me. Fonzo was the big brother of the kid who had chased me down with the toy microphone that led to my first fight. I looked up to them so much—academically, athletically, and in every other way. Although they were just one year ahead of me, they were the gurus of navigating MBA as Black students. I got advice on what to do and what not to do, what wardrobe alternatives I could get away with, and what teachers to request for the following year. They looked out for me. During free time and study halls, I would often be found in locations on campus labeled "Area of Refuge" with my guys; these became safe places for me, just like Pops and Granny's house.

The camaraderie at MBA was the most special part about my time there. Once I started participating in varsity sports, things were even better. The bonds I created at MBA were made stronger with the guys I went through the trenches with. Two-a-days and training camp for football were those trenches. I spent more time with the guys on the football team than anyone else. We got to a point where we would fight tooth and nail, in any arena of life, for each other. It is said that you become the average of the five people you hang around the most. When it came to making the choice of who to spend my time with, the answer was easy. I was blessed with a group of friends who inspired each other to be better versions of themselves. The bond between us was dear to me, and I still hold on to these relationships and will continue to do so for a lifetime.

My high school friends are still my most cherished friend group. Although we have gone down different paths and moved to different cities, our bond still holds strong. We talk nearly every day, and whenever we get an opportunity, we kick it just like we did when we were in high school. As if MBA hadn't blessed me enough, who knew it would also give me a group of lifelong friends. During the times when I felt most abandoned by family members and people in my community,

I was welcomed by my brothers who knew me, understood me, and loved me. Those relationships made up for many of the losses I experienced over the years.

In addition to the peers who became friends, I had coaches and teachers who also became dear to me. Coach Davis eventually became a father figure. He took me under his wing and taught me so much about life. At the time, he didn't have children of his own, and his father had passed away early in his life, so he knew the importance of having a positive male role model. Even though we came from vastly different worlds, it didn't affect our relationship. He welcomed me into his home, and he made sure that I felt like I belonged there. He encouraged me to do things I never thought I could do, which gave me so much confidence. He employed me to show me the meaning of hard work and helped me create better habits with the money I had earned. When he ultimately got married and had children of his own, I became their babysitter, but more like their big brother. Today, I feel like a part of the family and have so much love for all they have done for me over the years. He was very honored when I referred to him as my godfather on a call that I took during one of our dinners. I didn't even think about the term beforehand; I just knew he was more than just a coach to me. He was more than just the man who started BIM. He wasn't my blood, but he had won my heart, and that was not easy to do when I usually reserved my trust for women, having been raised mostly by so many strong ladies.

There were a number of teachers who had and continue to have a profound impact on my life. Madame O'Connell, whom I had to face during my trip to the honor council, became one of my biggest supporters. She taught me French for three years and could often read me like a book, despite my attempts to compartmentalize. She seemed to always know what to say when I was having a bad day and displayed more genuine and sincere gestures than anyone else I had ever met. I look at her like a second mother. The same could be said about Ms. Williams, another teacher I got to know during my senior year. As she often put it, she "loooooooved" me, and the feelings were mutual. I never felt the need to compartmentalize around her, because her unapologetic authenticity created a safe haven for me. There were so many people like that who made me feel so loved and supported during my time at MBA, and without them, I don't know how I would've made it.

While at MBA, I met one other person whom I now consider my brother. Blood couldn't make us any closer. De'Anté was two grades behind me, so as I was starting high school, he was just entering the seventh grade. When I saw him on campus, I was shocked because I had seen him before in a different context. The summer before school started, I was at the park playing basketball with some guys from the neighborhood. It was a hot day, and tempers were even hotter. I got into a heated altercation with a guy from the other team that began with some aggressive game play and ended with a face-to-face argument. Nothing more ensued. Little did I know that the guy I had gotten into the altercation with was De'Anté's cousin. De'Anté had been on the court with him that day, and we had had no idea that either of us were MBA boys.

Even though he was two grades behind me and the other guys, he always carried himself as an old soul. We'd often joke that he'd "been here before," meaning he had lived a previous life and was wise beyond his years. Over the years, De'Anté and I grew closer. I saw so much of myself in him. We had similar life stories and were both extremely guarded, which was never mentioned between us but understood. The little that we did share with each other further proved that we were very much aligned in our views on the world as a result of our experiences. We could always sense what the other person was going through on the inside without ever having to say anything. That worked for us because we were both dealing with the normalized trauma from our pasts, and verbal communication was not how we chose to express ourselves.

There were several defining moments in our relationship that solidified our bond and made me want to be the big brother he had never had. We had known each other a little over a year when he called me one day, crying. I couldn't understand what he was saying over the phone, but it didn't matter; I knew I had to check on him. I rushed down to his house. Police cars were everywhere. De'Anté came up to me and explained that one of his childhood friends had just been shot while they were all playing. He then put his head on my chest and started sobbing uncontrollably. I knew exactly how he was feeling, and I knew the only thing I could do was be there, so I tried to absorb as much of his pain as I could. Fortunately, the gunshot wound wasn't fatal, but the trauma from experiencing that was more than enough to haunt any child forever.

———

Before my time at MBA, the first Black person I knew who had gone to the school was a childhood friend, Shug, who claimed that the only reason he was there was to play sports. He used to tell us why he left MBA. In his words, once he broke his arm, they decided to kick him out of school. He added that if they didn't have a reason to use you on the field, they didn't need you there anymore. Having eventually gone to MBA, I know that's not the full story, but at least that was my mindset when I first entered MBA.

I seemed to be plagued by sports injuries, the thing I wanted most to avoid. It started with excruciating migraines that reduced me to tears nearly every day in my first year at MBA. While I believed they were a result of football-related activities, I was told that I simply needed more sleep and to eat breakfast, so I made adjustments. In track, I often pulled muscles. Sometimes I would push through the injury, and other times it was too debilitating. When one of my teammates asked a coach why I ran the way that I did, with a limp, the coach responded, "That's how some of *them* run; it's a habit." I assumed "them" referred to Black people, and that got under my skin, though I never said anything. I kept running in fear of getting kicked out of school for my injury. Again, looking back, this was unreasonable, but it was the idea that had been planted in my head.

When I was a tenth grader, I started to experience a nagging injury that persisted for several years. It felt like a knife was being stabbed into my groin with every step I took. After a while, the pain got so bad that I could barely put any pressure on it. I eventually went to a specialist and found out that I had a condition called osteitis pubis, or inflammation of my pelvic bone and surrounding muscles as a result of repetitive physical activities. I had played an entire football season on it, so I was forced to go through extensive physical therapy and eventually got several series of cortisone shots. I was out of commission for a total of nine months.

All through high school, the pain lingered. I hated practicing during any season because I felt like practice was just making me worse, since I never got any rest. It was more bearable during games because I would do things that I was unwilling to do every day for practice. I would take a few ibuprofen pills and a couple of painkillers so that I wouldn't feel the pain. With the adrenaline that came from playing a game, my pain was also alleviated temporarily, which allowed me to play a little better. It was not a healthy habit. During halftime, I would rush to the locker room to throw up because the medication made me feel so bad. Sometimes after that, depending on how I felt, I would take a few more pills to finish the game. That was the routine for every football game during my high school career. I am grateful that I never developed an addiction to those medicines.

When we approached graduation, a letter we had all written on our first days of school at MBA was returned to us. I had forgotten about it—on the first day of eighth grade, I had been asked to write a Hopes and Dreams letter to the head of the school, describing what I would like to get out of my MBA experience. To paraphrase my letter a bit more eloquently, it read: "I'm so thankful that I got into MBA because it will give me a better chance of going to the NBA. With the skills that I build here and through all the exposure I will get, colleges will be much more likely to offer me a place in my pursuit of making it to the pros." With all the opportunities the school presented and the talents I already possessed, my eighth-grade mind thought that sports were going to be my only way out of the hood. As I read that letter as an eighteen-year-old senior, I couldn't help but laugh. So much had changed in those five short years, and I now had a new outlook on life.

As much as I loved basketball, I almost never played it in high school because I felt that I needed to be spending that time working to help provide for my family. When Coach Davis heard about my plans, he expressed that he didn't like that my reality was so different from that of many of my peers. He felt guilty that I was in a learning environment among so many students with privilege, while I was also forced to do things like babysit and find part-time jobs outside of school. He took me home that day and explained that if I wanted to play basketball, I should. Before I got out of the car, he handed me a crisp one-hundred-dollar bill and said that as long as I continued to do well in the classroom, I wouldn't have to work a part-time job. The cash was followed by supplies and computers for school. Eventually, cars were given to me to help me get to and from school.

At the time, I was unaware that the gift I had just received was a violation of the Tennessee Secondary School Athletic Association's (TSSAA) rules and would eventually cause an investigation surrounding unlawful recruiting at my school. A year after I graduated from high school, an article was published by the *Nashville Scene* titled "What a three-year public records fight revealed about the TSSAA's financial aid rules and the school that broke them." The writer discussed the details behind the investigation into MBA's improper recruiting and financial aid problems. The article went on to list numerous individuals who had contributed to the issue at hand. While no students were named, most could be identified if you attended the school during those years. I was one of those students.

The release of that article shook things up at the school. Coaches were fired or stepped down, championships were vacated, and reputations were tainted. It upset me because I knew the parties involved. The children were great students and were in the school to receive a better education. It wasn't merely about athletics. The benefactors were kind-hearted individuals who wanted to provide a better opportunity for children who wouldn't otherwise have gotten the chance, like Coach Davis had done for me. Too often, the picture was painted that good athletes who were Black were *only* at the school to play sports. As one of those Black students who was also a good athlete, I resented that unfair and limiting belief. I felt that I exemplified the school's ideal of Gentleman, Scholar, Athlete.

———

During my time at MBA, my lifestyle changes were drastic to my family and friends because I spent so much time away from them. There were a number of reasons I didn't come around much, but the main reason was that I was always busy. People didn't understand how demanding my schedule was. A typical day from my senior year of high school would look like this:

7:00 a.m.: Drive to school and eat breakfast or get treatment

8:00 a.m.: Advanced Placement English

9:00 a.m.: Advanced Placement Calculus

10:00 a.m.: Study hall

11:00 a.m.: Honors French III

12:00 p.m.: Lunch

1:00 p.m.: Government and Economics

2:00 p.m.: Study hall

3:00 p.m.: Chorus

4:00 p.m.: Practice

6:30 p.m.: Drive to my girlfriend's house to do homework and eat dinner

9:30 p.m.: Drive home

10:00 p.m.: Finish homework

12:00 a.m.: Sleep

Being around family also meant that I would be approached for money by adults. If it wasn't that, people from my neighborhood were always reaching out to involve me in things that I knew I had no business doing. Old friends would pull up in stolen cars and ask if I wanted to go joyriding, which I always refused. It didn't take long before their faces appeared on the nightly news. I would get approached on Facebook as well. I received inbox messages from dope boys in the hood, asking if I was ready to make money or if I was ready to start in the family business of selling drugs. I was never tempted to do any of that, but it made me want to distance myself as much as possible.

Driving to my girlfriend's house after practice was something I did nearly every day. I know my girlfriend's mama hated that I was always there, but I loved being there. I didn't want to be home. Every time I walked into my house, I just felt so much tension. Not that there was always something going on, but I knew that at any moment, I could hear somebody screaming or crying. At my girlfriend's house, it was peaceful. I dreaded going home so much that I would try to fall asleep while I was there. Sometimes, instead of going home, I would find a safe place to park my car near school and just sleep there until the next day.

If I wasn't at my girlfriend's house finding peace, I was at the house of one of my classmates or coaches. The first time I went to a house on "the boulevard"—referring to Belle Meade Boulevard, home to some of the country's wealthiest families—I walked in and realized that the guest bedrooms were larger than any apartment I had ever lived in in my life. They had plenty of rooms, an entire guest house, beautiful artwork, fine china, and antiques. I felt like I couldn't touch anything, which was anxiety inducing, but after a while I became comfortable in houses like that. Spending time with my friends was nice because there was so much structure. Schedules were shared and coordinated, meals were served at predictable times, and there was actual silence. I loved it. It was such an escape from what I was used to.

As much as I tried to keep family life at home and school life in Belle Meade, there was undoubtedly some overlap. Rarely did I ever feel the same sentiments in both places because they offered such different experiences. But as life would have it, the same trauma and hardship that I knew in my family world soon became inescapable in the other world that had once been close to paradise.

The summer after my freshman year, I started to experience so much death around me. Shug, the first Black boy I had known to attend MBA, got into trouble. In the mix with the wrong crowd, he and some of his new friends gang-raped a woman. Following the rape, he was murdered in the park by one of the victim's family members. That loss shook me up because he had been just fifteen years old. I hadn't known anyone close to me who had been murdered that young, and the impact still remains with me and my friends and family members who knew him. I refused to go to the funeral because I didn't want to accept that he was dead.

Following that, it was like death was all around me. Before I was eighteen years old, I had started collecting funeral programs. It was like my library of angels who sat in my closet and watched over me. In rapid succession, my great-grandfather and great-grandmother, the patriarch and matriarch of our family, passed away because of old age. My great-uncle died of health complications that may have been a result of prior drug use. My great-aunt died of old age. Another family member died of suspected AIDS. I had a cousin who took a man's life for breaking in and robbing his house. He spent time in prison, and after his release, he beat an elderly man to death. He was placed back in prison and probably won't live another day as a free man for the rest of his life. Right before I graduated, I had another cousin who was murdered at the young age of twenty-six. His death occurred a few days after I last saw him at a Thanksgiving gathering in 2008. His funeral hurt me the most. It pained me to hear the cries from family members. No sound compares to the screams of a mother who weeps as she is forced to bury her child. At that moment, it felt like life was more fragile than fine china.

The tragedy didn't end with my family. A humble individual who worked as a janitor at MBA was brutally murdered. Ironically, he had escaped war-torn Sudan as a Lost Boy, only to be shot in Nashville, Tennessee. A friend from school, who was one of my biggest fans on the football field, committed suicide. After graduation, a bright classmate of mine passed away from a drug overdose. It seemed like death was ever-present and around every corner. I couldn't escape it in the best of neighborhoods.

After I graduated, I received a phone call from my advisor at MBA, Coach Brock, that changed my world forever. He calmly expressed that Coach Davis had tragically backed over his two-year-old daughter in the driveway, killing her on contact. My heart dropped. She had been like my baby sister. How could something so tragic happen to such a good family? I had so many questions. At her funeral, I waited impatiently to see the man who had become like a father to me. I tried to keep it together for his sake, but as soon as I saw him and was able to hug him, I broke. I hurt for him. I hurt for his daughter. I hurt for his wife and other children. It was such a tragic loss that continues to haunt many people.

Around the same time, a younger Black child from MBA died from unconfirmed causes, but many were led to believe that it was a suicide. I remember when and where I was when I found out. I was sitting in the car, dropping De'Anté off at his house. Scrolling through Facebook, I saw the kid's name preceded by the dreaded three letters I had grown too familiar with—RIP. I lost it. I had mentored that kid and tried to address some of the issues that the school had noticed he was facing. We had many conversations about life and what it looked like to live happily. After hearing about his passing, I couldn't help but wonder what he had actually been going through. Had he found peace? Was he happy? I'll never know. After all that death, I became numb to the pain.

———

When it came time to start applying for colleges, I was very thankful that I had MBA and the college counseling office, because my parents knew nothing about the college application process. Had I not had the help of the college counseling office, I probably wouldn't have gotten into any of the colleges that ultimately accepted me. My former

English teacher and favorite college counselor, Ms. Serrano, helped me with everything, from critiquing my résumé to helping me craft impressive essays.

One of the biggest dilemmas I faced during that time was the external pressure of people wanting me to go to places that I didn't want to attend. Throughout high school, I had built a great résumé for myself. I had proven that I could adapt to a rigorous curriculum, maintain great grades, participate in athletics and the arts, and rack up tons of volunteer hours. Those accomplishments had attracted several Ivy League schools. At the top of the list was Harvard. Beginning my junior year after football season, I started getting letters from a coach at Harvard that would always end with the phrase "Think Harvard." I loved getting those letters because I felt they signified that I was actually going to make it out. It was a promise I had made to myself on the first day of school. Not only was I going to make it out; I was also going to have an opportunity to go to one of the most prestigious universities in the entire world. Given where I started, it was surreal to think that Harvard was even a possibility. And although it was an extreme honor, I wasn't ever excited about it. I honestly didn't want to go there at all.

Everyone else had different plans for me. The head of the school, Coach Davis, my position coach, and even my college counselor pressured me to commit to playing football at Harvard. The narrative would have been such good publicity for the school. Headlines would have read, "First-generation college student defies all odds to attend the most elite Ivy League institution." It would've been a hell of a story, but it wasn't the story I wanted written at the time. I wanted to stay in Nashville and knew that I could get a world-class education at Vanderbilt University. More than hoping I could play for the team that I had encountered in my first ever all-star game, Vanderbilt felt like the right place for me. Upon learning that I wanted to be at Vanderbilt, people told me that I wasn't good enough to play in the SEC but that I would do well in the Ivy League.

Because most people's first reaction to hearing that I attended MBA was to ask if I played sports, I felt that if I were to attend one of those schools, I wanted to do it on merit alone. I hated being viewed in this way because I was so much prouder of my academic achievements than anything I had ever done athletically. Additionally, after my injuries, I had lost my passion for football, so I didn't want to continue to play in college. Nevertheless, I was cornered in the hallways, invited to fancy dinners, and intimidated into accepting an offer from an Ivy League school. Oftentimes, those situations would leave me feeling gut-punched and on the verge of tears because I felt like I didn't have a choice of my own.

Harvard had offered me a scholarship, but it wasn't a full ride. I would have to commit to paying $12,000 a year to receive a Harvard education, and my scholarship would pay for the rest. In my naive and ignorant mind, I thought that there was no way I would be able afford $12,000 a year for four years, which would ultimately come out to $48,000. We didn't have any money. We couldn't even afford to pay for the monthly $189 for MBA. My limited knowledge about college meant that I didn't even know that student loans were an option. I also knew that being far away from my family and not having the resources to come back whenever I needed to would make it difficult for me to go away for college. And my parents didn't have an opinion on the matter.

I had to do something to make sure that the people who wanted me to go to the Ivy League schools wouldn't have an argument. When it came time to taking the standardized tests, I intentionally did poorly. I wasn't a great test taker to begin with, for reasons that I would later discover were out of my control and steeped in cultural bias, nor did I take any prep courses to help. Simply put, I did not put forth my usual effort when it came to the tests. I even fell asleep on purpose a few times after randomly answering questions in a hurry.

In hindsight, it was immature and shortsighted of me to sabotage myself. But I was seventeen years old and making those decisions without much or any input from my family, the people who meant the most to me. And what all those people who wanted me to go to Harvard failed to do was see the decision from my perspective. I was the big brother in a family full of fatherless children. That was the case on both my mama's and dad's side. Five children including myself, three mothers, zero fathers. The numbers were even more alarming when I included the other siblings of my siblings who weren't directly related to me. My siblings needed a positive male role model in their lives, not an image of one whom they never got to see. They needed me to be there if anything came up, and I wanted to be there for those times. I was so passionate about being there for my younger brothers and sister that I was willing to turn down the grandest of opportunities, an Ivy League education, which I knew would be a huge sacrifice for me. So, I had basically made up my mind that I was going to go to Vanderbilt. I hadn't gotten in yet, but that was what I wanted and that's what I set my intentions on.

After applying to a ton of universities, many of which were Ivy League schools to appease those around me, I either didn't get in or got waitlisted at the schools that had been pushed so heavily on me. Without expressing any interest in playing sports there, it had greatly lowered my chances of getting in. I had known that all along, but it still took a lot of weight off my shoulders. I could finally tell people who were pressuring me that I hadn't gotten in, so there was no reason to press the issue. Ultimately, I got accepted to Vanderbilt University, which solidified the case for me that I was going to stay home for college.

Throughout all this, I learned that it is important that your dreams be *yours*. You can't be forced by anyone else to chase a dream you don't believe in. If that is the case, your willingness to work hard will not manifest in the same fashion as if you were pursuing something you truly desire. Someone else's dream could become your nightmare. The best results come from a burning passion within to achieve your own version of greatness. Only you can define what that is.

———

A tradition at MBA was to wear your college T-shirt one day in the spring for a group picture. On that day, after spending five great years at MBA and accomplishing so many achievements, I was left with a sour taste in my mouth. One of my coaches looked at my shirt that flaunted Vanderbilt University with a perplexed look on his face. He proceeded to ask me the one of the most annoying question I've ever gotten, "Wait, you're smart?" In my head, I ran through all of my high school accomplishments that he should have been well aware of and that transcended my athletic ability: scholarship presented by the Department of Education, Jack Diller Education Award presented by the Nashville Predators, Joe L. Word Courage Award presented by the National Football Foundation, Student-Athlete of the Rivalry Series presented by the Marines, Gentleman Scholar Athlete of the Year (x2), Gold Medalist on the National French (x3) and Latin (x2) Exams, French Honors Award for highest GPA (x3), College Algebra and Trigonometry Award for highest GPA, Algebra II Award for highest GPA, class president my junior year, Cum Laude Society, graduating in the top 10 percent of my class, member of chorus who received Supreme (highest recognition) at the state competition, and several other private scholarships and grants.

In addition to my achievements, I knew I would be off to college in a few months and starting a whole new chapter in life with more opportunities than ever before to accomplish even more amazing things. Not knowing how to respond to such a disrespectful question from my coach, I rolled my eyes and headed in the opposite direction. toward one of my dreams, becoming a high school graduate.

The only accomplishment I was short of achieving while at MBA was admission to its most elite honors society, Totomoi, which recognizes students whose leadership and character are exemplary and of the highest order. After being told that I was an ideal candidate for Totomoi, I still needed to apply to make it official. However, I never did for several reasons. The induction ceremony felt cultish to me. Current members would pace around the auditorium before slapping newly inducted members on the back with all their might to let them know they were in. The name of the society sparked curiosity, which led me to research its history. I found out that Totomoi was the name of the estate owned by the Tinsley family and later purchased by MBA where the campus was located. This estate was named after a plantation in Virginia that the Tinsley family also owned. And that plantation was named after Chief Totopotomoi of the Pamunkey tribe. The MBA web page dedicated to Totomoi specifically states that "in the 1600s, Thomas Tinsley had negotiated *cooperatively* with the Native American Chief Totopotomoi for the sale of this property in Virginia." Further research uncovered that Thomas Tinsley had allegedly participated in Bacon's Rebellion for the right to essentially go to war with Indigenous people over land and resources. That was one of my first realizations of the whitewashing of history, and it didn't sit well with me. My ultimate refusal to apply to the society was based on the reasons that Totomoi represented the opposite of everything it promoted, namely honor, character, and inclusivity.

CHAPTER EIGHT

ESCAPING THE FIRE

I learned that it was extremely important to have dreams and aspirations. To see something become reality, you have to think it. But a vision without action is merely a dream. If all you do is think about your dreams, you will never see them come to fruition. You must put in the work—and the work is what separates the good from the great. Many people have good ideas, aspirations, and dreams, but the ones who implement a plan to accomplish those goals are the ones who succeed.

While it is good to have ambitious dreams, they can be intimidating at the start. How do you eat an elephant? One bite at a time. You run a marathon one step at a time. Many times, people have grand ambitions, which is a great thing, but the thought of accomplishing the end goal is so far from where they are that it makes it seem impossible, so they get discouraged and quit. Life should be a continual process of improvement. Improvement does not mean perfection. Don't let perfection be the enemy of progress. If your goal is to be perfect, you will never be satisfied with your results, no matter how much you improve.

If your goal is to be better than everyone else, you will always fall short. Instead, being better than you were the day before should be the goal. To combat feeling discouraged, you have to think about the small bites of the elephant, the individual steps of the marathon, and you must celebrate those achievements. Too often, we focus so hard on how it will feel to celebrate once the ultimate goal is accomplished that we forget to celebrate the incremental steps that lead up to it. Small victories deserve celebrations.

Since I was a young boy, my goal was to be better than what I saw around me. I didn't want to struggle in the ways that we struggled as a family, and I definitely didn't want to put my future family through that. That feeling first presented itself as a desire not to have a child while I was in high school. I saw how hard having me was on my parents, particularly my mama, so I set that as one of my personal goals. I also had a goal of actually graduating from high school, because that was something neither of my parents had achieved, and I saw the effects it had on their lives as adults. Their opportunities were limited, even though they would both obtain their GEDs later. While these two goals of mine may not seem like huge accomplishments, setting and achieving them in the face of the adversity I had endured proved to be extremely ambitious. I could've easily fallen victim to repeating the same cycle that I had been born into, but instead, having those seemingly small ambitions led me to more major accomplishments.

Seeing how limited my wildest ambitions were as a child makes me wonder what more I could have accomplished if I had dreamed bigger. What if I had had different motivating factors, such as a family member who was a doctor or a CEO? Would achieving more than that have been my goal from the beginning? I went on to accomplish the goals I had set for myself early on, but I didn't stop there. I continued to reevaluate and challenge myself to reach greater heights with the new perspective that I could accomplish literally anything I set my mind to. Therefore, my newly developed goals were wilder, bigger, and scarier. Knowing where I had started allowed me to continue to fight for my desires, despite the perceived impossibility of my future goals, no matter how much they scared me.

Do not place limits on yourself. In cases where they are present, your visions and goals must be far bigger than your limitations. Had I been limited to the goals that I set for myself when I was a naive child with few experiences in the world, chances are you wouldn't be reading this book. By removing limitations, you open yourself up to possibilities beyond your wildest imagination. Allow your dreams to scare you, but don't allow that fear to cripple you. Sometimes fear is the only force stopping us from attaining what we want in life. By removing fear, we allow ourselves to take action in pursuit of our goals.

If you isolate my life to certain time periods, frankly, it wouldn't be unique at all. There are millions of children who grow up and experience the same types of childhood traumas I experienced. In many cases, the circumstances are worse. Those people have probably read the first half of this book with the normalization mindset and thought, *That's just how life is*, unaware of any other ways of living. But the combination of my experiences proves to be quite unique. A poor child surrounded by violence and crime in the hood with teenage parents, one of whom is in prison, usually repeats the cycle. If they are lucky, they are able to break parts of the cycle, but the steps are usually gradual, taking generations to correct.

Never do you expect the same child from the hood who was taught to break into houses at the age of five to thrive in all aspects of life at a prestigious private school. Nor do you expect the same child who has seen multiple dead bodies to be sought after by many Ivy League universities. You certainly wouldn't expect the same child who was swinging around a pistol unaccompanied as a toddler to be admitted to and shine at a top-twenty university. But that child did, and that child was me. And that was just the beginning.

———

As fall approached, I geared up to start at Vanderbilt University. I had always had a passion for cooking, so I signed up to work in the dining hall, in hopes that I could cultivate my culinary skills. The move-in date for dining hall workers was earlier than the general student population, so my dad helped me to get my room in order before I was to report to orientation. While I would've typically been anxious about such a transition in the past, my new confidence and desire to finally be independent created excitement for what was ahead.

I didn't know a soul in orientation, so I sat in the back by myself. There was a group of people from Memphis who all knew each other, so I made friends with them. They were smart, they had backgrounds to which I could relate, and they were just cool to be around, particularly this one guy, James Quick. He was the only white boy in the group, but we seemed to be on the same wavelength regarding our interests, goals, and, most of all, senses of humor. We both wanted to cook, but to our surprise, they didn't let students do any cooking. In fact, the dining hall jobs didn't have anything to do with preparing food. All we could do was be a cashier, server, cleaner, or stocker. Since we weren't allowed to be cooks, we both decided to work in the "munchie mart." We had made an instant connection and literally saw each other every day because we worked together. We became tight. It didn't take long for us to start opening up about our pasts, and it was apparent to me why he was so cool—he was just like me. Our stories didn't parallel each other, but our responses to the hands we had been dealt were very similar. He always possessed a positive outlook on life—no matter how bad things got, he knew he had the ability to make them better. He was driven to making his current and future life much better than his past through hard work and determination. But he balanced life well too. Although he was extremely bright and serious about school, he knew how to maintain a social life. I saw so much of myself in him. I probably could've guessed that first time we met that we would end up being best friends, and that was the case.

James and I bonded throughout our college years, especially when I introduced him to the music I made. Like my mama blaring Mary J. Blige, who possessed the ability to put my mama's feelings into words, I found solace in music. If I wasn't listening to an artist who spoke about the struggle and overcoming the odds, I was expressing my creativity and emotions through my own words. James had never attempted to write a song, but by the time we graduated, he had probably made a few albums' worth of music. We often collaborated on songs. If there was ever a time we couldn't express how we felt in everyday conversations, mainly due to our humor that we inserted into every waking moment as a defense mechanism, it came out in our music.

I never knew the creative journaling that I had adopted as part of my songwriting would change someone else's life until, six years into our friendship, James sent me a song titled "Invincible." His song discussed the evolution of our friendship from its inception and the impact I had had on him. Without realizing it, I had been teaching him and helping him develop traits that I was still developing myself, like confidence, vulnerability, and authenticity. He spoke of changing the trajectory of our lives instead of being defined by where we had come from. He recalled the time when his mother had passed away while we were still college students. After returning to campus following the memorial service, he spotted a napkin with the message "I love you" that I had left for him in his room. Although a small gesture, it helped him get through one of the most difficult times in his young life. As I listened to his song, tears rolled down my face. Without truly knowing the extent of his actions, he too had been the support I had needed through some of my toughest times as well. Beautifully crafted, a series of bars summed up the impact that we had on each other and the impact that music had on both of us. It would also set the standard for our future friendships with new people in our lives:

From that night, raps became my life wrapped in a diary.
They helped me get through tough times like my mom when she died on me.
But I know you would ride for me, and I knew you could fly for me.
I knew I could trust you, there was no need for no privacy.
You may not know it, but you influenced a part of me.
Fuck it, you changed me, excuse the language—just pardon me,
But it doesn't cover it hardly how immensely and largely,
You touch part of the heart of me.

———

Partway through my first semester of freshman year, I started to desperately miss playing football. When I wasn't in class or working, I would go to the rec center and work out. And I never failed to end up on the fence, watching the football team practicing. Even though I had initially thought I was done running up and down the gridiron, those feelings changed quickly once the season started. Vanderbilt had a tradition of letting all the freshmen students run down the field at the start of the first home game in what they referred to as the Gold Rush. It was then that I knew I didn't want to be a regular student. In my mind, I didn't want to look back on my college experience and think *what if,* so I decided I was going to do what I had to do to get back on the field.

A few weeks later, I found myself in the athletic facility in a meeting with a coach, discussing the possibility of my walking on to the team. He asked about my high school experience and found out that I had played at MBA just a few miles down the road. There were many ties between the two schools, so I knew that boded well in my favor. In fact, the athletic facility I was sitting in had been named after the great-grandfather of my high school's head coach, Daniel McGugin. Needless to say, the meeting went well, and the coach told me that he'd call me in a few days for a follow-up. When he did, he told me that he had spoken with Coach McGugin, who had told him I was one of his favorite players and people of all time. He followed that by inviting me to join the team for off-season workouts. I was elated.

Starting football meant that I no longer had the time to work my part-time job at the munchie mart with my new best friend, but it was a sacrifice I was willing to make. Academically, football actually provided the structure that I needed and was used to from high school. Prior to joining the football team, my grades were mediocre, which I wasn't used to after being a high achiever in the classroom all my life. I realized that I had more free time than I had ever had in my life, but I wasn't using that time to study more; I was much more interested in socializing and meeting as many people as I could on campus. For that reason, my grades suffered. However, during my second semester, because I was on a tighter schedule, during the little free time I did get, I spent it knocking out my work and studying. That first semester was a wake-up call for sure.

Playing football was probably the highlight of my undergraduate years. Not many things can top tens of thousands of fans cheering on your team while you run down the field. Just like in high school, the camaraderie among all my teammates was something that I still cherish. I had heard many horror stories about how walk-on players were treated at other schools, but Vanderbilt was different. From the administration to the training staff and the coaches, all the way down to the other players, everyone treated me with respect. This was highlighted when I went to the head coach, a soft-spoken, white-haired older man named Bobby Johnson, and asked to wear my high school number.

I started the conversation by saying, "Hey Coach, I know I'm a walk-on, but ..." He cut me off and told me it didn't matter if I was the best player on the team or the worst and that he would do his best to accommodate my request. Those words taught me so much about his character and made me love him more than I already had. It gave me an example of how good organizational culture should look. The best way to gauge culture in your organization is by asking the person at the bottom of the totem pole how they feel, and that will tell you everything you need to know. At that moment, I was at the bottom, but I felt like an equal. Right before the season started, Coach Johnson announced his retirement. It was weeks before our first game, so the school didn't have time to find new coaching staff to replace the current one. There were rumors that Coach Johnson had retired when he did to give his staff a complete year to find new jobs, because he knew that if he had retired earlier, everyone else would have been replaced. If true, that was just another way he showed his compassion for everyone he cared for. This was the community I had become a part of, and it felt amazing.

When the next season came around, I found out quickly that it was hard to get any playing time as a five-foot-nine, 165-pound defensive back walk-on on a team that struggled to win two games. Finally, during one of those wins, I was about to get my first opportunity to touch the field, but there was one issue: I had broken my hand two days prior. My hand had been aching previously, but I hadn't realized how badly injured it was until I tried to put on my glove the day of the game. It was virtually impossible, so I went to the head athletic trainer and asked him to look at it. He knew it was broken within seconds and asked me what happened. We had had a walk-through the Friday before the game, so there was no way it could have gotten hurt then. The story I told him was that I had hit it on someone's pads or helmet a few days ago but had tried to play through the pain. I could tell by his eyes that he thought the story was a lie. He went on to explain that I had what is referred to as a boxer's fracture, which usually comes from punching something, but he pretended to go with my story for the sake of it. In reality, I had indeed punched something, but I was too embarrassed to admit that.

What had actually happened, a few days before the game, was I punched my dresser in my bedroom out of anger and frustration. My high school girlfriend was visiting from her school, and things had been rocky between us basically since I had started college. We were drifting apart, and I didn't take it well. I got emotionally and even physically abusive with her. What started as an unhealthy need to control her every move turned into violent shoves and chokeholds in the latter end of our relationship. I don't have many regrets, but I do regret the way I treated her at the end. I had suspicions that she was moving on to other guys, mainly due to my deep insecurities that arose from my trust and abandonment issues, as I now realize, but nothing gave me the right to cause the harm that I had done to her. Knowing the lifetime of trauma I may have caused her has never sat well with me. While the physical bruises would go away, the emotional scars could be everlasting. What made it even worse was that I had vowed that I was going to be better than my dad when it came to how I treated women. Instead, I had done the same thing he had done to my mama and so many other women. I had let myself down and caused someone immense pain in the process. After our relationship came to an end, I renewed my vow that I wouldn't ever put my hands on another woman. When I reflect back on my life, it's probably the worst thing I've ever done to another person. I know that I can never change the past, but I can work to change the future. Learning from my mistakes, understanding and loving myself better, and finding healthy ways of expressing my emotions have helped me become a better version of myself.

After I had lied to the athletic trainer, he rushed me to get treated. "He might actually play this game," he explained to one of the other trainers, because the team we were playing was horrible, "so we need to make sure he is ready to go." After that, I stepped into a room where my naivete surrounding college football went out the window. The plan was to inject Toradol, an extremely effective painkiller, into my hand so that I wouldn't feel anything underneath the splint that was being used to keep my fingers in place. At the same time, I saw a starter on our team getting the same treatment to his ankle, which was rumored to be broken. My first thought was, *Damn, I could've used this in high school on my hips*, but that was followed by, *There's no way this is safe. My hand may be fine, but his ankle is going to be busted forever.* I later found out that Toradol shots were common in both collegiate and professional football. Win at all costs. By halftime, we hadn't established enough of a lead to justify putting me in, but the pain had returned and was worse than before. I got another round of shots to be ready for the next half and still didn't get to play. All that for nothing. I wouldn't get another opportunity to play again for the rest of the season.

After the end of yet another horrible season of 2–10, a new coaching staff was introduced to the university. It was a complete one-eighty. The head coach, James Franklin, was a younger, charismatic Black man who exuded so much confidence and passion. He ignited a fire for our team on the football field, around the university, and in the city of Nashville. It was a stark contrast from the soft-spoken, older, white-haired Coach Johnson. And although the two differed in a number of ways, I loved them both just as much for their commitment to making their players better men, on and off the field. That next season was amazing. We were finally competitive in nearly every game we played in, and eventually we made it to a bowl game. In fact, five out of the seven losses that we had were by six points or fewer. It wasn't ideal, but it still showed that we could actually play at a high level, which hadn't been the case the two years prior.

During spring and summer training, I proved to be a valuable member of the team. I impressed the new coaching staff and earned the skill player Iron Man Belt, an award given to the hardest-working player in off-season training, as judged by the strength coaches. I even earned a starting role on special teams. When the first game of the season rolled around, I had just one important task: be the first person down the field on kickoff, and don't let the kick returner outside of me. I can't tell you how hyped I was to know that I was actually going to be able to say that I had played college football in the SEC and that I was more than just a practice dummy. In that game, I recorded my first tackle, but most important, I got to live out one of my childhood dreams. Ever since I was ten years old playing in an all-star game in the Vanderbilt stadium, I had envisioned actually playing there on Saturdays and hearing my name being called by the announcer. I did that.

The year progressed. I played a little more and sat out a couple of games because that was the nature of not being a star player. Toward the end of that year, I started to feel unsatisfied with how I was going about my college experience. I had entered the university knowing that my efforts in the classroom were going to be my ticket to a better future, and although football helped to bring some structure back to my college life, it had become a burden in the pursuit of my long-term goals. Although I still maintained honor roll, my grades had suffered compared to what I was used to because I wasn't putting in the time to study properly; football had all of my attention.

Despite rules of amateurism, college athletics is big business. Student-athletes put their bodies at risk each and every day for entertainment without being adequately compensated for their work. While universities and the National Collegiate Athletic Association (NCAA) make billions of dollars, student-athletes are compensated with a "free education." However, a deeper look shows that, oftentimes, the value of that education compared to the hours spent "working" would suggest that student-athletes are compensated less than minimum wage. Additionally, many student-athletes are unable to take full advantage of their education due to the demands of their sports. Many universities force student-athletes into majors or paper courses that are not in their best interests. While the academic side of Vanderbilt often operated as if sports didn't exist at the university, the athletic department still demanded more than a fair share of our time.

Additionally, "optional" football workouts and practices during the summer made it difficult to commit to any internships, which ultimately affected my job-search process. So, after careful deliberation, I decided that after the final game, it was time for me to hang up my cleats for good and step into the next phase of life. It was one of the most difficult decisions I had ever made, but it was necessary for me to continue to chase the goals that were most important to me. I didn't know it at the time, but that decision would weigh on me and bring out emotions that I didn't even know I could feel.

———

After my football days were over, I was able to focus on the real reason I had gone to college—to get a world-class education. My grades skyrocketed, and I finished my last three semesters on the Dean's List, something I hadn't done in my entire college career before that point. With a new perspective on my future, I was able to take the drive and focus that I had dedicated to football and apply that to the classroom and beyond.

In all of my college career, I retook only one course due to a horrible grade, and ironically, it happened to be the course that directly relates to my current career path. The course was Money and Banking. The first time I took it was during my last semester on the football team, which was one reason for my inability to grasp the concepts, but the other was my own hubris. When I signed up for the class, I thought, *Easy A; I been makin' money my whole life.* It was a naïve and narrow-minded view. Because I had so much confidence in my own knowledge of money, I neglected the study materials and thought my common sense would help me excel. What I failed to realize was that my view of money had been shaped in a household and community where there was no money. And although I had been marginally more knowledgeable about money than those I had grown up with because of my experience at MBA, I was still ignorant in the grand scheme of things. That class humbled me, but I took the class again the next semester and did well. I was taught a great lesson that there is a whole world of knowledge, especially as it relates to money and wealth, that nothing in my experience could have prepared me for. It made my thirsty to learn even more.

I quickly discovered that college was not only about getting good grades. The experiences were what proved to be most beneficial. An education from college wasn't going to teach me everything I needed to know about the real world or my future job, but what college did teach was me how to think about and see challenges as opportunities for solutions. Knowledge is power, and the more we know, the more we are able to accomplish, not only for ourselves but also for the world as a whole. Knowledge can be obtained in a number of ways, but experience is one of the best teachers. When navigating life, seek to find lessons in everything, whether good or bad. If you fail, don't consider it a failure; instead, consider it an experiment. Experiments can't be passed or failed. You simply use an experiment to collect data, so you can apply it elsewhere later in hopes of a better result.

College also provided a social aspect that cannot be replicated in any other arena of life. Being surrounded by thousands of determined young adults who are finding their way in life and striving to be better than they were the day before pushes you forward to do the same. On top of making sure my grades were back on track, I made an effort to engage with my peers outside of football. I reengaged with my old friends who had grown used to seeing me less because of my football commitments, and I began to associate more with other students on campus. Similar to how I approached my first semester, I met so many people, but unlike freshman year, I was doing so in a more productive manner. It was an adjustment from primarily socializing to a focus on networking.

We all know the cliché "It's not about what you know, it's about who you know." Well, I like to take that a step further by saying, "It's not only about who you know, it's also about who knows you." Many opportunities open up in life when the right person knows about you and your reputation. Networking is a skill that allows that to happen.

I cannot stress enough the importance of networking. Networking is connecting with people. I like to think networking should be done in the most genuine manner, with quality trumping quantity. There are master networkers who can work a room and leave with hundreds of connections, and there are people who are too shy to look up from their shoes. I've been both and everywhere in between. The times when

I've allowed myself to connect with a just few people on a deep level have provided the best opportunities for me.

While networking is extremely important, it becomes one of the hardest things to do when you are battling mental health issues such as grief or depression, which I found out early in my career. Operating in a financial services business requires a lot of networking and dealing with people on a daily basis. Because of some of the battles I was facing in my personal life, there were many days when I would be so overwhelmed that I couldn't get out of bed. Sometimes I tried to avoid personal contact altogether. If I did attempt to do work, it was halfhearted. I called people at times when I knew they wouldn't be able to answer. I rescheduled meetings or canceled them with little notice. Being alone was my way of coping. And I know if I've felt that way, many others may have also felt this same way at some point in their lives. Just know that you are not alone. Know that is okay to not feel okay. Rejecting invites or leaving functions might be the best medicine for times when you need to recover. There is nothing wrong with that.

Finally, college challenged my perception of what it means to be Black. Nearly all my life, I had been programmed to think that to really be Black, you had to come from a certain background or be associated with things like the hood, Ebonics, living in poverty, going to certain schools, having a dysfunctional family structure, and so much more. I know the treatment I received from going to a predominantly white high school and being considered less Black for it played a huge role in that belief. But I came to realize that my concept of what it meant to be Black was socially forced upon me in the name of systemic racism, which forced me to see Black as inferior. Similar to Ibram X. Kendi, as he chronicled his own personal journey of self-discovery in his best-selling book *How to Be an Antiracist*, I had to learn to embrace the positive aspects of my Blackness while unlearning the negative associations that growing up in America had taught me.

In an African American Studies class, my eyes and mind were opened to how flawed my views were. We read a book called *Who's Afraid of Post-Blackness: Forty Million Ways to Be Black*, which forced me to reconsider my personal definition of what it meant to be Black. A Black person who is educated, articulate, from a good neighborhood, has both parents, and lives in abundance isn't any less Black than any other Black person. I let go of these flawed views. Our uniqueness as a people is our beauty. I will forever embrace it.

In the spirit of reflecting, I now realize that, for years, I had been repeating a lie about my transition from my predominantly Black middle school to my predominantly white private school. The lie, "I was the only Black person in my grade the first year," simply wasn't true. There was, in fact, another Black student in the class, but because of my flawed ways of thinking, I didn't consider his Blackness to be "Black enough," or rather Black at all. A brilliant half-Black and half-Asian young man walked the halls with me every day with what I now assume was an even more complex approach to his personal identity as a biracial individual in that environment. But I had never acknowledged his Blackness. I didn't get to know him well because he left the school after my first year, but I wish I had done so. Perhaps we had more in common than I realized.

———

To my surprise, one of the people I met haphazardly during college would turn out to change my life forever. On a typical day between classes, I was sitting outside the dining hall with one of my teammates, waiting on the next class period to start. Out of nowhere, our conversation was interrupted by a girl named Katie who was sitting near-by. "Who doesn't like the Olympics?" was the first thing she said to me. She had mistaken my reference to a pair of Retro 7 Air Jordans named the Olympics for the actual Olympic Games. It just so happened that a few days prior, another friend had asked me if I knew this girl because she was a local who had attended a school I had actually played against. At the time, I didn't know her, but I decided to befriend her on Facebook anyway. She was beautiful, and I knew that one day, I would somehow meet her. But I never thought it would happen the way it did. Three days after virtually befriending her, she interrupted my conversation in person. And three days after that, she entered my life to stay.

We talked for hours about life, wondering how our paths had never crossed before that point. I learned about her family's history, and I shared with her some of mine. She was shocked when I told her where I had gone to high school, because I was so far from the image she had had in her mind when it came to people from MBA. I was sure to debunk the myth that all everyone there were privileged, rich, entitled, white boys. She surprised me at how opinionated she was about top-ics that I rarely discussed, like politics and the inequalities our world faced. One of the things that stood out the most about her was that she challenged me to think. Bringing to the table such articulate arguments about everything under the stars, she was able to keep me engaged in conversations I had never had before. After talking to her for just a few hours, I knew being in her presence was going to make me a better version of myself.

Like an angel, Katie came into my life in the midst of some trag-ic losses, when all I needed was someone to talk to. She was good at that. I eventually opened up to her about some of the tragedies I had faced. On the heels of my cousin's murder, I was also grieving the loss of Coach Davis's daughter. Her death had occurred just five days before we met, so the emotions and pain were still heavy on my heart, although I tried to mask it most of the time. Unlike anyone I had ever met, I felt a sense of comfort with her that allowed me to talk freely about how I was feeling. Even though it hurt to expose myself like that to someone, because I had never done it before, it also felt like a weight had been lifted off my shoulders.

Before Katie, De'Anté and James were the only two people to whom I had come close to revealing deep personal issues. Among the three of us, we had experienced similar traumas and hardships in life, and we could sense that in each other. It was easier talking about the struggle with them because there was never a sense that they would judge me—since all they had to do was change a few names and places and basically tell the exact same stories about their lives. But Katie was different. Her life had been essentially trauma-free, but I got the same comfort knowing that she was never judging me. She equipped me with a vocabulary and scientific research that helped me express my traumatic past, especially as it compared to other people with similar experiences. She took the information I had barely retained from my Psychology 101 course and made it practical to my actual life.

Prior to meeting her, I hadn't had much alcohol in my life (other than with Pops when I was a child), but when I turned twenty-one, I started to drink. That opened up a whole new box of emotions that I hadn't ever expressed. At parties, where everything seemed to be going well, I'd suddenly feel a sense of grief wash over me and break into tears. I couldn't explain it. I would go from dancing and singing to sulking in a corner in a matter of seconds without any warning. It was then that I realized just how much all the trauma I had internalized over the years was affecting me.

One thing that I hadn't given a second thought to when I was playing football was how painful it would be to leave the game behind.

Football had opened doors to a new life and given me a sense of accomplishment, while helping build me into the man I had become. Although I had made the choice to leave football behind, it was a huge loss that I was subconsciously grieving. So much of my identity was tied to the sport, and the football field had become my safe haven in a world full of drama. How was I going to replace something that was so near and dear to my heart for half my life? I didn't watch a single football game the entire year after I was done playing because I couldn't bear the fact that I would never step foot on the field again.

That's when I opened up to Katie even more. She was there to listen and give me advice. She removed the stigma that I was weak for having those emotions and made me feel like everything I was feeling was valid. After a while, I had gotten to a point where I had just accepted the losses in my life. For the first time, I was expressing true emotion, and it felt good. That feeling of comfort quickly grew into love, and that love soon grew into trust. That was huge for me. I knew I had loved before, but I can't honestly say that I had ever truly trusted anyone before I met my angel, Katie. Our relationship continued to grow stronger over the years. We became best friends and lovers. Although my fear of allowing someone so close to my heart caused me to default back to my shell and push her away at times, her understanding and love remained unwavering.

She seemed to take so much of my pain away, pain that I didn't even know existed because I had never known a life without it. Imagine being born in a fire pit, and for your whole life, you've lived in that fire pit. During the years you are in the fire, you grow so accustomed to the pain that you don't even know you are burning. It's only when you are pulled from the fire that you realize just how badly hurt you are from experiencing that life of pain. It's not until you escape the pain and experience bliss that you realize how damaged you once were. That's what it felt like for me to finally find joy. I had finally escaped the fire. For so many people living in this pain and who constantly surround themselves by other people in the same situation, they are unable to realize their circumstances. That was the case for most people in my family. My mama and dad, having been confined to one type of lifestyle, had never been pulled from the fire. They were still in the environment that was causing their pain; thus, they were far less able to recognize it.

The tables were reversed just a couple of years into our relationship, when Katie's dad was diagnosed with ALS, an uncurable and often fatal neurodegenerative disease that leads to muscle atrophy and impacts your ability to make voluntary movements. She had been my support through so much that I had been through, and it was my time to step up for her. When I talk about the relativity of trauma, I think of that moment for her. She had been blessed with a peaceful, nontraumatic upbringing for the most part. However, with one heavy blow, the most traumatic thing that could have happened to her did. When I first met her, I could already tell how close she was with her father, but their relationship was stronger than I had realized. The possibility of losing someone so significant meant that she and her family were going to need the strongest support system around. The tragic news brought about strength and unity despite the uncertainty of the days to come. Just like we had done in my times of need, we bonded closer in hers.

CHAPTER NINE

I AM THE ROSE

ollege had proven to be a success. Yet again, I had been placed in an unfamiliar environment compared to anyone who had come before me, but I had made the best of the opportunity and thrived in multiple aspects. Leading up to graduation, I had met hundreds and maybe even thousands of people who came from different backgrounds with different stories and different perspectives to add to my view of the world, including some dear friends and loved ones. I had received a world-class education, learning from some of the most highly regarded educators. I got to play football at the highest level collegiately for a coach who, I would argue, will go down as one of the best in history. I joined a network of alumni that stretches across the entire globe, full of successful people in their respective fields. And most important, I continued to grow into a better me—one who was more self-aware than ever before.

I majored in economics, which was a popular major for folks who had aspirations of working on Wall Street for prominent investment banks. I didn't share those dreams, because I honestly had no exposure to what they were. Many children were following in the footsteps of their parents in their career choice, but I was basically paving the way for myself. It wasn't until my senior year that I started to seriously consider career opportunities. While the summer leading up to my senior year was productively spent interning at the Nashville Entrepreneur Center, where I was able to consult with a number of different start-up companies, I knew it would take some time before I was ready to become an entrepreneur myself. During my senior year, I started to ask my peers about their postgraduate plans. By that time, many of them had already had one or two internships with investment banks where they wanted to work. While I saw my lack of internship experience as a disadvantage for me, I believed I could overcome it and still land a job at a similar firm. I was wrong.

It was nearly impossible to get the job offers that my fellow classmates with internship experience received. Then, one day, my future plans became clear. I was sitting in an accounting class during the second semester of my senior year, and recruiters from Vanderbilt's Owen Graduate School of Management came to pitch the Master of Accountancy (MAcc) program. It felt too good to be true. In just one year, I would finish with a master's degree from one of the country's top business schools, have unrivaled exposure to the Big Four accounting firms, get experience with a ten-week paid internship, and pass the CPA exam all before starting with one of those Big Four firms. Not to mention, the MAcc program had the highest pass rate in the country for the CPA exam. I was sold.

I never wanted to have a career in accounting, but from my time at the Entrepreneur Center, I knew that learning "the language of business" would bode well for me in any future endeavor. So, I applied. Just as soon as I pressed *enter* on my application, I was called in for an interview. The very next day, I was accepted. That day was full of joy. Not only was I a few months away from being the first person in my family to attend and graduate from college, but also I was headed to business school to receive a master's degree. I felt like the sky was the limit.

The summer prior to starting the MAcc program, I had a moment when my judgment failed, and I feared it would jeopardize my plans. During a drunken night at a bar with my brother Jarrett, an incident occurred where I felt disrespected. I was hit in the face by another patron for stumbling and bumping into them, and I reverted back to my childish ways, which resulted in an altercation where I swung back. Unlike childhood fights, adult ones came with serious consequences, and just as soon as my fist landed, those consequences came to my mind. My instincts were to run—and that's what I did. There I was, Vanderbilt grad who had never been in any trouble, with a future as bright as the stars, running away from bouncers and police officers through the downtown streets of Nashville. While I was running, I felt so ashamed. Flashes of my dad running from the police appeared in my head. I had always strived to be better than him, and at that moment, I had failed myself.

On foot, they stood no chance of catching me, but I slowed down as I approached a busy intersection at Broadway and Second Avenue. Just as soon as I did, a cop on a horse stopped me. I surrendered and threw my hands in the air. When the bouncer who was chasing me finally caught up, he put me in an unnecessary headlock that I'm sure he got some pleasure out of. The police officers put cuffs on my wrists. The feeling of them clamping down and pinching my skin was something I had never thought I would have to experience. After that, I felt the pain that so many Black men suffer. Without knowing much at all about what had just taken place, the police assumed I was a criminal. Two officers on separate horses told me to raise my hands as they put a baton in between my arms and held either end of it. The grip of the handcuffs squeezed tighter, ripping the skin off my wrists as they lifted me up off my feet. I complained about the discomfort, and an officer glared at me and shouted, "Shut the fuck up, or it will get even worse!" Again, unnecessary behavior because I had given myself up and had been cooperative.

Up until that point, my encounters with the police had never resulted in any physical harm. I was used to being stopped and harassed for walking or lounging outside with friends. I had been pulled over a number of times for no reason other than to let the officer "get a look at [my] face" or because "[my] tags are set to expire next month." While I knew all those occasions were a result of racial profiling, I usually went on about my way emotionally rattled but physically unharmed.

However, as I looked up at the officer that night, so much fear and terror ran through my mind and body. If I hadn't shut up, how bad would it have gotten? Knowing that so many young men who looked just like me had been beaten and even killed for far less than what I had engaged in that night, I couldn't help but think, what if it had escalated? Would someone have been there to record it? Would anyone have stepped in and stopped the abuse? Would the police have justified their actions because I had been running? Would they bring up all of my past wrongdoings in the media? Would my name be preceded by a hashtag or the dreaded three letters? Would it cause protests? Riots? More violence? Would I be here today to tell this story? The thoughts alone haunt me.

I was eventually put in the back of the police car and asked about the incident. The officer asked me if I had ever been arrested.

"No, sir," I told him, and I believed that was true.

"Why are you lying to me?" he asked as he brought up incidents from my childhood that I had been told would never be a part of my record.

"I have never been in handcuffs or in the back of a police car, and I have never been told that I was being arrested or read my rights, sir." I thought it was bizarre that my minor childhood transgressions were even being discussed.

Among the offenses he began to name were several citations I had received for fighting in my teenage years. I had received another citation for indecent exposure for having sex with a girlfriend in a car when I was fifteen. As he read that offense to me, I had a flashback of that day. The officer had pulled up right next to my girlfriend's car and flashed a light on us, though the fog on the windows blocked his vision. When we got out of the car, he asked me for identification. Because I was only fifteen, I didn't have a license or anything other than a school ID. He didn't accept it and told me that he was going to take me downtown to the detention center while he allowed my girlfriend, who happened to be white, to call her parents to pick her up. I shook my head as my heart dropped to my stomach, but I never showed the pain I felt from the injustice. I had always feared being fingerprinted and falsely accused of an unsolved crime that the police wanted to close. I had seen that happen once, and that was one too many times. When he saw how badly the thought of my arrest was making my girlfriend cry, he had a change of heart and allowed me to call my parents as well. My dad had just gotten out of prison, and I knew he would be more understanding than my mama, so I called him to come and get me. I didn't receive a lecture on the ride home; instead, my dad and I shared a resounding message: fuck the police. Police had been a source of trauma for both of us at that point. Thankfully, I had been saved by the tears of a white girl.

Feeling that the officer was trying to provoke me, I said, "I never tried to lie to you, but I also never knew that I had been arrested. My apologies." Taking the blame didn't seem fair to me at all. In a moment of clarity, I asked the officer if my current arrest would negatively impact my acceptance into business school. He didn't have an answer for me, but that became the only thing I could focus on. After getting my statement, the officer cited me with disorderly conduct and let me out of the car. Disappointed in myself, I went home and had a long night of reflection. The next morning, I physically exhausted myself in punishment and as a way to get back on track. I posted a picture on Facebook on June 15, 2013, after my workout with the caption: "Just ran 5 miles while jump roping then two 400s. Gotta get back FOCUSED!" At the time, only Jarrett and Katie knew why. The charge was eventually expunged from my record and had no effect on my pursuit of higher learning.

———

"My name is Reggie Ford, but you can call me Ford Mustang. No, I'm not a big, strong, fast muscle car, but I'm driven, and to understand me, you have to know what drives me. I have three key motivators: my family, competition, and people telling me I can't. Everything I do is for my family, to see that those who have come after me can have a better life than I've had. As a consummate competitor, I always want to win. And when people tell me I can't, all I want to do is prove them wrong. One thing that people told me I couldn't do was play Division I football because I was too small, weak, and slow. Ultimately, I got the opportunity to play football in the SEC at Vanderbilt. One day, my coach pulled me aside and told me that I'd played big, strong, and fast and gave me the nickname Ford Mustang."

The quote above is a paraphrased elevator pitch that I delivered in my first communications class during business school. Instead of going the traditional route of regurgitating my résumé, I wanted to express creativity, which resulted in my receiving the best grade in the class.

Drive is something that isn't taught; you are either born with it or you aren't. Sometimes in sports, we describe drive as "having that dog in you." When you "have that dog in you," you do whatever you have to do to accomplish a goal. The obstacle for most people is finding the drive or "the dog" within themselves. To find it, you have to find your passion. For me, my passion has been helping my family and making believers out of disbelievers. Everyone has different passions. Find yours and unleash "that dog" within you.

One misconception is that drive has to be nonstop. One thing I am adamant about is taking breaks and finding time to rest. Sometimes high achievers believe that to reach new heights, you have to be "on" twenty-four/seven, and that rest shows weakness. To the contrary, rest is essential. Self-care is vital. To be the best version of yourself, you have to recover.

The MAcc program was everything it was advertised to be. The class size was small, so we had a tight-knit group. Everyone was brilliant and ambitiously working to achieve the goals they had set for themselves. Some had aspirations of making partner at a Big Four accounting firm, while others were using the MAcc program as a springboard to other opportunities. I fell into the latter group, but I was willing to go through the process as the creators of the program had intended. My goal was to shine in the networking opportunities with the Big Four accounting firms, land an internship, get a full-time offer, and pass the CPA exam all in one year. And that is exactly what I did. I was recognized by the business school as an Owen World Shaper, an honor given to those who not only succeed in the business world but also shape the community for the better.

Through my hard work, intelligence, positive attitude, and ability to connect with the team, I landed a full-time offer with one of the most prestigious companies in the world, a Big Four accounting firm.

They often bragged that it was more difficult to get a job there than it was to get into Harvard based on acceptance rates. Not only was I employed by a great company, the Fortune 500 clients that I worked for were also amazing, which allowed me to receive world-class business experience. The work was extremely demanding and fast-paced during certain parts of the year. It was a great start to my career. On top of that, some of the people I met became a part of my family. However, after a few years, I realized that my passion lay elsewhere.

I grew up in a socioeconomic condition that was marked by a cycle of poverty. From my perspective, this phenomenon has been exacerbated due to financial illiteracy and lack of awareness surrounding wealth accumulation. Given that I had come from that type of situation but was now in a position to recognize the glaring holes of knowledge, I felt that it was my responsibility to help others realize the financial power they could also possess. For that reason, I decided that wealth management would be the best route for me. When I was ready to leave the job, I came across a quote by Steve Jobs that spoke to me:

> *Your work is going to fill a large part of your life, and the only way to be truly satisfied is to do what you believe is great work. And the only way to do great work is to love what you do. If you haven't found it yet, keep looking. Don't settle. As with all matters of the heart, you'll know when you find it. And, like any great relationship, it just gets better and better as the years roll on.*

After reading that quote, I knew it was time for me to move on from the accounting firm.

I joined a wealth management firm in Nashville that catered to some of the wealthiest families in the state and across the country. The firm was located in the heart of Belle Meade, less than a mile away from MBA, so feelings of my time in high school reemerged. I often felt out of place, but I knew there was much I could learn from being in that uncomfortable environment. If my life had taught me anything up to that point, it was to become comfortable with being uncomfortable.

Socially, it was more difficult than MBA. Out of the entire firm, I was one of two Black employees. The other, Frederick, was an older Black man in his sixties who had been forced to assimilate in an industry that rarely gave men who looked like him opportunities. After college, I had gained a new sense of awareness for the issues plaguing the Black community, so much so that I began to see injustice everywhere. But it was as if the Belle Meade bubble was blind to what I was feeling—even Frederick, at times.

During the moments of the deaths of Freddie Gray, Philando Castile, and Alton Sterling, I wished to be in an environment that would allow me to grieve properly for the deaths of yet another Black person who didn't deserve to die. During the Charlottesville protests, I wished to hear my coworkers in the breakroom denouncing white supremacy and recognizing the challenges that Black people and other people of color faced in this country. In response to the NFL and Colin Kaepernick's protests of police brutality and racial inequality, I wished to hear my managing directors using their privilege, power, and influence to develop strategic solutions to the systemic issues by which I had been directly affected.

Instead, I heard nothing about the deaths. Not even the deaths of Jocques Clemmons or Daniel Hambrick, who had been murdered by police in our own city of Nashville. I heard no one denouncing white supremacy or the mass shooter Travis Reinking, who before being fought off by a local hero James Shaw Jr., had killed Akilah DaSilva, Joe Perez, Taurean Sanderlin, and DeEbony Groves, the cousin of one of my childhood best friends at a Nashville Waffle House. I heard nothing about what the organization was doing to combat the issues that had prevented me from thinking clearly due to my constant sense of grief. What I did hear were comments that riots weren't the answer, that disrespecting the flag was not a productive form of protest, and that professional athletes should be grateful for their large paychecks, followed by the question, "What more do they want?"

I wish they had heard my response when I said, "*They* want to get your attention because there is a terroristic threat to the survival of people who look just like me only because they were born Black. They got your attention, but I think you missed their point. Now that you know, they want you to educate yourself to the systemic problems that have plagued our society so that you can begin to sympathize even though you will never know what it truly feels like. Then, they want you to act in a manner that promotes change and that will break down the systems of oppression that have created the unjust and inequitable world that has afforded you the privilege of believing that the reason they are kneeling is about a piece of fabric instead of the loss of lives. They want you to be committed to the necessary changes until the more than four hundred years of painful history is actual history and not a continuation of the present." They didn't hear that, though, because I had only said it to myself in my head. I wish I had spoken up.

While blind, deaf, and mute to those issues, the environment didn't contain an ounce of hatred toward me. Like my time at MBA, I was welcomed and loved, but I felt isolated. That isolation sometimes turned into bitterness, which made it difficult to motivate myself to attack every day with the tenacity that had landed me the job in the first place. I attempted to introduce clients and candidates to join the company as an attempt to alleviate the feelings I had. My efforts were often in vain. More disheartening was that many of our clients and even some of my coworkers were large stakeholders in CoreCivic, formerly known as the Corrections Corporation of America (CCA), the second-largest privately held prison company in the United States. Growing up in Nashville, CCA was a household name. Not because we were investors in the company, but because we knew so many people who had been locked up there. It wasn't until I got to the firm that I saw the monetary value that private prisons provided wealthy people. They were literally becoming wealthier as a result of more people being imprisoned. It made me think of the people like my dad, who had essentially paid their quarterly dividends several times over during their periods of incarceration.

As hard as it was to face my new reality, I endured it because of the benefits I was afforded by being there. The work that I was performing on a daily basis was totally different from the work I had done at my previous company. I was learning a new skill, and that intrigued me. Through all of my training and education, I had never truly learned personal finance or wealth management. While I was familiar with a number of concepts, I had never had a real understanding of wealth until working there. My goal was to endure it for as long as I could and soak up the knowledge that was so often withheld from people like me.

The one glimmer of familiarity was Frederick. I had the pleasure of getting to know him during the recruitment process as he had been tasked to take me to lunch a couple of times before I signed my offer letter. He had an uncanny ability to connect with people from all backgrounds and appeared so genuine. I loved that about him. He made me feel comfortable. A lot of days, when I felt like I couldn't turn to anyone else, I would go to his office to seek counsel. He always broadened my mind, even when we had differing opinions. He also expressed how I too had opened his eyes to issues that he had so often overlooked. For instance, he didn't find it problematic that clients would frequently mistake me for a former Black intern, DeShaun, despite not working in the same department or looking anything like him. He initially didn't understand why I had taken the day off after the 2016 presidential election that had divided our country in ways I had never witnessed in my short life. There was one person who understood my reason, but he didn't even know me. His name was Michael Emerson, coauthor of *Divided by Faith: Evangelical Religion and the Problem of Race in America*, who stated, "The election itself was the single most harmful event to the whole movement of reconciliation in at least the past thirty years."

As was often the case, after we debriefed, which was a healthy exercise for both of us mentally, he often was left reevaluating the way he had normalized so much of his career's experience. Despite our different views, our relationship grew so much that he started sharing deep personal aspects of his life. It helped me understand and respect him even more than I already had. Our bond grew into a father-son type of relationship, which I cherished. Similar to the area of refuge that I had with Granny and Pops, Frederick's office and our many conversations kept me sane and motivated in a world that was tough to navigate.

———

Within months of working at the wealth management firm, I was recognized as one of Nashville's Black 40 under 40. At twenty-six years old, I was one of the youngest honorees of the award. The appropriate response to receiving that award should have been a display of pride that I was being recognized for the hard work I had put in my entire life. Instead, I barely acknowledged the achievement because it felt like a consolation. I knew that the world would devalue the honor because of one word, *Black*. I hadn't achieved Nashville's 40 under 40, which was hoisted up on a pedestal and presented in the *Nashville Business Journal* each year. Instead, my award was not as highly touted and presented in a young Black-owned publication, *STAYONTHEGO Magazine*, which many people hadn't heard of.

Although my playing days were over, I kept in touch with a number of former teammates, some of whom were professional athletes in need of financial advice. Since I was in the business and had experience working with high-net-worth families, I was equipped with the knowledge to provide the advice that they needed. In helping them, I realized that they were part of the majority of people who had little knowledge when it came to their personal finances. It worried me, especially considering how notoriously professional athletes managed their finances. I used the opportunity to write a detailed article on why professional athletes go broke, which garnered a lot of support and sparked my desire to become a solution to the issues that they faced.

During the day, I was helping well-established millionaires, trust-fund babies, and generational-wealth beneficiaries to grow and maintain their wealth. At night, I was researching about or working with professional athletes to help them achieve financial freedom and sustainability. I quickly realized that there was a financial literacy problem that needed to be addressed. Although I added true value to my clients in the day, I was so much more valuable to these less financially equipped professional athletes.

The passion grew so much that I decided I wanted to help more professional athletes become better at managing their money. While I had initial plans of doing it at my firm, there was little interest in my doing so, and the cultural fit, I felt, would be a barrier to the story I wanted to tell. I decided I wanted to start my own firm. Although I loved working with my traditional wealth management clients, I felt that they would be taken care of with or without my help. On the other hand, I thought that my knowledge and life experiences would resonate a lot better with professional athletes who were young and often from communities similar to the one I had grown up in. Having seen how Pops's relatively high income was squandered away due to a lack of knowledge on how to manage money, the passion to prevent that in others turned into a burning desire. The idea of starting a firm finally came to fruition, and I called it RoseCrete Wealth Management.

RoseCrete derives its name from the metaphor of the rose that grows from concrete. In a poem, Tupac Shakur describes how marvelous it is that a rose has grown out of a crack in the concrete. With no sunlight, little water, and poor soil, the rose is faced with the most extreme adversity, yet it still manages to blossom into a beautiful flower. People coming from the toughest conditions can fight in the face of adversity and become a success. As Shakur wished in his poem, our society should recognize those people and also recognize that they may be a little rough around the edges because of their beginnings. But even though you can see those rough edges, when you find out where they've come from, the blemishes become irrelevant. The journey and results are what matter most.

Everyone faces adversity, but it's not the adversity that defines a person; it's how they respond to that adversity. Like the rose, many professional athletes have faced obstacles, both on and off the field, to reach their degrees of success. Despite the highly unfavorable odds of making it to the professional level, they thrive. For some, the odds of making it out of their neighborhoods alone are even more astounding. The metaphor was also a representation of my life. The success that I was experiencing was seemingly impossible, yet I was living it. RoseCrete was created to celebrate that—not only in my story, but in the stories of so many others like me.

Just as soon as I launched RoseCrete, I was interviewed by a writer from *Forbes* who decided to feature me and RoseCrete in an article about the importance of financial literacy. It blew my mind that I was even being considered for a feature. When the article finally published after months of back-and-forth with the writer and editor, it brought tears to my eyes. At the time, I hadn't accomplished nearly anything compared to what I knew I could do, but the recognition was beyond my imagination. It was the feeling I should have possessed when I landed on Nashville's Black 40 under 40.

After the article was published, I was also nominated for *Forbes* 30 under 30, a set of lists presented by *Forbes* magazine of some of the top entrepreneurs, entertainers, and creators in the United States and Canada. Although I ultimately did not make the list, the nomination proved to me that I was on the right path. Shortly after the nomination, I was featured in the Top 100 in *Finance Magazine*, which was a huge honor for me. And although I hadn't "made it" yet by any stretch of the imagination, it started to feel like I was finally moving in my purpose. Dreams that I hadn't even been able to fathom when I was younger were coming true.

I would not be where I am without the opportunities I have been blessed with. Time after time, people have witnessed potential in me, sometimes when I couldn't see it myself. My obligation was to see that I made the most of those opportunities. Opportunity alone will not turn dreams into reality. You must take full advantage of those opportunities when presented. If not, they could pass you by. It takes hard work to reap the rewards of a good opportunity, and when the work isn't there, an opportunity becomes a thing of the past—what once was or what could've been. Opportunity may never knock. It might only knock once. If and when it does, be ready. Stay ready so you don't have to get ready. And if it doesn't knock, create an opportunity for yourself. You'll savor the prize that much more if you create something out of nothing. And for those in a position to help someone else out, present the opportunity. It could change a person's life forever.

———

Money is interesting. When you have it, it is less of a constant concern. When you don't have it, that fact consumes you. Having an abundance of a resource can either make you wasteful or ungrateful. When you have so much of something that you can't run out of it, you simply don't think about it as much. Conversely, the lack of an essential resource becomes all you can think about. If you were suffering from a lack of oxygen, it would be difficult, nearly impossible, to think about anything else when all you are trying to do is breathe and survive. Living in poverty is similar to that.

I've been running from poverty my entire life. Although poverty is defined by the lack of money, it is so much more than that. Because money is such a necessary resource in everyday life, not having such a vital resource creates many issues. A lack of money can give rise to stress, which can result in long-term health issues, both physically and mentally. It can lead to abuse, because frustration builds up and takes over to a point of helplessness. It can lead to poor education and job opportunities, which perpetuate the cycle and keep the impoverished where they are.

Having seen the effects of a life in poverty, I knew I wanted to end that cycle. While many people who are living in poverty lack the opportunities to change their circumstances, I was fortunate enough to be presented with countless. Taking advantage of each of those opportunities was important not only for me, but also for the millions of people who continue to suffer.

I've always felt that education is a good equalizer to help bridge the gap. For that reason, I consider myself a lifelong learner, and as of late, a lifelong educator. I continuously educate myself on as much as I can so I can apply and pass down that knowledge. In addition to general education, financial education is a tool that will help build up more financially independent people. Hopefully, it results in generational wealth for many more families.

While I don't hold money and wealth as the highest of all virtues, primarily because I've seen the evil that the greed for money brings, I do recognize its power. Wealth buys more than material possessions. It buys us a seat at the table to make decisions that will impact communities. It influences politics and laws and regulations that impact our education, criminal justice, and financial systems. Those spheres, in turn, can impact our mental health because money can sometimes buy peace of mind. With fewer life stressors that financial stability and economic empowerment can lead to, many issues that have plagued me and those I love would have less of an impact on our daily lives. While money isn't everything, it does affect nearly everything. This fact of life is just one reason why I am constantly running from the poverty I was born into and running toward wealth while trying to bring as many people with me as I can.

CHAPTER TEN

BLM

Throughout this book, I have alluded to the most glaring form of trauma I have faced in my life: racism. The aggregation of my life's experiences has helped me to formulate a growing racial consciousness that has given me a new vocabulary to discuss racialized trauma. I have experienced life from polar-opposite sides of many social spectrums, yet one thing has remained constant—I am a Black man in America. Stating that phrase in that manner shows the disconnect that I have with the country I have always lived in and pledged allegiance to, all because of the color of my skin. It just doesn't feel natural or right to say I am an American man. I'll admit that I have been blessed and privileged to avoid some of the evils that racism brings. Some would argue that this simple fact could have turned me further away from the fight for justice since those issues have had less of an impact on my life compared to others of my race. Instead, it did the complete opposite. I've realized that my blessings and privilege mean that I have to fight even harder for a greater cause that is so much larger than myself. Although things seem better for me from a myopic perspective, I still can't escape the horrors of racism.

To those who know me, I am Reggie D. Ford, a friend, family member, colleague, or acquaintance, but to many who don't, I am just a Black man in America. That comes with a host of negative responses: being forced to buy a pack of gum when the store I enter doesn't have the item I want to prevent being patted down and accused of shoplifting, which makes me feel *untrustworthy*; risking running out of gas to avoid exits or gas stations that present Confederate flags or give me a "bad feeling," which leaves me *anxious*; unwarranted traffic stops or questioning that leave me in *fear*; unnecessary invasion of privacy and physically forceful behavior from those who are supposedly there to serve and protect me, which leave me *distrustful* and in *pain*; harassment for congregating with my friends and brothers that leave me feeling *angry* and *irritated*; strange stares as I walk around my current and childhood neighborhood that has now been gentrified as if I don't belong, which make me feel *unwelcome*; comments that qualify any redeeming quality I have with the phrase "... for a Black guy," which leave me feeling *inferior*; prejudices that cause people to fear that I have the intent to commit a crime at any given moment, which make the true intent of my character feel *unknown*; and more comments that downplay the fact that the foundation of our country was built on racism that still exists today, which make me feel *unheard*, *belittled*, and *ignored*.

And I'm one of the lucky ones—and trust me, I'm *grateful* for that. The truth is all these negative feelings that have resulted from the racism I've faced have contributed to the life of trauma that I have lived.

———

Not long ago, I learned the story of a young man that moved me to tears. Kalief Browder was sixteen years old when he and a friend were cornered by the police, who asserted that they fit the description of thieves who had stolen a backpack days before. Though he denied having any involvement in the crime, and there was no evidence of the contrary, he was arrested on the spot. His bail was set at three thousand dollars, but with the aid of a bail bondsman, the amount his family needed to free him was nine hundred dollars. In the two weeks it took for his adoptive mother to raise the funds, his bail was denied because the judge considered Kalief to be in violation of his probation (from a previous arrest) by simply being arrested again.

Kalief's biological mother suffered from a drug addiction, which forced Kalief into the care of Child Protective Services. He was later taken in by a woman who had raised more than thirty children whom she had given birth to, adopted, or fostered throughout her lifetime. Though Kalief had seven biological siblings, he grew up with six siblings, some of whom were biological, all raised by his adoptive mother.

Prior to the aforementioned arrest, Kalief was charged as an adult with third-degree grand larceny for joyriding in a stolen bakery truck. He pleaded guilty to the crime but later admitted to only being a bystander. He was placed on probation for five years.

As an innocent child who had yet to be tried for the alleged crime, he was detained on Rikers Island, one of the most violent and corrupt prisons in the country. After more than two months, he had his first trial and was offered a plea bargain, which he rejected to maintain his innocence.

During his time in prison, he was starved, beaten, and tortured by correctional officers and inmates. Two years of his young life were spent in solitary confinement, where the trauma and torture began to have a great impact on his mental health. He was denied mental health treatment, even after four suicide attempts, despite his many requests. He spent a total of three years in prison and rejected more than a dozen plea bargains as he continued to stand for justice.

When he was eventually released with all charges thrown out against him, he got his GED and enrolled in college, where he maintained a 3.562 GPA for his first semester. Because of his mental health, he skipped a semester of school.

During the years after his release, he appeared on television shows across America, telling his story in the fight for criminal-justice reform while pursuing a wrongful-imprisonment lawsuit against the New York City Police Department, the Bronx district attorney, and the Department of Corrections. His public notoriety made him a target on the streets. Police surveilled him, while people from his neighborhood plotted against him. He was shot in the stomach and later stabbed in the face in two separate altercations, but he continued to push forward.

On May 11, 2015, after returning to school, Kalief submitted a paper for a class titled "A Closer Look at Solitary Confinement in the United States." In the paper, he discussed the need for alternative forms of punishment instead of solitary confinement because, as he stated, "the mental health risks it poses are too great." A month later, Kalief Browder hanged himself. May he rest in peace.

I tell Kalief's story because it highlights perseverance through severe dysfunction, as well as the racist system that led to his tragic death. While his family fought an unjust criminal justice system, racist practices that have existed for centuries were the ultimate culprit.

Before Kalief took his first breath, he had been dealt a bad hand. Being born to a mother who was addicted to drugs was an immediate strike against Kalief, over which he had no control. Going back further, I can't help but think about what had led to her addiction. She may have inherited and experienced so much trauma that drugs became a coping mechanism. Instead of her addiction being treated as a health issue, it was criminalized and went untreated to the point where her children were taken from her.

After birth, Kalief was placed in an impoverished home with parents who would eventually split up. Despite the saintly efforts of his adoptive mother, she lacked proper resources to address the issues that Kalief had been born into. Because of a housing system that forces groups of oppressed and traumatized people to live among each other, feeding off of each other's mistakes, he got into trouble in his neighborhood. He was enrolled in an education system that wasn't equipped with the tools and resources to provide the services and guidance he needed to be a successful student.

Racial profiling by police who were emboldened by an inherently racist stop-and-frisk ordinance allowed for him to be arrested without cause just for walking the streets as a Black person. He faced an unjust criminal justice system that punished him for not having the money to post bail. He was unconstitutionally denied a speedy trial and detained and treated as a prisoner in a system that claims that people are innocent until proven guilty.

After being placed in an institution that should instead be used to rehabilitate people, he was traumatized more. He was placed in a twelve-by-eight-foot cell for twenty-three hours a day for over two years and was failed by both our prison and health care systems, which caused his brain to experience irreparable damage.

Upon release, there was no system in place to help him transition back into life outside the institution that had broken him. He was reinserted in the same traumatic environment as before and preyed on by other impoverished people who saw him as a target because the perception was that he had money.

Kalief Browder may have hanged himself, but he was not responsible for his death. The system that allowed for all of this to occur is to blame. And that system had a greater negative impact on him simply because he was born Black.

———

Discussions about racial equality have become politicized, which makes them extremely polarizing. People view things as all or nothing, which keeps their minds closed off to growth. Truthfully, racial equality is far from political. One of the most disheartening things to witness is how divided our country is on basic morality issues of whether or not certain types of people *matter*.

Gordon Allport, who is considered the father of personality psychology, wrote the classic *The Nature of Prejudice*. He writes about two men who are walking down the street. As they are walking, they see a third man across the street. One man says to the other, "You see that man over there? Well, I hate him."

The other man says, "But you don't know him!"

He answers, "That's why I hate him."

For a second, I want you to think about the person or group of people you love most. Maybe a family member or a close friend or possibly a significant other. Now I want you to realize that that person was once a stranger to you. Each and every one of us comes into this world as a solitary individual, unfamiliar with the next person. Yet, we have an amazing gift, the capacity in our hearts to love.

As years go by, we forget about the gift and neglect the strangers around us because of our teachings, prejudices, or jaded experiences. With those negative beliefs put aside, just imagine how much better the world would be if we treated strangers more hospitably.

Many of us have been taught to live by the Golden Rule: treat others the way you would want to be treated. However, the Platinum Rule should be the standard: treat others the way *they* would like to be treated. Albert Einstein once said, "Any fool can know. The point is to understand." Understanding takes patience and an active ear to know what someone else has experienced and why they feel the way they do. The first step to understanding others is to understand yourself. Listen to and be honest with yourself.

To understand someone else, you must work to be a better communicator. Solid communication is the key to any relationship. Each party must understand the other to avoid any confusion. When you understand others, you are better equipped to sympathize with them. Instead of focusing on why someone doesn't share the same views as you about life, you should make it a point to see life from their perspective. You can both respect and disagree with others; the two are not mutually exclusive. Just because someone has a varying opinion about something doesn't mean that they are unworthy of your respect. Take a walk in their shoes, and it may open up your mind to new ideas.

———

In his best-selling book *My Grandmother's Hands: Racialized Trauma and the Pathway to Mending Our Hearts and Bodies*, Resmaa Menakem attempts to guide the healing process of racialized trauma in our minds and our bodies. The book also confronts the impact of trauma as it moves through generations. In doing so, he explains how our bodies carry their own form of trauma and require their own healing processes.

For Black bodies, Menakem utilizes his HIPP theory to explain the traumas faced. HIPP is an acronym for historical, intergenerational, persistent institutional, and personal traumas. Black bodies don't just experience trauma in a personal sense; they also experience the trauma as it relates to genocide, colonization, and slavery, as Menaken details. That historical trauma is decontextualized in our minds because we may be so far removed from it or we suppress it. However, our bodies experience the same responses as if it had happened to us. That response can be witnessed in the communal outcry when one Black person is slain on a video that is spread across the world.

For white bodies, Menakem explains that the trauma arises from the implication in such heinous atrocities. When left unaddressed, it prevents the acceptance of racial injustice and thwarts the buildup of stamina to combat the issues that have resulted in white supremacy. It presents itself as white fragility, the discomfort and defensiveness on the part of a white person when confronted by information about racial inequality and injustice. Until the truth is accepted and stamina to discuss these issues is enhanced, there will be no healing in a cross-communal sense. Menakem also discusses the healing process that blue bodies—the police—must go through. When each of these healing processes take place, communal healing can be addressed.

There is truth to Menakem's theory. In looking at my own trauma and how it has affected personal relationships in my life, no healing can be accomplished if all parties aren't willing to take the steps to heal on their own first. Once we heal on an individual level, then and only then can we come together and heal broken relationships.

———

The damage that the media and propaganda have inflicted on our country as it relates to race, while not irreversible, has persisted for years. Take for instance the 1915 film *Birth of a Nation*, perhaps the most influential film to perpetuating the racist society that we know today. From the beginning, the movie opens up with "A Plea for the Art of the Motion Picture." From just the language of the plea, much of the movie is foreshadowed. The makers of the film demand that they be uncensored in showing "the dark side of wrong," referring to northern white abolitionist and rebellious enslaved Black people who opposed "the bright side of virtue," or the southern white slave owners and the Ku Klux Klan.

The plea also demonstrates how Christianity has played a significant role in perpetuating these racist ideas by its mention of the freedoms of the written word in the Bible. I have always had a complicated relationship with Christianity. Living within the Bible Belt, it is often presumed that you are Christian, and my upbringing held up that belief. However, as I grew older, I grew distant from Christianity. There were pivotal moments throughout my childhood that led to my departure from the Church. Most events were rooted in the hypocrisy and judgment I witnessed firsthand, which left me feeling anything but loved and included. I know and love many people who identify as LGBTQ+, but my upbringing in the Church had me believe that their way of life was wrong. Having been raised by strong Black women my entire life, I never truly understood the degradation of women in the religious context either. Ultimately, I couldn't accept the evil that I saw from those who claimed to be the most Christian but who caused more harm than good. I've always recognized the power that faith has in people's lives, so I respect all religions, even though I don't subscribe to one myself.

From a historical context, enslaved Black people were first handed redacted and altered bibles by the same people responsible for their oppression and told that it was a sin to desire liberation from their masters on earth. Jesus could save their souls, but they had to sacrifice their bodies and minds, only to be liberated at death. I saw that mentality played out over the course of my life. People who had been gifted with so many talents felt that life was out of their control, as opposed to thinking that God had provided those talents and the ability to capitalize off of them.

In *The Color of Compromise: The Truth about the American Church's Complicity in Racism*, author Jemar Tisby discusses how Christianity, instead of confronting racism, has played a huge role in perpetuating it throughout periods of history. Following the emancipation of enslaved Black people, the Jim Crow era began and was marked by extreme discrimination and racism that was often enforced through violence. Like what can be seen in *Birth of a Nation*, the perpetuators of that discrimination and violence often utilized the Bible as justification. While Black people, and Black churches, were fighting for their lives, white Christians and churches sat idly by, allowing the abuse to continue.

Tisby describes the period following Jim Crow as the era of institutionalized racism. This is the period we have been in since *Brown v. Board of Education* legally dismantled Jim Crow but only disguised racism. During this time, racism became covert and embedded in institutions, policies, and ideas. In 1981, Lee Atwater, political advisor to presidents Ronald Reagan and George H. W. Bush, highlighted this adaptation of racism in an interview. He states, "You start out in 1954 by saying, 'Nigger, nigger, nigger.'" He goes on to say that once the N-word became unacceptable to use, society's racism shifted to the abstract with policies such as cutting taxes, forced busing, and states' rights. He admits that through those implementations, "Blacks get hurt worse than whites."

Coincidently, in 1954, the words "under God" were added to the Pledge of Allegiance that I, my parents, and my grandparents were forced to recite every day. Throughout history, the institution of Christianity—while promoting ideals of love, compassion, unity, justice, and peace—stood by as if Black people didn't matter.

While religion or faith is a necessity and has a great purpose in the lives of so many people, I fear that it has not only aided in the perpetuation of racism but also in unaddressed mental health issues. A belief in God has helped countless people through challenging times and has saved many lives, but when dealing with ever-present mental health conditions, prayers alone will not heal the wounded—just as prayers by themselves won't end racism. Some form of healthy intervention must occur to combat the issues that we face.

———

In the midst of a global pandemic due to the coronavirus outbreak, there is evidence of how even the novel virus has had a disproportionate effect on Black, Indigenous, and Latinx people when compared to white people. In fact, according to the COVID Tracking Project, Black people are dying at two and a half times the rate of white people.[22] Black, Indigenous, and Latinx peoples living in densely populated areas, requiring the need of public transportation, having a lack of access to or utilization of health care, and working essential or high-risk jobs are all cited as reasons for the disparity. The impact of COVID-19 extends to many other areas of life, such as the education and wealth gaps that also have negative impacts on these communities. COVID-19 has also presented challenges for survivors of domestic violence and abuse, as stay-at-home orders have likely forced them to remain in close proximity to their abusers. The National Domestic Violence Hotline has resources and guidance for anyone who may be in an unsafe environment.

While COVID-19 has had a huge impact on the course of everyday life, it has also sparked the rise in concern regarding racial inequality. Normally, people are busy with work, watching sports, or simply living life, which distracts them from events like the murder of George Floyd. In an unprecedented time of stay-at-home orders, millions of people around the world gave their undivided attention to a video that epitomized the system of oppression in America. While staring directly at the camera with his hand in his pockets, former Minnesota Police

22 The COVID Tracking Project. "The COVID Racial Data Tracker." *The COVID Tracking Project*, 2020, covidtracking.com/race.

Department officer Derek Chauvin knelt on George Floyd's neck as he begged for his life. As a spectator of the video, I felt hopeless because there was nothing I could do to prevent the murder that was occurring on the other end of that camera—a feeling that I have often had in regard to racial inequality in America.

Ahmaud Arbery was murdered while jogging. Breonna Taylor was murdered while sleeping. George Floyd was murdered while shopping. Countless other Black people have been murdered for similar acts of simply living. Following these tragedies, the world opened its eyes to the issue of racism more than ever before. Over two thousand US cities and more than sixty countries all over the world protested in support of the Black Lives Matter movement against police brutality and racial injustice, making it the largest protest in the history of the United States.[23] As the conversations continue, my hope is that the real issues aren't neglected in place of symbolic gestures. While support is needed from allies who sympathize with the plight of Black Americans, major reform is required before the issue of racism is behind us.

Racism is more than merely racial slurs and hate crimes. While these behaviors are generally unacceptable in society, racism is much deeper than what can be seen by the naked eye. It is the unjust system of discrimination on the basis of race that permeates every crevice of our society dating back to the *founding* of America. It is the system that didn't include Black people, who were viewed as subhuman property at the time, in the Declaration of Independence when it stated that, "All men are created equal." It is the system that educates us that although Indigenous people first lived on the lands that we call the United States of America, it was discovered by a white European man. It is the system that uses documents written hundreds of years ago by

---

23 Buchanan, Larry, et al. "Black Lives Matter May Be the Largest Movement in US History." *The New York Times*, The New York Times, 3 July 2020, www.nytimes.com/interactive/2020/07/03/us/george-floyd-protests-crowd-size.html.

a small group of white men to determine the legality of a large nation of people from all walks of life. It is the system that allows for mass incarceration of people of color as a way to disguise modern-day slavery due to a loophole in the Thirteenth Amendment. It is the system that results in higher mortality rates for women of color during labor than their white counterparts.

Deep breath.

It is the system that allowed white servicemen to return from wars and benefit from a GI Bill that Black servicemen were largely deprived of. It is the system that recognizes a white mass shooter as mentally unstable but fails to extend the same grace to a whole race of people who are born into environments that would drive anyone insane when they commit less egregious acts of violence. It is the system that links educational funding to property values in a given area that generally increase the whiter a community is. It is the system that controls the outcome of elections by strategically drawing lines around voting districts and devising voting laws that affect a targeted group of people. It is the system that permits unequal educational and employment opportunities. It is the system that views any pro-Black movement as a threatening political effort to overturn the nation. To combat racial injustice, it takes recognizing the problems and addressing the root cause of those problems.

Deep breath.

James Baldwin once said, "To be a Negro in this country and to be relatively conscious is to be in a state of rage almost all of the time." That constant rage turns into insanity. To be deprived of the most basic forms of equity for centuries has caused an entire race of conscious individuals to be angered beyond rebuke to a point where it has affected their psyches and passed down their traumas generation after generation. Mad mothers and frustrated fathers raise or abandon children who repeat the cycle because of the injustices that are out of their control, all the while trying to present an air of strength. The injustices are so far out of their control that they avoid addressing them because, for centuries, their efforts have been in vain.

A remedy for these psychological traumas requires a remedy of the system. Since the founding of America, racism hasn't disappeared; it has just evolved. The issues of the system are so embedded in our everyday lives that they, like the mental health issues that I faced as a child, have been normalized and accepted as the way the world is. In a similar process of turning pain into peace, America has a lot of work to do to combat these issues. That is, if the true goal is liberty and justice for all.

———

In response to George Zimmerman's acquittal in the shooting of seventeen-year-old Trayvon Martin, the Black community was enraged. Of the many people who went to social media to vent their frustrations and anger of the unjust judicial system that allowed for a Black boy to be killed with no repercussions, Alicia Garza, Patrisse Cullors, and Opal Tometi took to Facebook and declared that Black lives matter.

While the movement has grown in popularity and is viewed as a political movement in some people's eyes, it is far from that. It isn't political. It is a statement that needs to be heard, believed, and proven because, for so long, that has not been the case. Some people may believe that Black Lives Matter is an organization, but Black people all over wish that those people would just believe that Black lives matter.

When I first heard about the death of Trayvon Martin, I reverted to normalizing the tragedy. By that time, I had experienced enough murders in my personal life that I didn't want to absorb the pain of the death of someone I didn't know. When people flocked to the streets to protest, I sat idly by as I begrudgingly recounted the number of friends and family members whose deaths didn't get national attention. In a selfish and naive manner, I was jealous. However, more maturity and clarity has helped me to realize the larger issues.

As I experienced a totally different world than the one I had grown up in, I was often the only Black person in the room. From the classrooms to boardrooms, I recognized that my Black skin was different, and it made me wonder. I wondered whether my colleagues would have looked at me the same way if I hadn't been so fortunate as to have attended MBA. I wondered if I was truly liked or if I was merely being tolerated. I wondered how everyone would treat me if I was a random Black man on the street. Every day was, and continues to be, a battle of wondering if I—as a Black man in America stripped of my name and accomplishments—matter. And that feeling is emotionally draining and health damaging.

REALIZATION

Many people tell me that my life is a success story, but I disagree because success is relative. Success is something that should be determined on an individual level. Success for me will look different than success for someone else. However, success should not be defined as monetary worth. If you derive your success from money alone, you will never be happy or satisfied.

While I don't feel that my life is a success story, I do feel that my life is an inspiration story. There are some people who will find my accomplishments, or lack thereof, to be unsuccessful, and that is totally fine. But I doubt that there will be many people who will find my story to lack inspiration. Success is relative, but we all can recognize inspiration when it is present.

After learning bits and pieces of my life's story, one of my best college friends and teammates told me that I had a proverbial PhD in dealing with trauma and masking emotions by the time I ever stepped foot on a college campus. His comment made me reflect on the traumatic experiences I had endured all before the age of eighteen. Childhood trauma isn't uncommon, but I was surprised by just how much I had been exposed to compared to many others.

There have been many studies surrounding childhood trauma and the impact it has on the overall well-being of children throughout their lives. One of the most popular methods for studying this type of trauma is by looking at adverse childhood experiences. The Centers for Disease Control and Prevention (CDC) describes adverse childhood experiences as such:

> Adverse childhood experiences, or ACEs, are defined as potentially traumatic events that occur in childhood (0–17 years). For example, experiencing violence, abuse, or neglect, witnessing violence in the home or community, or having a family member attempt or die by suicide.

> Also included are aspects of the child's environment that can undermine their sense of safety, stability, and bonding such as growing up in a household with substance misuse, mental health problems, instability due to parental separation or household members being in jail or prison.

> ACEs are linked to chronic health problems, mental illness, and substance misuse in adulthood. ACEs can also negatively impact education and job opportunities. However, ACEs can be prevented.

I was already well into adulthood before I discovered ACEs. However, by identifying them, the proper steps may be taken next to address their negative effects.

In 1998, CDC-Kaiser Permanente published a study that investigated the impact of ACEs on physical and mental health problems in over seventeen thousand adults. During the study, the adults were given a survey asking about their ACEs, ranging from physical and mental abuse to neglect and household dysfunction, and those findings were compared to the current health statuses and behaviors of the adults. Scores of the test ranged from zero to ten, with ten meaning they had experienced the most ACEs. Of all the participants, 36.1 percent had reportedly experienced zero ACEs, 26 percent had one, 15.9 percent had two, and 9.5 percent had three.[24] The results of the remaining 12.5 percent of participants were defined as those who had experienced four or more ACEs.[25]

According to recent research from the CDC, about 61 percent of adults surveyed across twenty-five states reported that they had experienced at least one type of ACE, and nearly one in six (about 17 percent) reported they had experienced four or more types of ACEs.[26]

The research shows a strong correlation between ACE scores and health outcomes. Generally speaking, the higher the score, the worse the health outcome. For example, compared with people with an ACE score of zero, those with an ACE score of four or more were twice as likely to be smokers, twelve times more likely to have attempted suicide, seven times more likely to be alcoholics, and ten times more likely to have injected street drugs.[27] People with an ACE score of six or higher were at risk of their lifespan being shortened by twenty years,[28] as

---

24 Centers for Disease Control and Prevention, Kaiser Permanente. "The ACE Study Survey Data" [Unpublished Data]. Atlanta, Georgia: US Department of Health and Human Services, Centers for Disease Control and Prevention, 2016.

25 Ibid.

26 Centers for Disease Control and Prevention. "Preventing Adverse Childhood Experiences |Violence Prevention | Injury Center | CDC." Centers for Disease Control and Prevention, 3 Apr 2020, www.cdc.gov/violenceprevention/aces/fastfact.html.

27 Van Niel, Cornelius et al. "Adverse events in children: predictors of adult physical and mental conditions." *Journal of Developmental and Behavioral Pediatrics: JDBP* vol. 35, 8 (2014): 549–51. doi:10.1097/DBP.0000000000000102,

28 Brown, David W et al. "Adverse childhood experiences and the risk of premature mortality." *American journal of preventive medicine* vol. 37, 5 (2009): 389–96. doi:10.1016/j.amepre.2009.06.021.

well as three times[29] the risk of getting lung cancer. A person with seven or more ACEs had a three-and-a-half-times greater risk of developing ischemic heart disease, the number-one cause of death in the US.[30]

Nadine Burke Harris, MD, author of *The Deepest Well: Healing the Long-Term Effects of Childhood Adversity*, describes in her book just how the brain, and subsequently the rest of the body, is affected by adverse childhood experiences while offering ways to prevent, screen, and treat the effects for better health outcomes. In the book, she uses the analogy of walking in the forest and suddenly spotting a bear. (Please note that there is much more science involved, but I will spare you those details.) At that moment, the stress responses in your brain, referred to as your fight, flight, or freeze responses, kick into gear. In an instant, your heart beats faster and stronger, your airways open up to allow more oxygen flow, and blood is forced to the large muscle groups in your legs that are used for running and jumping. Other parts of your brain may activate and tell you that fighting the bear might not be the best decision, so you decide to run. You make it all the way to your cave, where you feel safe, and the stress-response systems finally turn off. But what happens when you can't experience safety in your cave because the bear is living with you in the cave? Your fight-or-flight response is constantly triggered day in and day out, to a point where it no longer becomes lifesaving but rather health damaging.

As an adult, I performed the test to determine how many ACEs I possessed. I initially discovered that I had experienced nine ACEs in my first seventeen years of life that I could vividly remember. Through discussions with Katie, who is a pediatrician and who has studied the impacts of ACEs for many years in hopes of better understanding and

---

29 Brown, David W et al. "Adverse childhood experiences are associated with the risk of lung cancer: a prospective cohort study." *BMC public health* vol. 10, 20, 19 Jan 2010. doi:10.1186/1471-2458-10-20.

30 Dong, Maxia et al. "Insights into causal pathways for ischemic heart disease: adverse childhood experiences study." *Circulation* vol. 110, 13 (2004): 1761–6. doi:10.1161/01.CIR.0000143074.54995.7F.

treating her patients, I came to realize that I had in fact experienced all ten ACEs. The one in question related to sexual abuse. While I do not think or remember that I was ever molested or raped, I have been able to uncover memories of unwanted sexual behaviors from women who were more than five years older than I was at the time (five was an arbitrary number used during the initial study). With a poor understanding of what constituted sexual abuse, coupled with the misogynistic society in which I had been raised, I took pride in these sexual experiences that honestly have had negative effects on me.

I am careful to state that I either don't remember or can't think of past traumas because it is an important distinction from never experiencing them. It is common for those who have gone through such traumatic events to suppress those memories as a defense mechanism. It is my theory that if we could somehow extract all the memories from those seventeen thousand adults in the CDC-Kaiser Permanente study, we would find that the number of ACEs experienced was greater than what the participants were able or willing to report. My parents and their parents have never taken the ACE study to determine their scores, but I would venture to say that they too would report having high ACE scores. They have been the root cause of many of my ACEs, which makes me believe that ACEs and lifetime trauma are passed down through generations if not intentionally combatted.

My ACE score suggests that I am at risk for many negative outcomes in life, yet I have overcome so many of the odds stacked against me. ACEs can have lasting, negative effects on health, well-being, and opportunity. While my long-term health may still be greatly affected, I have been able to cultivate a life full of abundant opportunities and healthy relationships. Those achievements didn't come without challenges, though. I have, at different points in my life, exemplified the characteristics of a person with a high ACE score, such as self-isolating and destructive behaviors. However, having beaten so many statistics, I have a sense that anything I want to do in life is mine for the taking. I will not be defined by my adversity. Instead, I will utilize lessons learned from my adverse past to my benefit, in hopes of a better future. I strive to not pass down my ACE score or my trauma to my younger siblings or any future children I may have.

Some would argue that my life experiences should have made it more difficult for me to succeed. When we are young, we develop survival tactics that are meant to keep us safe in the face of danger. In this case, that danger was the trauma, violence, and threats from my everyday life. A common response may be to attack (fight) when threatened. Perhaps the need to keep the peace by avoiding confrontation (flight) or shutting down (freeze) is the technique we choose. While those protective measures aid us from potential harm, holding on to those mechanisms can turn us cold and bitter or threatening. I have experienced the latter, yet I've been able to focus my energy on the positives more times than not. Having said that, I invite more people to join me in letting go of some of these protective measures that keep us from opening our hearts and our minds. Realizing those actions that you have normalized and unpacking why you've "always felt a certain way" about something takes a lot of self-discovery. You may be in a new location, a new relationship, or just in a new phase of life where you no longer have to fight to survive. If you are in a position where you no longer require those tactics for survival, the healing process should begin. It is a difficult process, but the results can be liberating.

———

The first time I realized that my feelings and behaviors had words to describe them was in Psychology 101 in college. All the emotions I had reduced to happy, sad, or mad actually had better descriptors. After meeting Katie, I realized that it could be normal to identify as having a mental health condition. Katie was and is one of the strongest women I know, and she often shares her emotions. She combined the vocabulary with practical application as it related to her own life, which forced me to reflect on my own experience.

Spazzing out at seemingly trivial things and my recurring nightmares were actually posttraumatic stress disorder episodes from triggering events, instead of just random occurrences. My past actions and behaviors started to make sense to me when I was able to reconcile them with my mental state.

As a young boy, I had always considered myself to be shy. I now realize that what I had called *shyness* would have been better described as *anxiety*. The need to perform well to avoid punishment put me on edge. To avoid sounding stupid or making a mistake, my brain went into overthink mode, which caused inaction and sometimes the inability to speak.

Episodes that I would have normally called slumps that forced me to distance myself from my friends and family were bouts of depression. I realized my initial inclination to fight was a factor of not having the words to properly describe how I was feeling.

My desire to be alone and avoid community was a fear of abandonment and rejection. Feeling rejected by my parents, family, and even society at times made me want to avoid that feeling. The best way to prevent being rejected by others is to not depend on others; therefore, I became extremely independent. Even my work ethic and drive were defense mechanisms to escape the pain and focus my mind on other things besides my mental health issues.

I began to realize that my distrust and mistreatment of women was due to unresolved issues between me and my mama and the traumatic exposures from my dad. As I became racially conscious at MBA, I realized that even my Blackness was a form of trauma.

All of this was applicable to me, and it was also applicable to my parents, as well as their parents and so many more generations before them. The little that I know about my parents' past would suggest that they too endured many of the same mental health issues that I face without ever knowing it.

However, realizing that there were issues and having a vocabulary to discuss them didn't mean that they would suddenly disappear. And just because I'd realized them didn't mean I was ready to seek treatment for them. Realization was just a part of the journey toward liberation. It was going to take more maturing for me to make that leap.

CHAPTER ELEVEN

STICKS AND STONES

After graduating from college, I got my own apartment and had to get all new services and utilities turned on in my name. One that stands out the most was the cable and internet service. I had always looked forward to getting my own apartment because I knew that when I did, I would be able to do things any way I wanted. I was very excited about having my own space for once. But while I was on the phone with the cable company, my excitement went out the window.

"We are unable to come out and service you because you have an unpaid bill of $123.46," the customer service representative told me. I was perplexed because this was my first time ever calling them on my own behalf. I didn't know how I could have had an unpaid bill. I probed to find out more.

"When was this bill from?" I asked her in hopes of getting some clarity.

"2007."

I chuckled because I realized what was going on. I politely told her that I had been sixteen years old in 2007 and had no way of legally signing a contract to have services provided by them. She didn't budge and told me that because the balance was tied to my name, I would have to pay it off before they would come out. I conceded because I realized that I was not getting anywhere with her. After I gave her my card number to process the payment, I hung up the phone, furious that this was how I was going to have to start life on my own. I immediately called my mama to let her know how angry I was for putting a bill in my name and letting it go unpaid. It wasn't uncommon for people in my community to put bills in the names of their children who weren't old enough to get a driver's license. I knew for years that my mama or Big Mama had bills in my name, but I had never thought it would impact me. I was wrong. The Black Tax was back in full effect.

Because I was the first person in my family to have a salaried job, there was a perception in the eyes of my family that I was rich. In my first year of employment, I had either loaned or flat-out gifted family members and a few close friends with thousands of dollars. It was always a hundred dollars or so here and there. I got requests from so many people that it started to add up to a point where, after my bills, I barely had anything for myself. However, as somebody who had "made it," I felt and was forced to believe that it was my obligation to provide for everyone else. It was like a form of survivor's remorse that I like to call "high achiever's guilt." Instead of enjoying my success for what it was worth, I often felt guilty that other people I loved couldn't join in on my enjoyment. It was the same guilt I had felt for even considering going away to Harvard for college and leaving my family behind in Nashville. It was the same guilt that came over me whenever I boarded yet another international flight, knowing that no one in my family had even been on a plane. It was the same guilt that made me think that even though I had earned everything I was experiencing, I still owed it all to my family and those who had come before me.

My parents and siblings were at the top of my list of people I would do anything for, so I made sure to help them out financially whenever they needed it. I recognized the financial burden my younger siblings put on my mama, so I wanted to alleviate that strain as much as I could. My generosity helped make birthdays and Christmases more bearable. When it came time for items that they needed like computers, braces, glasses, private school applications, or anything that I felt would benefit them from an educational standpoint, I would provide support with no question. With the lack of support from their fathers, I knew I had to step up and do my part. That included being present whenever they needed me to show up for something.

Apart from the financial support I provided, my siblings knew that they could always call on me when things were too much to handle. When fifteen bullets went through Kevin's house in a drive-by shooting, I was the first person he called to come calm his fears. Though I don't always have all the answers, my presence gives my younger siblings a sense of security and hope that things will be okay in the future, just like Granny and Pops' presence had done for me. However, there came a dark time in my life. My brother Jarrett had lost hope that there was going to be a brighter future, and it brought me so much pain to see him suffer.

After a few unsuccessful attempts at completing college, several criminal charges that had a lasting impact on his employment opportunities, and a few out-of-wedlock children, at the young age of twenty-two, my little brother had had enough. He also had just lost two of his closest childhood friends, one to murder and another to the prison system after a rape trial that garnered national attention for years. I knew Jarrett was battling his internal demons and thought that our conversations were providing him hope that there was a better tomorrow, but in retrospect, that was not the case in his mind.

During a work trip in Cleveland, Ohio, I woke up to a text that was unlike any other I had ever received in my life. It was an actual suicide note from Jarrett. In the letter, he addressed his daughters, mother, sister, Kevin, and me. Before finishing the letter, I dropped my phone and curled up in bed, full of agony. After reading the words "I've decided to take my life," I knew that the world had become too much for my brother to handle. The shock from that nearly killed me.

I somehow built up the courage to continue reading the letter and got to the point where he addressed me. His message to me was about how much fun we used to have in my dorm room during my college days. Initially, I was hurt that that was the most memorable thing he could think of, but when I stopped to think, those days were actually some of the best days of my life too. For the first time, we were free to do whatever we wanted and to be ourselves without any fear. It was our protected space. Most times, Kevin and Jarrett would come stay with me during school breaks when no one else was on campus. We had food, an Xbox, a computer to listen to and record music, and each other. It was a perfect setup.

After I gathered myself, I called Jarrett's mama. I got her on the phone, and she was actually with Jarrett, who hadn't gone through with the suicide attempt. I was relieved but still worried. I told her I was going to fly back to be with him as soon as I could. She told me to calm down and said that it wasn't that serious, as she was sitting in earshot of my brother. This infuriated me. I had just awakened to news that purported my brother had killed himself, and nothing was more serious to me at that point. After hanging up with her, I called the police to see if they could somehow find him and save him. Because I was calling from Cleveland, there was confusion as to why I was calling about a person in Nashville, so I hung up on them and called Katie who was in Nashville. She eventually got through to the cops, so they could send someone to help Jarrett.

The ambulance eventually got to my brother and took him to the hospital. His mother seemed to be upset that he had been forced to go, which didn't make sense to me, but I attributed it to pride. Perhaps her reaction was a case of the "Black don't crack" mentality and her own normalization of these issues through the trauma she had endured. I was able to get a flight back later that day, and I immediately went to the hospital to see Jarrett. When I saw him, I grabbed him and hugged him closer than I had ever had in my life. I felt his heartbeat against my chest and thought to myself that I had been so close to never feeling that sensation ever again. At that moment, there was nothing I wouldn't do for my brother, and I sensed that he knew that.

The few weeks he was in the hospital, I made an effort to see him every single day and to also invite other people who I knew loved him. The love and support gave Jarrett a renewed sense of hope. He's since grown from that period of life and is working every day to be a better version of himself. When I see him smile, it gives me life. Everything above and beyond that is a bonus. I'm just glad that he's here with us today.

———

Whenever I'm asked what my hobbies are these days, the first thing I mention is hot yoga. Not many people look at me and immediately think I'm a yogi. When it comes to forms of exercise, they generally assume I lift weights like I had done for football for so many years. Although I occasionally perform those activities, I practice yoga religiously. I stand behind it 100 percent because of all the positive effects it has had on my life.

Despite the misconceptions about yoga, it has become more than a form of exercise for me. Yoga is defined as the cessation of the modification of the mind, a difficult task to accomplish, which is why each session is referred to as a practice. But during my practices, so much inside me changes. When I get on my mat, my heart rate slows, and my blood pressure seems to drop. As a young Black man who has concerned many doctors about my borderline high blood pressure, the health benefits of yoga have been remarkable. As someone who used to run into 220-pound men at full speed for fun, the passive nature of yoga levels me out. For someone who has many qualms about organized religion in our society, the yoga studio has become my place of worship, so much so that I've now become evangelical in my approach to recruiting people to come practice with me because of its healing powers.

The ancient Chinese philosopher Lao Tzu once stated, "If you are depressed, you are living in the past. If you are anxious, you are living in the future. If you are at peace, you are living in the present." Living in the present is probably one of the hardest things to do. With so many distractions, it may seem nearly impossible to focus on the now. We often feel like we are wasting time if we aren't actively doing something, so we neglect the time to just stop, think, and check in with ourselves.

When I first started practicing yoga, I never realized just how busy my mind was at every moment of every day. Not once in my life had I paused and focused on my breathing. Inhale. Exhale. Our subconscious minds handle breathing for most of our lives, so we never have to focus on it. But when we take the time to concentrate on our breathing and the thoughts that enter our minds, we start to get in tune with the who, what, how, and why we are. That's meditation. It creates a strong mind that can overcome many obstacles.

When practicing meditation, try to rid your mind of any thoughts. The moment you try to do that will be the time when you realize that turning off your mind is the toughest task in the world—so, practice. For thousands of years, people have been practicing. It's not something you will ever perfect, and that should bring some peace of mind. Thoughts are just your brain's way of using ideas, images, sounds or emotions to capture your attention. When those thoughts arise, recognize them, then work to remove them just as quickly as they had come about.

Being in nature also helps mindfulness and meditation. Without the distraction of technology, you are able to relax and connect with yourself and the natural world around you. Go on hikes, sit on the beach, listen to the rain, look at the stars. Do it all without distractions and see if it helps you. If you can't practice in nature, a quiet place will do the trick. Make a habit of checking in with yourself at least once a day. You deserve it.

There is science to back the benefits of yoga that I have personally experienced. Dr. Bessel van der Kolk, clinical psychiatrist and author of *The Body Keeps the Score: Brain, Mind, and Body in the Healing of Trauma*, describes in detail his definition of trauma, as well as ways to combat it. More than a memory or series of thoughts, he argues that trauma is a feeling of your body being stuck in heartache, terror, or an intolerable state. Because he feels that trauma is a sensation that is felt, he believes the best way to address it is by reclaiming your body.

Dr. van der Kolk explains that when you do yoga, you allow yourself a safe space to explore your body and how it feels. Knowing that you may find yourself in an uncomfortable position, you are able to bear it because the sensations are only temporary. After a round of breaths, you are able to return to comfort to safely explore further. Similarly, when your body is in an intolerable state of trauma, you learn through yoga that even that feeling is temporary. By building the courage to explore your body, you train yourself to explore your mind. Throughout his countless studies, he has found that a steady yoga practice has proven to be more beneficial than any medication in treating trauma.

As I think about some of the most memorable moments I've had on my yoga mat, I remember how one of my teachers would always say, "Place one hand on your heart and one hand on your navel. Your heart signifies life. With every beat, you are reminded of what it feels like to be alive! Your navel, this is your first home. When you were one with your mother, this was your life, your food source, your everything."

Every time I hear those words, I think of my mama and how close we used to be, figuratively and literally. I used to live inside my mama, but now we rarely ever see each other. People used to say we acted more like brother and sister than mother and son. I enjoyed that dynamic. We were best friends. We used to talk and laugh and cry together, but now we barely speak to one another.

———

It's hard to lose people in your life to death or to prison. Unfortunately, I happen to be familiar with both of those fates. What may be worse, though, is losing someone who is still alive and completely free.

As a young adult, I experienced early successes that even I wouldn't have thought imaginable, coming from where I had. I had defied all the odds stacked against me. I was having the type of success that many parents dream of their children having. Of course, I expected my mama, who had raised me from a baby, to be extremely proud of all my major life accomplishments. However, with each milestone I hit, my mama and I grew further apart.

As I began high school, tension started to arise between us, which isn't uncommon for teenagers and parents. I was learning and experiencing more than anyone else in my family had ever done, so I wanted to share some of the things I had learned. Early spats started as a result of me questioning her parenting style toward Secret and Demo. After experiencing her parenting style for myself, on top of witnessing an alternative way of doing things from many of my friends' parents, I decided to voice my concerns. Those conversations always ended the same way, with my mama telling me that I couldn't tell her anything because she had been responsible for raising me and that she wasn't going to raise her children like white people.

I quickly began to realize that no matter what type of advice I gave her, her rebuttal would be along the same lines of "I raised you, so what could you possibly tell me?" I bit my tongue more than I wanted. After I moved out, I had no plans of returning, and I got through my visits without any issues. I liked that arrangement. I loved coming over to joke around as a family or to check in with my siblings and see how they were doing in school or what their latest interests were.

However, one day stands out in my memory because it caused a domino effect regarding the fallout between me and my mama. Soon after I started my job at the accounting firm, I went over to help my mama put together a piece of furniture for Demo's room. When I got there, Big Mama and Thomas were there too. While watching me assemble a bookshelf, Big Mama asked me if I was a millionaire. I thought she was joking because she knew that I had just graduated from college, and I hadn't done anything to suggest that I was a millionaire. I was a twenty-three-year-old with a good job, but I was far from a millionaire. I was actually broke.

Whatever had made her think that also made her adamant that it was true. Even my mama looked at me as if to say, "Well, are you?" They weren't joking and wanted an actual answer from me. I just chuckled, shook my head, and told them that I wasn't. In my mind, I was upset for a couple of reasons. First, I didn't like the way they were asking me the question. It felt like I was being shaken down by a bully for my lunch money. They were counting my pockets, and that made me uneasy. Secondly, I was disappointed that their concept of money was so flawed that they could think I was a millionaire.

The conversation died out, and I eventually forgot about it. Apparently, *they* hadn't. A few days later, I received a voicemail from Big Mama about how rude I had been in my reaction to their interrogation. She told me how I didn't care about anybody but myself and that the only redeeming quality about me was that I was smart. A similar sentiment I had heard from my mama a number of times.

I was blindsided by it all. I felt like I was being attacked for nothing. So as not to react out of emotion, I decided not to respond immediately, to give myself time to calm down. During my moments of reflection, she left me another voice mail saying that the least I could do was respond to her out of respect. She continued by telling me that I was low-down, just like my dad, and that no matter how much money I had, I shouldn't treat people the way I was doing. That one hurt. I knew the pain my father had caused her and my mama through the years, and to compare me to him meant that she must've thought horribly of me. I worked hard to disassociate myself from the wrongdoings of my father. The last thing I wanted was to be compared to him in that manner.

After receiving that message, I responded. She didn't answer, so I left her a voicemail that I wish I hadn't. But for so long I had been voiceless, and I felt that I needed to stand up for myself, especially since I knew that I hadn't done anything to deserve those comments. In the heat of the moment, I attacked her with the same amount of hate that she had shown me. This eventually led to a severed relationship between us that lasted for several months and was never fully repaired.

Later that year, she texted me to make amends. We both apologized and expressed our love for each other. On Thanksgiving, I proposed to Katie after several years of dating and invited everyone in my immediate family to celebrate with my future in-laws, except for Big Mama. Our relationship didn't seem the same, and I wanted the day to be filled with love. That same day, my dad showed up high from the night before. It was the first time he had ever met my future in-laws. Part of me wished that I had invited Big Mama instead of him, but I couldn't take it back.

After hearing about my engagement, Big Mama sent me a sweet message saying that she knew my new fiancée, Katie, would be the one and how happy she was for us. That Christmas was the first time I had seen her in almost a year. It was brief, but I was able to tell her that I loved her.

Shortly after Big Mama sent me those mean voicemails, my mama basically did the exact same thing. She called me and told me how I hadn't done enough for her and that I was extremely selfish. The messaging aligned closely with that of Big Mama's, so I felt that they must have been feeding off of each other. Unlike Big Mama, my mama called early in the morning, before I was even awake, yelling into the phone about how I had neglected her and my siblings. I wasn't unfamiliar with the morning calls. Historically, they were about Demo or Secret and how they were misbehaving, but this time I was the topic of her rants. Sensing the negativity and knowing that it was far from the truth, I decided to just not speak to her. I didn't like the feeling I had gotten from responding to Big Mama about similar accusations, so I kept to myself. Instead, after several months of not talking, I decided to write a letter to my mama. I have always been better at expressing myself through writing, so I felt that would be a good way to let her know how I felt. Things seemed to go back to normal after that. I hoped to receive a letter or something from my mama that would show me her true feelings, but I never did.

———

When I had seen Big Mama on Christmas, she told me that she had been feeling sick. Just fifteen days after Christmas, she attempted to drive herself to the hospital. As she opened her car door, she fell to the ground and died. I got the call while I was at work, but I let it go to voicemail. I still remember where I was standing when I opened my phone to listen to the message from my great-aunt.

"Hey, Reggie, it's your auntie." She paused for a few seconds before continuing. "Um—" and like ripping off a Band-Aid, she just let it out. "Big Mama just died."

I fell to the floor and lost control of all the papers in my hands that I was preparing to deliver to a colleague. I felt a pain in my heart and stomach that I had never felt before, while my whole body trembled. I didn't know what to do. I didn't know who to go to.

I eventually gathered myself after a few deep breaths. While holding back tears, I went to Frederick's office to tell him the tragic news so that he could relay it to whoever needed to know. My plan was to get out of there as soon as possible. It so happened that another colleague was in his office, and they both could tell that something was wrong. As I told them, I broke down for the first time after hearing the news. They prayed over me and told me to go do what I had to do. Right before I left, I went and told the CEO. He gave me the biggest hug, and I left.

On the ride home to tell Demo and Secret, all I could think about was my mama. I knew she didn't have much contact with many people in her family, so I doubted she would have known before me. I thought to myself, *How do I tell her? Do I wait to see her in person? Do I call her now? How will she take the news over the phone?* I decided that she needed to know sooner rather than later, so I called her while she was at work. In tears, I cried out, "Mama, Big Mama just died." She was quiet. It must have been a shock to her, but knowing her, she wasn't going to show much, if any, emotion around her coworkers. After a few seconds of silence, she simply said, "Okay," and hung up.

When I got to my mama's house, my cousins had already arrived to inform Demo and Secret, who were crying uncontrollably. Seeing everyone so upset was extremely tough for me. We all hugged each other and tried to share encouraging words, but it was mostly filled with tears. We eventually got a call to go to the hospital, where members of my extended family were. To identify the body, they required my mama to be there. She refused and explained that she didn't like the feeling of being in hospitals, especially after Popeye's passing. Looking back, that may have been a trigger for her own traumatic experiences. I also knew that she didn't want to be in an emotional and vulnerable state around her family members, so I knew she wasn't going to come. I left the hospital angry because the doctors wouldn't allow me to see Big Mama one last time, but there was nothing I could do.

I eventually saw my mama later that evening when our extended family gathered at my aunt's house to discuss the arrangements. My mama was reluctant to even come to that, but she did. Big Mama didn't have any form of life insurance, so it was up to us as a family to foot the bill for her final expenses. In a roundtable discussion, all eyes were on my mama. It felt like an interrogation, with everyone asking her how she was going to make it work. I started to get angry again. At that moment, it felt like the burden was being put on my mama, so I tried to avert that attention. I asked if they could give her some time, as she had just lost her mama. *And her only true friend,* I thought to myself.

When it came to the discussion about money, everyone was silent. That infuriated me more than anything. A room full of siblings and nieces and nephews of Big Mama, and no one was willing to pitch in a few bucks, or at least it felt that way. Then my great-uncle said he would put in a thousand dollars. Another family member said five hundred dollars. My mama had a handful of money that she had earned that day cutting hair and said she had that to offer. It hurt me knowing that it was every dollar she had to her name, but it showed me how big her heart was that she was so willing to give it up for her mama. Taking in Thomas was another huge commitment she made that highlighted her love. One of my aunts looked at me to ask what my contribution would be. In my mind, I had already been prepared to pay the whole thing myself, as I figured I would have had to anyway, so I told her I would make up the difference. We had finally come to a conclusion on how we were going to pay for the funeral.

My mama's brother, one of Popeye's son's, who was in prison at the time, heard the news and reached out to me to share his condolences and offered to help out in any way he could. From prison, he arranged for a significant amount of money to be delivered to us to alleviate the financial burden. Seeing the family come together to make sure that Big Mama would have a nice memorial service restored my faith in them after the negative emotions that had initially taken over.

Big Mama had a beautiful service, and so much love was shown by family and friends. I knew, though, that her death would continue to be tough for my mama. Over the years, she and Big Mama had become best friends. They talked nearly every day about everything. They had a special bond. It was a bond that my mama didn't share with anyone else, and I knew that void would always be hard, and probably impossible, for her to fill.

———

As I got older and more aware, I began to notice that my mama didn't have many friends, and she had also stopped associating with family members. She had socially isolated herself from everyone and seemed to always find reasons to not let people into her world. Even our relationship was shallow. Never did we talk about anything more than other people or what was going on in the given moment.

Her social isolation never affected how I lived my life, but it was concerning. However, when it came time to plan our wedding, it had a huge impact. Because of my mama's feelings toward certain people, she gave me an ultimatum. If those people were invited to our wedding, she would refuse to attend. This resulted in my not inviting half of my family, but it was a sacrifice I was willing to make. I didn't think it was a sacrifice I should have been forced to make, but if it was going to ease my mama's worries, I was going to do it.

Having appeased my mama on her guest list demand, I thought the tension would be released for the big day, but it began with stress. The last guest to arrive, and late to boot, was my mama. After she eventually arrived, things finally started to go as planned. Because she had not attended many weddings, I was hoping that she wouldn't recognize a tradition that Katie and I had decided to scrap. Katie's dad had passed away from ALS several months before our wedding, so she would not be able to perform the father-bride dance. So as not to make the night any more emotional than it already was or to raise any unwanted questions, we decided not to do the mother-groom dance either. Luckily, she didn't make a fuss about it. The wedding went on without a hitch and was a joyful collision of all of my various worlds. Under one roof, my Black family was introduced to Katie's white family. Christians mingled with agnostics and Muslims. Rich people danced alongside poor people. Gang members shared drinks with board members. College graduates locked arms with high school dropouts. It was beautiful.

However, several days after returning from our honeymoon, I heard what my mama did have a problem with. She was upset that she and I didn't have a single picture with just the two of us. For me, the entire wedding had been a blur of being pulled left and right, and it hadn't occurred to me. But instead of simply asking me for a picture the day of the wedding or showing up on time before all the festivities kicked off, she had allowed it to fester so that she could bring it up later. I didn't understand it. It was like she just wanted something to be upset about.

While she was upset about the pictures, I found myself upset too. When we returned from the honeymoon, Demo texted me, asking when I was going to return his tuxedo. I had rented him the tuxedo to save my mama money because I knew it was something that she hadn't factored into her budget. It had been about two weeks after the wedding, which meant that we would've had to pay for it twice over in late fees. I had explicitly given him and my mama instructions to return it the day after the wedding, but my mama's response made things worse. Instead of owning up to it and saying that it was a mistake, she blamed me and told me that since I had been the one who rented it, I should've been responsible enough to return it—disregarding that I had hopped on a plane right after the wedding to go halfway across the world to enjoy our honeymoon.

Her response upset me, and it had nothing to do with the money. The store didn't even charge the fees, thankfully. I was more so upset at her lack of responsibility to do something as simple as return it, her lack of accountability to own up to her fault, and her lack of gratitude, seeing as I had done her a favor. It was bigger than the tuxedo. Her response was the way she had always responded to things my entire life. Going out of my way to do something nice turned into me being berated for how everything bad that happened was my fault. It caused tension and unwanted negativity, so again we went a while without speaking.

Over time, I started to feel that my mama had begun resenting me. Any good gesture was looked at as insufficient. Instead of "thank-yous," I got "fuck-yous." I was told that I never cared for anyone but myself.

I was called selfish for not recognizing her depression fifteen years prior as a child. I felt like I was already going above and beyond my call as a child, providing for not only her but also my siblings as well. She even went as far as to say that she didn't want me around my siblings because I would be a bad influence. That stung because I was striving so hard to be a positive role model for them. Sometimes, it felt like I was being blamed for the shortcomings of her baby daddies, when in reality, I stepped up and was more of a father to my siblings than any of them had ever been.

Instead of celebrating my successes, she held contempt for me and challenged my character, as if I had had to sell my soul to the devil to make anything of myself. In her eyes, everything she had sacrificed for me to be able to receive all those opportunities had also taken her away from her goals and dreams. I know this because she told me, "My life would've been so much better had I aborted yo' ass," in a string of voice mails that contained many other hurtful comments, but that trumped them all. It eventually led to a prolonged severance of our relationship yet again. I just couldn't handle the roller coaster that it was and wanted to give myself space to heal.

Sticks and stones may break your bones, but words will rip your heart out.

Having escaped the dangers of violence in my neighborhood, I thought the fear of bullets was behind me. I was wrong. My mama shot more metaphorical bullets at me with her words that hurt more than anything I had ever felt in my life. I recognize that her past traumatic experiences have played a huge role in our relationship. While I can admit that, it doesn't make the pain hurt any less. While I can recognize the trauma at play, it does no good if it goes unaddressed.

No child deserves to ever hear those words, especially from his own mother. It's a parent's responsibility to make all the sacrifices in the world to see that their child is given as many opportunities as possible at whatever cost. No child made the choice to be born. No child asked to be here. Resenting your child because of their success does nothing to better your life; it just serves to break down a child who is doing what you wanted them to do when you set them up for that success.

When I didn't know where to turn, I went to a safe place. Teary-eyed, I drove to Granny's house and told her about what I had just experienced. Seeing my pain made her weep. It was the first time I had ever seen her cry tears of sadness, but she did what she had always done best. With a huge embrace, she let me know that I was her baby and that I had nothing to worry about.

After hearing my mama's words, I thought to myself, *What if she had gotten that abortion? What would've transpired had she severed the ties between us? Would her life have been better off?* Possibly, but there is no way to determine that for sure. I can tell you what would've been different, though. None of what I had accomplished in life would have come true. Most important, I wouldn't have been able to touch my heart. Nor would I have been able to touch my first home, my navel, as my yoga instructor often prompts. If the time when I had been one with my mother was the time she decided her life would've been better off without me, my first home would've become my last.

It became extremely difficult to accept that my mama carried so much resentment toward me. However, I extended grace in hopes that, one day, the emotional wounds that she had and the ones she had passed down to me would heal. I knew the type of relationship we could get back to, based on past experiences—a time when we were both in a phase of normalization—and I clung to that while yearning for my mama to experience her own mental health journey toward liberation.

CHAPTER TWELVE

WORST CHAPTER OF MY LIFE

When I had the gun pointed to my face as a twelve-year-old, my focus was on my breath and keeping my eyes open. I feared that if I blinked, it would be the last time I would ever close my eyes. Thoughts raced through my mind rapidly as I experienced the worst emotional pain that I had ever had to endure up to that point. Life was only just beginning for me. While the emotional damage from that event still haunts me, it pales in comparison to the mental and emotional agony I have endured as an adult.

We had the memorial service for Big Mama on a Monday in 2017—Martin Luther King Jr. Day, to be exact. The year had not gotten off to a great start. That same week, Granny told me that she had been diagnosed with lung cancer. So much had changed in such a short period of time. More childhood friends had passed that year, but at that point, I had built up an emotional budget for those kinds of deaths. One death had not been included in my budget, though. In December of that year, my soon-to-be father-in-law passed away after a few years of battling ALS. The compassion that I had for my then-fiancée, Katie, who was enduring her own grieving process, grew immensely. The totality of everything that I was experiencing was emotionally draining.

Granny took to treatment well, and her cancer shrank. Although the chemotherapy and radiation were negatively impacting her body, both internally and externally, she continued because there was light at the end of the tunnel. She was going to be cancer-free after it was all said and done, or at least that's what it looked like. My dad and I had bonded together stronger after hearing the news of Granny's diagnosis. We were so hopeful that she would come out on top because of the positive signs. We told each other that she was a fighter and that we didn't have anything to worry about. And she fought—and we didn't worry. It was all working out in our favor.

Throughout the treatment, Granny would tell us how ready she was to be done with it all, but she never presented any real signs that it was causing her much discomfort. Black don't crack. Her face had become more swollen, but that was the only sign we could see. It wasn't until she called me and asked if I could cut her hair, knowing I had been a barber on campus during college, that it began to feel real. As bad as I wanted to say no because I didn't want to accept that cancer was affecting her, I agreed. I cut her bald, but I kept one of her braids just to have forever in case her beautiful hair never grew back.

She was nearing the end of her treatment after two years, and the cancer had nearly disappeared. During an appointment with her doctor in November of 2018, she found out that the lung cancer that had previously been gradually shrinking had failed to shrink to the point of remission. The next month, Granny complained of dizzy spells and severe headaches. As we sat on the couch watching TV and gearing up for the holidays, she received a call from her doctor. I heard her say "okay" a few times before hanging up. Based on her initial reaction, it appeared that everything was normal. She then let out a huge sigh and grumbled, "Well, ain't this some shit." Although she had seemed calm on the phone, inside she was screaming in frustration. She had just been told that her lung cancer had spread to her brain.

To act quickly, she agreed to have a procedure to remove one of several tumors. Surgery was scheduled for December 27. In preparation for the surgery, Granny wanted to get her arrangements in order, in case things didn't go as planned. Granny named me as power of attorney (POA) and my dad as contingent POA. She drew up her last will and testament, bequeathing her house to me, which she later signed over to me, and her cars to my dad. As for her cash, she had plans of leaving it all to me because, as she told me, she didn't want my dad to get anything. "All he do is criminal shit, and I'm sick of it," were her exact words. I wasn't shocked to hear her say this because she had shared similar sentiments many times before. However, I was surprised that she was willing to eliminate him from receiving anything.

When Granny went to the bank to update her beneficiary designations, she tried to avoid a family member who was a personal banker, but her desk opened up first. After small talk and trying to avoid talking about her recent diagnosis, she explained what she wanted to do. As she started telling the banker that she wanted to name me on everything in her account, she had a feeling of guilt and decided that she wasn't going to cut my dad out entirely. Instead, she named me and my dad as beneficiaries, 90 percent and 10 percent respectively. When the banker asked why, we both just shook our heads. Knowing my dad's past, she understood exactly what we meant.

The last pressing issue on Granny's mind before her surgery was finding a facility to take care of her after the operation because she wasn't comfortable being home. She had searched for multiple places but was unsuccessful at finding a place that was available or affordable. Thus, she went into surgery without any around-the-clock care established.

Everything was happening so fast that I became emotionally numb. My response, when trying to avoid the pain I was in, was to occupy myself with busy tasks. It felt reminiscent of the times as a child when I would occupy my mind by fidgeting with whatever I could get my hands on or biting my nails to focus on anything but the pain. It was the response that had previously helped me do well in school, sports, and early in my career by working harder and longer than I probably should have. Helping Granny accomplish her presurgery goals was my way of preserving some normalcy. In the past, Granny would always solicit my help for anything that required the use of a computer: downloading music, searching for lottery results, finding online bingo games, and even helping her create a résumé after her diagnosis so she could find part-time employment after being forced out of work. I found joy in those tasks because if I could take my mind off the actual reason we were doing them, it reminded me of how things used to be between us.

———

Her surgery was successful, and she spent some time recovering at the hospital. I was so relieved. However, after being discharged from the hospital just a couple days after the surgery, Granny's new state of mind emerged, which was concerning to me and my dad, who had moved back into the house to help take care of her. Paranoia and obsessive thoughts regarding her blood sugar levels and her personal finances took control of her mind. As she put it, the State was going to take all of her money and take away her provider rights. To ease her anguish, I showed her on her computer that everything from a finance perspective was in order. While I was at her computer, something told me to check the search history. What I found were dozens of failed attempts to log in to the bank's website and at times of the day that clearly showed that she hadn't gotten any sleep. In between worrying about managing her diabetes, she had been constantly trying to prove to herself that "the State" was in fact taking all of her money.

Prior to her surgery, in hopes that it would remind her that she wasn't at risk of being insolvent, I gave her a visual representation of all of her accounts by creating a balance sheet. As a financial advisor, I frequently performed this type of work for my clients to simplify their complicated financial affairs. On the same sheet of paper, I made a budget for her as well. It listed her forms of income and all of her expenses. After her expenses, she still had a surplus, which I wanted her to see to ease her worries. I also made sure to mention that I had created auto payments for each so that nothing would slip through the cracks. Everything was on autopilot, and all she had to do was rest and recover.

However, a damaged and drug-induced mind doesn't act rationally. Granny began worrying about her insurance and Social Security benefits. She was convinced that everything surrounding her retirement was being mishandled. For her, retirement had happened in the blink of an eye. One day she had been enjoying work, and the next she was on short-term disability to start her cancer treatment. Short term turned into long term. Long term turned into no possibility of returning to work. From many talks with her over the years, I knew she would've worked forever if she could. Retiring was hard on her, and she wasn't in a mental space to understand it all. "See, you young, so you don't understand all this retirement stuff. It's gon' drive me crazy, though," she often told me after her surgery. I tried to be as sensitive as possible while also reminding her that I professionally specialized in many of the things that were agitating her the most. She didn't believe me and spent all of New Year's Eve searching for an attorney to provide her peace of mind.

———

January 1, 2019—the start of the worst year of my life. When I woke up to a call from my dad, there was no exclamatory "Happy New Year!" wish. Instead, I heard shock in his voice. "She ain't doin' good. Somethin' wrong. I'm gettin' ready to take her to the hospital," he said. Before he could explain, I hopped out of bed and headed over to see what was going on.

When I got there, he was warming up the car. He had a blank look on his face that matched his voice on the phone. It was like he was in a trance. I rushed in the house to figure out what was going on with Granny. As I approached her room, I saw her on the bed through the doorway. Her body was stiff as a plank. I dropped to my knees because I thought she was dead.

After a few seconds, I saw a slight movement. Relieved, I walked into the room, but what I saw reignited my fears. Her eyes were bulging out of her face, and she was sweating profusely. Her lips were pressed together tightly, and she wasn't able to speak. Trying not to alarm her any more than I thought she was by crying, I looked her in the eyes and smiled. I rubbed her hair and told her that I loved her and that we were going to take care of everything. As I was staring into her eyes, she made an attempt to talk. "I'm sorry," she said. One of her bulging eyes winked and she repeated, "I'm sorry." I reassured her that she had nothing to be sorry about. The wink made me curious. Thoughts were running through my head. *Was it involuntary? Was she trying to tell me something? Why is she apologizing?* I was so upset and perplexed, but I tried to remain calm and strong for her and my dad.

The ambulance eventually arrived and took her to the hospital. When we reached the emergency room, it was revealed to us that this was, in fact, not a complication from her surgery—she had attempted to commit suicide by overdosing on insulin. We found out that a root cause for her suicide attempt was a steroid she had been prescribed that was used to prevent her brain from swelling after the surgery. Psychosis was one of the side effects of the steroid at a normal dosage. After reading the instructions from her recent discharge, it wasn't clear to anyone—me, my dad, the nurses, Granny—how much she was supposed to be taking. Actually, it was quite misleading. She was taking eight times the amount the doctors had intended for her to have. I couldn't believe that a medication so powerful didn't come with clear instructions.

I was furious to know that everything we had just experienced could have possibly been avoided with proper medical attention. The brain surgeons who had studied their entire lives to do some of the most complicated procedures in the world had literally failed to provide simple instructions on how many milligrams of medicine to take. I was reminded of the countless medical experiments that had been performed on Black bodies over centuries that resulted in the distrust of the medical establishment in the Black community. I thought to myself, *Did her doctors care for and respect her body as much as they would have, had she been white? What if Granny had died?* They would have ruled it a drug-induced suicide, and I would have had to live with the trauma of never knowing what had truly happened to my grandmother, while no one would have been held responsible for their gross ineptitude.

"I wasn't supposed to be here. Why am I even here right now? I don't understand," Granny boldly stated as we entered her room for the first time. She wanted to "go home to be with [her] mama," who had passed away years ago. Hearing that shook me. After telling her that she was just confused as a result of the surgery, she snapped back, "No, I ain't confused; I'm pissed off," in a voice that only an old Black lady could make. It hurt so badly to hear her talking about killing herself. My dad couldn't take it, so he left the room. I went closer and laid my head near her arm on the bed and started to cry more. This ordeal was unlike anything I had ever experienced in my life as it related to Granny. She had always been full of joy and life, but it seemed like that had come to an end.

As she patted my head to console me, she asked in a calm voice, "You must've not seen that note I left you then?"

"Nah, what note?" I responded as I wiped the tears from my eyes.

"Go look on my bed. I laid it all out there," she explained. She had written a suicide note and left it for me to find. In all the haste, we had overlooked it. On the way out of the hospital, I saw my dad outside, pacing and smoking. Seeing him hurt broke my heart. I couldn't imagine the pain, guilt, and fear he was experiencing.

As I sobbed in the car with Katie, I cried out, "I wanna see my mama!" I hadn't so much as talked to her in six months, with the tension between us. But at that moment, life felt so fragile that the beef between us became immaterial. I called her and she answered. "Mama, I miss you. Can I come see you today?" She said yes. I told her I loved her as I hung up. Getting her to say it back was always like pulling teeth. My belief was that it stemmed from the abandonment and lack of love she felt from others. But that day, she told me she loved me too.

Before we got home, we stopped by Granny's house so I could find the note. I looked for a long, elaborate letter, but what I found proved to me that she had been far from her right mind when she wrote it. On a notepad, I read:

Front	Back
Dated 1-1-2019	*Don't want to put*
This is too much	*Little Reggie —*
AIG has taken off	*through all this*
my rights <u>provider</u>	*~~Reggie~~*
Do not want to do	*Regions - Little Reggie*
Radi [sic] & chemo	*Remove CD money*
Love Little Reggie	*unlocked*
& my son Reggie	*Little Reggie has all rights over*
who don't <u>understand</u>	*property & my*
I want to be home with	*finances*
Mamma	
Love Granny	*Granny*

On one hand, she was being irrational with her paranoia, but at the same time, her refusal to continue radiation and chemotherapy along with her desire to protect me from experiencing all that went with it made perfect sense. Even in her degraded mental state, she wanted to protect me from the pain of witnessing further trauma.

It was the worst start to a New Year I'd ever experienced. That night, I went and saw my mama, Demo, Secret, and Thomas. Hugging my mama felt weird because I felt so distant from her, but I needed it. I told them about what had happened, but we didn't dwell on the topic. We mostly talked about Demo's obsession with nature and wildlife. At twelve years old, he was like an encyclopedia for anything that lived in the water, plants included. Before the night was over, we played with a few toys and a telescope that he had gotten for Christmas. With that brief moment of happiness, the day ended much better than it had started.

I was six months into starting my company, and I was beginning to feel like it was a horrible decision. In all of my preparation, I failed to account for my personal life taking such a toll on me. As hard as it was to accept, I thought it was time to go back and get a steady job. I figured I wasn't cut out for the entrepreneurial lifestyle. To boot, I was in my first year of marriage, another undertaking that required just as much work as my business. I started to worry that my wife would resent me if I failed and wasted time doing something that wasn't fruitful. I hadn't hit my goals for the end of the year, for many reasons: my prospecting efforts were thwarted, depression had sunk in, my relationship with my mother was nonexistent, and my grandmother was dying. I got to a point where I didn't want to talk to anyone or even get out of bed. Many days, I just lay in my dark room and sulked.

I would sink into an even greater depression in the weeks and months to follow. On a drive back from a business trip in Mobile, Alabama, I received a call from Granny's oncologist. I was informed that even with additional chemotherapy and radiation, the prognosis for Granny would be the same as if they were to not treat her at all. They went on to say that they were going to put her on hospice care and that they presumed she would have just six months to live. My heart stopped. I tried my best to keep my composure as I was driving on the interstate, but all I wanted to do was bury my face in my lap and cry my eyes out. In a short three-minute call, my entire life was turned upside down. I started thinking about all the tough times I had had when Granny would be there to hug me close to her chest as tears rolled down my face. While I drove, I wanted nothing more than to feel her embrace, especially since there was now a defined timeline on how much longer I would be able enjoy it.

I began to take care of Granny effectively by myself in the following weeks. In that time, severe family dysfunction took rise. My dad and Granny's siblings used manipulation as an attempt to obtain money from Granny. In my rare absences, they guilt-tripped me for trying to balance work with taking care of Granny, although they weren't employed. I was forced to keep the peace when multiple homicidal threats among them occurred as a result of misunderstandings and poor communication regarding Granny's care. I was emotionally manipulated from all parties involved, especially my dad.

After disappearing for days at a time, my dad came to me, shaking his head. "I can't do it. I can't be here and watch my mama die." He told me that if she died, he would kill himself because he would have nothing left to live for, as he repeated, "I have to disappear. I have to disappear. I can't sit here and watch this." When I told him to be strong, his rebuttal was that I should take my own advice once he went through with killing himself. Without any clear indication of what the future held, he left again.

At the time, my dad lived in Huntsville, Alabama, but he had decided to move to Nashville to stay with Granny full time. After being gone for several days, he and my great-aunt and great-uncle, Lucy and Lonny, came up from Huntsville together with all of his furniture on a trailer. Because they had all arrived to take care of Granny, I was relieved, as that meant I could finally go home, take a shower, and get a good night's sleep with Katie. Just as I fell asleep that night, my phone rang. It was my dad, who calmly asked, "Reggie, please tell me you took this money out this closet?"

"Nah, I don't know what you talkin' 'bout."

He replied as if his fuse had just been lit, "I swear to God I'm 'bout to kill these motherfuckers! They tryna steal from my mama, and now they stealin' from me! It was two thousand dollars in that closet, and she got that shit, and now she tryna act dumb. I'ma shoot they ass, Reggie!" I tried to defuse the situation, but there was nothing

I could do over the phone. I hopped out of bed and headed back over to Granny's.

By the time I arrived, my dad had left. I checked in with Lucy and Lonny to get their side of the story. They told me that my dad had assaulted Uncle Lonny and pointed a gun at them before fleeing in Granny's car. When my great-uncle Terry arrived, I called my dad to see where he had disappeared to. Suddenly, I heard Granny yell from her room, "Call the police on his ass! I'm sick of his shit!" That was exactly what Aunt Lucy did. I was still on the phone with my dad, who seemed to be shocked that they were actually involving the police. He told me that he wasn't going back to jail and that he would kill himself before he let that happen. Not knowing how to respond, I just tried to convince him otherwise. After the police arrived and questioned Lucy, Lonny, and Terry, they went to the police station to press charges on my dad. At that point, my dad was considered a fugitive on the run, armed and dangerous.

With everyone gone, Granny and I stayed up and watched *Cast Away* with Tom Hanks. It seemed so fitting because, at the moment, I felt like I had no one around to help me—like I was stranded on a deserted island. When Lucy, Lonny, and Terry finally returned, they dumped my dad's furniture on the front lawn and drove off without even checking on Granny. At that moment, I resented everybody. I resented my dad for his entire response to Granny's diagnosis. In her time of need, he had abandoned her and continuously manipulated me emotionally to get his way. I resented Lucy and Lonny, who hadn't lived up to their end of the bargain regarding their responsibilities and had disappeared, never to return. I resented Uncle Terry for going about his daily life nearly unfazed while my own life had been shaken up. I resented Katie for working and not being by my side when I needed her. I resented my mama for not being the nurturing soul I could turn to when I was down. I resented Granny and Pops for breaking up years before and disrupting my area of refuge that had transformed into the exploding powder keg that night. With that explosion, the defense mechanisms in my mind were reactivated, just as they had been when I was a child on high alert.

———

After the altercation, I became the primary caregiver to Granny. My days were consumed with, first and foremost, making sure Granny wouldn't try to commit suicide again, which meant that I didn't get any sleep. In between all the medical attention, I was actively investigating questions that she had about her finances and insurance. I spent countless hours on the phone with her former employer, insurance companies, banks, and service providers. All the attention I was dedicating toward Granny was physically and emotionally taxing, and it left me with little energy to devote to my company, my wife, and myself. I had neglected any form of self-care other than canceling or simply skipping meetings or networking opportunities for several weeks. I was living out my very own version of *Groundhog Day*.

Then one day, I got a call from a prospect who was ready to move forward with transferring more than a million dollars over to be managed by me. I was thrilled to know that he entrusted me with his hard-earned money, but the circumstances didn't allow for me to meet with him in person as I had wished. Luckily, our relationship was good enough for me to explain what was going on, and he more than understood. So instead of flying to meet him, I closed my first million-dollar account over FaceTime while sitting on Granny's couch in between taking care of her. The feeling was bittersweet. On one hand, I was so proud of myself for the accomplishment, but on the other, I was upset at my new reality. It was far from the celebration I had once imagined for such a major accomplishment. My mind had grown incapable of feeling the peaks of the highs as I fought not to feel the valleys of the lows. I couldn't even comprehend that I was in the worst mental state that I had ever been in my life, and it was only getting worse.

After a few days of taking care of Granny alone, I picked up the phone to call Pops. He knew nothing about Granny's diagnosis because she had asked us to keep it from him. When I explained everything, he said he'd come over immediately to relieve me. The next morning, I saw Pops cry for the second time in my life. I knew he was upset at the state that Granny was in, but he also voiced his frustration with my dad for a number of reasons: his criminal actions, not checking on Granny, and never making an effort to be better to her. Despite all the chaos, I witnessed Pops give Granny a kiss for the first time in a decade. For that brief moment, my area of refuge had returned. It brought a tear to my eye, but for the first time in a long time, it was a tear of joy.

Knowing that Pops and I couldn't take care of Granny and keep our sanity and health, I began calling around to nursing homes and assisted-living facilities. I knew that this was something Granny had originally wanted to have set up before her surgery anyway. I probably called twenty places and even solicited help from friends and family members. I finally found a place Granny could afford that was still pricey, available, and located just a few miles away. I took Granny there to tour the facility to see if she liked it. She told me that the place would be perfect.

I let the family know where she was, so they could visit her whenever they wanted. But because Lucy and Lonny knew where Granny would be, my dad refused to visit her in fear that the police would get him if he did, as he was still a fugitive. We had a conversation over text where he told me again that he was going to kill himself because none of us were taking him seriously. I couldn't understand what was going through his mind; he had gotten to a point where he wasn't making much sense.

When Pops arrived to relieve me for the first time, he told me that my dad had actually been hiding out at his apartment. This irritated me. For nearly a year, my dad had avoided Pops because, as my dad put it, "All that nigga want is some money." Knowing how generous Pops had always been to everyone, especially me and my dad, I resented those words. Particularly, I thought they were hypocritical because my dad was actually behaving in a way that suggested that all he cared about was what he had to gain financially in the midst of Granny's decline.

A few days later, I lost my father. In a similar fashion to my mama, it wasn't because he passed away. It wasn't even because he was back in prison. For the first time, I was real with him about his actions, and he didn't like that. Again, it happened over a text-message conversation. He was irritated at Lucy and Lonny for telling the family that he had stolen from Granny earlier in the year when she was hospitalized. My confirmation of his theft appeared to him that I had chosen the side of Lucy and Lonny, but in reality, I was choosing what was in the best interest of Granny. He responded by shooting jabs and implying that I was being a shady "businessman" in the dealings with Granny's finances, which he believed were rightfully his. With so much built-up frustration at the accusations, I responded, "Don't try to make it seem like I'm doing something wrong here. She said if anything happened to her, a.k.a. if she died. SHE STILL ALIVE!! It's still *her* money. Not yours. Not mine. And as power of attorney, I can tell you what to do and not to do with *her* money." He did not like that power dynamic.

Later that day, he texted me, "I love you so much dude . . . I'm just not in my right mind." I totally believed this, but I refused to respond because I still hadn't calmed down. His next message just an hour later read, "I just left my mama and she said I need access to her account … I need to know how much in there too …" At that point, I knew that the money was more important to him than our relationship. It was more important to him than making sure his mama was living out her last days on Earth as peacefully as possible. It was more important than anything.

———

A week after Granny moved into the assisted-living facility, family members who had neglected to help out when Granny and I needed them the most had opinions on how and where she should be living. During their visits, they planted thoughts in Granny's head to make her think she wasn't happy there. After a while, it started to show. When I'd see Granny every evening, she'd ask me when she would be able to return home. It was tough explaining to her this new reality, but I attempted to every time. My dad had an agenda of his own—to gain access to her financial accounts. The requests never made sense coming from Granny's mouth, and I could tell she had been coerced to ask me about them. The whole time, I continued to receive demeaning texts from my dad that labeled me the demon.

I continued to be there for Granny every day. After initially being terrified to leave the security of her assisted-living facility, she built up the courage to go out. I wanted her to enjoy every minute of life, so we did the things she liked to do. First thing she wanted was to get a manicure and pedicure, so we did that. We followed it with a massage and ended with a nice dinner. For the first time in a while, things started to feel normal. We kept up that routine on at least a weekly basis, which always gave us something to look forward to.

On my twenty-eighth birthday, we spent the entire day together and went to some of her favorite places. It was the perfect day, and it concluded with a steak dinner. As the night came to a close, my anxiety grew because I had a planned vacation the next day. Instead of being excited to go to Hawaii with Katie, I was nervous for multiple reasons. The biggest of all was that I knew there would be a possibility that Granny could pass away while I was gone. That was the absolute last thing I wanted to happen. Another reason was that I knew my dad and family would be able to coerce her into leaving her assisted-living facility. I voiced my concerns to Granny before I left her that night. She assured me that everything would be fine and told me to relax and enjoy myself because I deserved it. She even told me that I shouldn't bother to call because if she needed anything, she would call me. Having Pops there to watch over her also gave me some comfort. The next day, I was off to Hawaii.

As soon as we landed and got to the hotel, I called to check on her. She told me that everything was fine and to stop worrying and have fun. Enjoying my vacation was a much more difficult challenge than I had imagined. When walking the beach during sunrise or sunset, or hiking a beautiful volcano, all I could think about was Granny. I wished she could've been there experiencing it with me. I wished the paradise that was Hawaii was the reality I would return to when I got home. However, just as I had suspected, my dad and family did a number on Granny. When I returned from the trip, I rushed to see Granny to show her all the pictures we had taken. She smiled at a few of them, specifically a picture of Katie in a red dress, but her reaction was nothing like I had expected. I thought that maybe the disease had progressed and was affecting her ability to show emotional expression. It wasn't until a few days later that I found out what was actually going on.

The entire time I was gone, my dad had been working on her to get access to her financial accounts as before. She was even demanding her driver's license, which had been recommended to be suspended due to her risk of seizures. Because I had refused to furnish her with those items, she was furious at me. She was suddenly talking to me in ways that she had never done in her entire life. I was taken aback. During a visit with her hospice nurse, she continued to berate me and got to a point of cursing at me. I tried to remain calm and logically explain to her that if she wanted her things, I could bring them to her, but I didn't think it would be a good decision to leave the facility. Her argument was that she'd rather be home where she could have access to her security cameras.

I asked her, "So, you'd rather be at home with cameras and not be taken care of properly than to be here without cameras and be taken care of?"

"Yes," she barked back in the sassiest tone ever, with her lips pursed together.

I responded, "That just don't make sense to me. Who gon' take care of you every day?"

"I have brothers and a sister." She looked at the nurse, who'd only met one of her brothers once. "Call my brothers and sister, and we'll see."

I couldn't hold it in any longer. Her attitude toward me for something so unnecessary and something that had obviously been planted in her head by my dad frustrated me to a point where I was raising my voice to her and on the verge of crying while telling her that we had already tried to do it the way she was describing, but it hadn't worked because no one had helped out. "We've tried that, and look what happened. You over here mad at me because they've convinced you of all this shit, and it ain't right. Ain't nobody put in all the work that I have to make you happy. They doin' all this for some fuckin' money." I was interrupted by Pops, who hated to see me upset. I left extremely frustrated.

That night at ten, there was a knock on my door. I expected it to be the police telling me that my dad had been arrested or someone telling me that Granny had passed away. Instead, it was Pops, who had come by to check on me after the way I had stormed off. We talked for a while, and he apologized while reassuring me that I was doing the best job I could. He then told me that my dad and Granny had gone to the bank that day and changed everything to remove me from her accounts as power of attorney and beneficiary.

My heart immediately started pounding out of my chest. My blood was boiling, and I started breathing like I had just finished a marathon, but I didn't show any emotions to Pops. I hugged him and told him I loved him as he left. My first reaction was to turn to violence. The reaction I had resorted to so many times during my younger years re-emerged, as I knew no other way to express the immense pain I was feeling. However, when I got to my room, I saw Katie sleeping, and it reminded me of everything that I had to lose. As badly as I wanted revenge on my dad, I came back to my senses. Seeing Katie lying so serenely was a reminder that I had found peace and that I had to fight to hold on to it.

The next day, I rushed to the bank, where I found out she had gone to the day before. Without identification, she had been able to state her Social Security number, which allowed them to act on her account, despite having a letter on file saying that she was unable to make financial decisions in her condition. No other information could be disclosed to me.

After I left the bank, I went to see Granny, and she was still irate.

"Why are you so mad at me?" I asked her.

"Because I want my cell phone and license back," she explained to me.

"Okay, I'll bring them to you. What did you do at the bank the other day?" I probed to get more information. She told me that if I wanted to know, I should go to the bank and ask them. I informed her that I had just returned from the bank, but they wouldn't tell me anything.

"Well, if they won't tell you shit, you don't need to know shit. I ain't tellin' you nothin'."

Hurt by the tone in her voice, I simply nodded, got up, and left. I was intercepted at the door by Uncle Terry, who tried to calm me down. He told me that my dad had gotten a printout of Granny's bank statement that showed charges for the manicures, massages, and meals. He had convinced Granny that I had been stealing from her—and in her mental state, she believed him. She thought that I had betrayed her trust, and there was nothing I could do to convince her otherwise.

The thought that my dad had manipulated my sick grandmother's mind to have his way was too much for me to handle. If he had been willing to go that far, I had no idea what other steps he would take in the future to get his way. At that point, I started considering whether or not it was worth continuing to try to convince Granny of my innocence. After having sacrificed so much to make sure she was being taken care of, I was being treated like a criminal, all because of the actions of the actual criminal, my dad. I was left to make a decision. I could pursue conservatorship over Granny and continue to be viewed as the bad guy while trying to do what was best for her, or I could resign as power of attorney, giving her all of her possessions back and washing my hands of the situation, to save myself from the emotional toll I would be put through. I decided to give it the weekend to think it over.

First thing Monday morning, I got a call from Pops, who told me he had been ordered by Granny and my dad to retrieve Granny's possessions from me. That solidified my decision. I felt like everybody was conspiring against me, and I was fed up with it all. Pops pleaded with me to continue what I was doing, but I told him I couldn't take it anymore.

My dad went on a texting rampage. He accused me of stealing from Granny and of stealing the money that he had blamed Lucy and

Lonny for stealing. He finally ended by calling my wife a "white bitch," just to twist the knife a bit further. After he was finished with his rant, I simply told him that I was done with him and that his true colors had been shown.

I immediately decided to relinquish everything back to Granny. I went to visit her one last time. When I got there, she was just as mean to me as she had been since I returned from my vacation. On the verge of tears, I grabbed her face and gave her three kisses on the forehead as I told her I loved her. As I walked out, she said, "I have to do all this to get my shit back," in the nastiest attitude. I immediately started crying because I knew those would be the last words I would ever hear from her.

Pops tried to get me to stop and talk to him. "Lil' Reggie, lil' Reggie, come here. Hold up, lil' Reggie." I could hear the pain in his voice, but it wasn't enough to get me to stop. I hopped into my car and sped off. Five seconds later, I couldn't see the road because I was crying harder than I had ever cried in my entire life. I needed to pull over because my safety was at risk, but I didn't care about anything else at that point, not even preserving my life. The moans that I let out as I cried were sounds of true heartbreak. I had never felt such pain before. My world had come crashing down. I was broken on the inside.

With tears still fresh on my face, I headed directly to a meeting and tried to compose myself, to get through it without breaking down. I followed that meeting with another meeting, thinking that if I kept myself busy, I wouldn't feel the pain inside. I was wrong. I quivered with every word that left my mouth. In between every meeting, I cried, then quickly flipped the switch to appear presentable for the next meeting.

That day, after my meetings, I quitclaimed the house back to Granny in the spirit of wiping my hands of the situation. I was extremely hesitant because of what that house represented to me. Other than being my area of refuge for so long, it was also the first time in my family's history that someone had been able to pass down an asset, which was so significant in leveling the playing field where the odds are often stacked against poor Black families. Even then, I felt it was the best decision to make. I delivered the deed to Granny's mailbox. Tears filled my eyes, and as I shut the door, it felt like turning the page on the worst chapter of my life.

The emotions of betrayal and abandonment that I felt were reminiscent of the feelings I used to carry with me throughout my childhood. The roller coaster of a relationship with my dad had run out of tracks and come to a crashing halt. Granny, the most peaceful woman I had known my entire life, had turned into a source of trauma and chaos. Pops, the most selfless person I'd ever known, had become an innocent bystander who was forced to witness the relationships among everyone he loved fall apart as the love of his life was dying of cancer. While no one had been physically harmed, so many people were mentally and emotionally damaged forever.

CHAPTER THIRTEEN

SEARCHING FOR PEACE

Feeling abandoned and lonely, I called Jarrett and Kevin to brighten my spirits. After updating them on everything that had occurred, they were just as mad as I was. They immediately began to concoct plans of revenge on my dad, all of which involved violence. For whatever reason, the conversation shifted from planning our attack to describing what life had been like having him as a father. After everyone aired their grievances, we all agreed that life would've been so much better if he had never existed. The thought alone felt liberating to us. All the hurt and all the pain seemed to cease for just a moment.

Just a few days after I had emotionally freed myself, I had plans of decompressing with a client over drinks and dinner. As I walked through the doors of the restaurant, I received a call from a random number. "Is this Reggie Ford?" It was the sheriff's department.

"Yes, this is he," I responded, hoping they were calling to tell me that they had found my dad.

The lady on the other end of the phone gave me news that I didn't think I would ever hear. "I wanted to inform you that your grandmother has attempted to take an order of protection out against you, but it has been rejected for lack of basis."

To add insult to injury, my dad had convinced Granny to go to the police about me for no reason at all, even after I had relinquished all her possession back to her. Not to mention, he was still a fugitive on the run. I was amazed that he had the bravado to involve the police at all in his current situation.

I blocked out the majority of the night after that call. I was seeing red but tried to maintain my composure at dinner. After going through the motions, I planned to find my dad to confront him. I had already texted my brothers, De'Anté, and Katie, and apologized for what I was about to do. Luckily, my client foiled my plans and talked with me for several hours to calm me down. When he felt sure that I wasn't a threat to anyone, he took me home.

A few hours after I laid my head down that night, I jumped out of my sleep after a nightmare. In the dream, my dad had knocked on my door. As soon as I opened it, he apologized to me before shooting himself in the head. Part of me wished it had actually happened. My thoughts were becoming so disturbing, but I couldn't control them. Everything from the outside world that was impacting me was in control of my mind.

A few days later, Pops called to tell me that he too was removing himself from the situation because of my dad's actions. My dad was mad at him because Pops wouldn't believe the lies my dad was trying to feed him about me.

Several days later, I scheduled a doctor's appointment for myself. For the first time in my life, I mentioned to the doctor that I wanted to be proactive about my depression, knowing that Granny's death would be difficult for me. After asking a few basic questions, he decided that I didn't "qualify" for any medical attention and told me to just keep talking to my support system to deal with things. I left the doctor's office extremely disappointed. It had taken me an enormous amount of courage and vulnerability to bring up my mental health, and he had dismissed me. I like to think that if I had come into his office with my heart literally dangling from its arteries outside of my chest, he would have taken my cry for help more seriously—because that was exactly what it felt like for me.

Needing to release some stress, I wrote a song titled "Pray 4 Me." I wasn't sure if listening to it on repeat after I had finished it was hurting or helping. The song was my raw form of expressing pure anger with everything going on with my dad and Granny:

> *Why the fuck would I ever steal from a broke nigga*
> *Taking advantage of your mama, you a joke nigga*
> *Kill yourself motherfucker, here go the rope nigga*
> *Fifty years old and selling dime bags of dope nigga*

Those bars were a complete personal attack on my dad addressing his financial woes, his accusations against me, his manipulation of Granny, his suicidal ideation, and his drug dealing. The hook of the song requested that the listener pray that I refrain from doing anything irreversible to my dad in response to the ultimate betrayal.

———

Over the next few months, I tried to regain my sanity. Self-care was the highest priority for me, and that meant neglecting many expectations from the outside world. I canceled or flat-out skipped meetings that I had. I made sure to be present enough so as not to raise any concerns, but I was virtually coasting to work on myself.

Although I was working on finding my peace, I was often reminded of the things that I was actively trying to forget. Granny drove Nissan Altimas for as long as I could remember, and my dad was now in possession of them. Every time I saw a silver or green Altima, my mood would change. I became more vigilant and expected it to be my dad in the car. I even found myself following random cars long enough to prove that it wasn't him. What I would've done if it had been him, I don't even know. It was irrational, but it consumed me.

Every time I visited Pops, which was nearly every week, the first thing he would ask me, the peacemaker that he was, was whether I had talked to my dad. That question drove me crazy because I had made it clear that I wasn't going to speak to him again.

One thing that I continued to torture myself with over those months was checking Granny's banking information to see how much money was being spent. Nearly every day, I would log on and see transactions that were clearly not for Granny: dozens of ATM withdrawals, several charges to a pill clinic that my dad would get his drugs from, charges for auto parts, and so many more. Over the course of about two and a half months, nearly forty thousand dollars had been drained from Granny's account, and it infuriated me. I wanted to do something to stop it, so I tried calling the bank. They didn't seem to care too much about the unusual activity. I tried talking with Adult Protective Services, but they also didn't seem to care.

Even when I wasn't torturing myself, my dad still found ways to get under my skin. The NFL draft had come to Nashville for the first time ever, and people came out in record numbers. Seeing as I hoped to hear the names of some of the guys I had engaged with called during the draft, I was excited about the next couple of days. I decided that I was going to enjoy the festivities with Demo, hoping that his excitement would lift my spirits. I got him out of school early, and we headed downtown to enjoy ourselves. His eyes lit up brighter than the lights on the stage, which filled my heart. At a draft party later that evening, I received a text from my dad that simply said, "Punk bitch." It was unprovoked and unexpected, and it deflated me. I saw that Demo was getting tired, so I used that as an opportunity to escape the crowds and head home.

The day after the draft ended, I received another unwarranted text from my dad that accused me of doing more things than ever before, including stealing his dogs. It was so strange because he had fabricated in his mind these scenarios that painted me as the bad guy. It was unsettling because it showed just how unstable he was. He was in tremendous pain from the news that his mama was dying, and he wasn't helping the situation by altering his brain with opioids and other drugs. By combining that with the decades of trauma he had endured, it was clear why he was not in a good state of mind, but never in a million years did I think he would lash out at me.

Because of his instability, I wanted to protect myself, so I filed for an order of protection against him. I explained to the judge my reasoning, and he agreed to grant it. I could hear in his voice that he was sympathetic toward me. As I left, he apologized for everything that was going on. I thought to myself, *That's just life.* Leaving the sheriff's office, I thought I would be sad, but I wasn't. I was relieved. I knew my dad would finally know that I had gone to the police instead of assuming it, and I was okay with that. I knew that it was officially over between me and him.

One day when I was visiting Pops, I ran into Granny's hospice nurse, who had a patient in Pops's building. She lit up when she saw me, but that quickly faded as she told me that she was not supposed to be talking to me about Granny, as she had been instructed by my dad. She did, however, give me a few updates. According to her, things were getting ugly. Granny had begun wetting the bed and hadn't been her joyful self on her most recent visits. I had been prepared for those developments, but I never thought I would be on the outside looking in when it actually happened.

Over the next couple of months, Pops kept me updated on Granny, but mostly, he would tell me about the things my dad was doing. My dad finally turned himself in to the police and bonded out. He had neglected Granny and even left her alone many days. He also refused to follow medical orders because he felt he knew what was best for Granny. Yet, my dad's mental state continued to be unpredictable. Over the course of several weeks, he had outfitted a tiny storage shed in the back of Granny's house with new flooring, a television, and a heating and cooling system. With a large bag of prescription pills nearby, he would sleep in the shed instead of in the house. As I tried to make sense of it all, I figured my dad was reverting back to being confined to his jail cell, having been institutionalized for so many years. Perhaps as preparation for what he believed to be an inevitable return to prison, a search for comfort in the world of incarceration that he had once normalized, my dad had retrofitted the shed as his personal dwelling. In the midst of it all, he had also inexplicably bought several cars and a motorcycle. Many of his actions were strange, but they would often get excused by family members because he was "grieving" or because he'd "always been like that." I never understood why no one ever challenged him on his transgressions or why they failed to realize how his decisions impacted me.

———

On a ride to see one of my mentees, DeShaun, the former intern from my wealth management firm, graduate from Indiana University, I received a message that I desperately needed to hear. During the ceremony, I agreed to let one of DeShaun's friends, Aaron, ride back to Nashville with me. The four-hour drive started off with a little bit of small talk, and that quickly shifted to talking about our respective passions and business endeavors. In the midst of our conversation, after I basically gave him the story of my business career, he told me that I was a whole person. All the while, I had been holding back the most pressing issues that I was currently facing, and so that made me feel like an imposter. I took a deep breath and told him everything. Our four-hour drive turned into a six-hour conversation because we sat down outside of his house to talk for two more hours.

After hearing my story, Aaron gave me some key bits of advice that helped me cope with things better. He first prayed with me and hoped that I would find reconciliation in the relationships in my life. When I told my story, he had heard that I was able to recognize the deficits that Granny had mentally because of the disease, but he also challenged me to see that my dad was also suffering mentally and that I should have sympathy for him just as I had for Granny. It was tough for me to accept. But he was right. My dad's brain, too, had been altered by his life's experiences. Aaron reminded me that though I hadn't talked to my dad in months, I was still allowing him to get the emotional reactions out of me that he wanted through text messages alone. All those months, I had been telling myself the lie that I hadn't blocked his number so that he could incriminate himself. In reality, I was wanting to get upset by the things he was sending. By allowing him to continue to contact me, I was leaving the door open for him to provoke and hurt me.

After a truly heartfelt conversation, we parted ways. As soon as he got out of the car, I decided that it was time to block my dad's number, to regain some power. It felt like a weight was lifted off my shoulders.

In the midst of the most trying time in my life, we got a puppy. What I soon realized was that most puppies don't shed their first coat until around six months of age. It was a reminder for me that during periods of growth, we may have to shed things as well. To improve and grow into the person we want to become, sometimes it requires shedding bad habits, bad energy, bad thoughts, bad people, and bad experiences. While the shedding may come as an annoyance or even be painful, a better version of yourself awaits you on the other side.

On July 30, 2019, I got a call from my mama. When I answered it, she said, "You know your Granny died today, right?" My heart stopped. It was the first I had heard of the news. My initial reaction was to think that it wasn't true because I didn't believe my mama would hear about the news before me.

I called Pops, and he confirmed my worst nightmare. He was at the hospital with the rest of the family, and it made me feel so sad and lonely that I was not able to be there, when I was the closest person in the world to Granny. I couldn't believe that they were all okay with leaving me out. I wasn't a part of any decision-making process for her arrangements. No pictures of me were included in the slideshow, and I wasn't even named in her obituary. It was petty more than anything at that point, but there was nothing I could do about it.

Nine days prior, Pops had called and told me that Granny wanted to see me. I knew that must've meant she wasn't doing well. My dad was out at dinner, so Pops thought it would be a good time for me to come over. Katie and I rushed over to see her, and I was devastated by the state she was in. The cancer had taken a huge toll on her body since the last time I had seen her just a few months prior. All I could do was lie on her chest like I had done all my life whenever I would go see her if I was upset. Her breaths were long and spaced out to the point where I thought she had stopped breathing a few times. Her head was becoming a different shape as the tumors grew, and she could barely keep her eyes open. I kissed her and told her that I loved her, and she was able to make out the words, "I love you too, baby." Those were the only words she spoke that night. I will forever be grateful to have shared that last moment with her.

The day of her funeral, I wanted only to be around the people who actually loved me, so I refused to go into the church until the last minute. Instead, I stayed outside with Katie and a few friends who had come to support me. When I finally went in, I approached Granny in her casket. The closer I got, the harder it became to breathe. When I finally got to the casket after the longest walk down the pews, I lost control of my body. The pain of seeing her there was more than I was ready for. I sobbed uncontrollably as my legs gave out. After kissing her, I turned around and looked for a comforting face. And although my wife and friends were near me, the only face I could see in the entire church was Pops's, so I went to him and held him close.

During the service, I shuffled from being upset, to angry, to un-amused. I spent most of the time with my head down, looking at the beautiful picture of Granny on the program and thinking of how she would be reacting to the service. The thought made me laugh because it was far too over-the-top for her style. My laughter turned to sadness when they closed the casket. It felt like the last breath that I had in me left my body because I knew that I would never see her body again. I let out a moan and laid my head on Pops's shoulder. My sadness turned into anger when the morticians rolled her casket out and my dad walked behind it while crying. I was so angry that he had stolen the last months of Granny's life away from me without any remorse whatsoever. I had a panic attack, and I just wanted to hurt him. Fortunately, I was surrounded by my loved ones, who made sure I didn't dishonor Granny by doing anything rash. I eventually calmed down by staring at the picture of Granny. She would have just wanted me to let it go.

Over the next couple of days, I fell into the worst depression. Katie asked if there was anything she could do, but there was nothing I could think of. Although I knew I wouldn't feel that way forever, the pain at that moment was unbearable. The pain turned into anxiety for the simple fact that I had not gotten confirmation that the order of protection I had taken out on my dad was delivered. Nearly every few weeks, I got a letter from the sheriff's office stating that they had been unsuccessful at delivering the order of protection to my dad, so I figured that it would never be enforced. I hadn't heard from him, but I still wanted to know that it would be delivered. Pops hadn't heard from him since Granny's funeral either. My dad had needed Pops's signature for a life insurance policy, and once he obtained that, he stopped talking to Pops. That didn't surprise me, but it angered me.

When I was child, I had had no idea what a junkie was, but I had been quick to assume. If you looked and acted a certain way, that was the giveaway. As an adult, I watched as my dad turned into one before my eyes, but unlike what I had imagined, he presented himself well, probably better than he had ever done in his entire life. Deep down, he was broken. He always had an ability to appear better off than he was.

On my dad's birthday, I didn't see or talk to him. Instead, I went to the funeral of the father of one of my high school classmates. I heard reflections from my classmate and his sister about how supportive and loving their father had been, and it made me weep. Seeing the pain that ripped through their hearts for a man who had been nothing but a source of light, love, and inspiration made me feel hopeful and sad at the same time. I longed to have similar feelings for my dad, but I knew that I didn't have the same things to say about him. I started wishing that I could trade places with my friend. I thought to myself, *Why should his dad be dead after the love he provided his family, while mine is still alive, causing harm to so many people?* Life is unfair sometimes.

———

Meanwhile, things with my mama were coming to a head. She had been able to provide emotional support for me right after Granny's funeral, and on her birthday, I took her to lunch, where we spent quality time together. It seemed like we were about to mend our relationship, but two days after our lunch, things started to deteriorate again. By this time, my mama had socially isolated herself from almost everyone in the world for reasons deeper than what I will ever be able to comprehend. After I took my siblings to a cookout, despite my mama's wishes to keep them separated from our extended family, she felt disrespected and let me know it.

Over the next couple of days, she repeatedly called and berated me. It got to the point where she told me she wouldn't talk to me anymore because I was apparently against her in life and I didn't care about her. I thought she was blowing it way out of proportion. Finally, I couldn't take it anymore. The early morning voicemails were getting more and more disrespectful and flat-out hurtful. She even threatened to take me to court for defamation of character if I spoke about her to anyone.

She knew the right buttons to press to hurt me the most: bad-mouthing my wife for being white, making comments about never coming to any of my football games, threatening to keep Demo and Secret away from me, involving the police if need be, and the most painful—throwing in my face that Granny had "turned her back on me." Just days after losing the most loving and nurturing person I'd ever known, who had suffered through cancer, my mama was manipulating her memory against me. At my breaking point, I texted her while including Demo and Secret in our messages in full transparency. I told her that I loved her but that I wouldn't allow her to speak to me this way anymore. I followed it up by telling her that I wished she knew me better and that I was going to be working on myself and I hoped she would do the same. I cried the entire night.

As I reflect on my mama's behavior, I can't help but think of all the negative things she must have endured to treat me the way she did. She exemplified the phrase "Hurt people hurt people," meaning that those who are suffering inflict pain onto others as a defense mechanism. Could it have been something that Big Mama and Popeye did to her? If so, why did they behave the way they did? How far back did that type of behavior originate? In her breakthrough book *Post Traumatic Slave Syndrome: America's Legacy of Enduring Injury and Healing*, Dr. Joy DeGruy attempts to answer similar questions that I pondered. In the book, she describes the psychological consequences of the multigenerational oppression of Black people resulting from centuries of enslavement and institutionalized racism, which continue to perpetuate trauma. Through her years of studies, she found that those consequences result in the following characteristics: vacant esteem accompanied with feelings of hopelessness, depression, and self-destructive behavior; violence; and internalized and self-directed racism. Her studies were my reality.

I spent the better part of the rest of the year searching for peace. After receiving those calls from my mama, I didn't sleep for a month. I couldn't fall asleep even if I wanted to. That lack of sleep started to wear me down mentally. I couldn't think straight most of the time, which affected all aspects of my life. I hit a point where I completely broke down. I had a panic attack, which led to me lying on the floor blabbering incoherently and crying. That night was the first time in months that I actually got any sleep. Following that night, I found myself on the road to recovery.

I lost loved ones, trust, and peace of mind all in a matter of months. My mental health had deteriorated to the lowest level it had ever been in my life. I was so unfamiliar with the way my mind was responding to my circumstances, and that scared me. Instead of using my tribulations as fuel to elevate myself to higher levels like I had done so many times before, I folded. Similar to my opponent in my first fight, when my head was lifted up, it was clear that life had won. Feeling defeated, I knew that I had to focus on building myself back up.

After years of avoiding it, I finally sought professional help. I started with finding another doctor who took my cry for help seriously and prescribed an antidepressant. I also reached out to a therapist, which proved to be the most effective treatment for me next to my consistent yoga practice. After some bad side effects from my prescription, I decided to rely on other forms of treatment. Through all the work that I did for my mental state, I finally began to rediscover my peace, and it felt good. For so long, I had thought that it was soft to express emotions. I had thought it was weak to admit that I needed help. However, after getting the help, I now realize that allowing myself to remain broken had been the true problem.

LIBERATION

When you lose everybody, you are forced to find yourself. After the worst episode of my life that was filled with betrayal, emotional trauma, lost loved ones, and an overall decline of peace of mind, I was mentally broken. Admitting that I was broken and needed help was hard, but remaining broken would have been even harder. That was a fact I had to come to terms with.

Once I realized I had mental health issues to address, I neglected to do so for years. When Katie and I first started dating, she realized that I was facing many demons that affected our relationship, and she encouraged me to seek treatment. After initially being offended, I conceded because I trusted that her advice was only going to make me a better person. However, that trust faded when I found out that she had told her best friend that I had agreed to go to therapy. I defaulted back to being against the idea. I was embarrassed more than anything, but it presented itself as defensiveness and anger. The belief that showing vulnerability was weak lingered in my mind long after I had already become aware of my need for help. I feared the labels that would come with admitting that I was suffering from something I could have easily hidden. It wasn't until I physically could not hide what was affecting me mentally that I knew it was time to accept my reality.

The more I matured, the more accepting of my realized mental health issues I became. I accepted that I had had a traumatic childhood that has shaped the course of my life. I also accepted that those who had caused some of my trauma had also been traumatized themselves, probably by other people who had also been traumatized. One thing my therapist told me about the trauma of my loved ones was that I hadn't caused it, I can't control it, and I can't cure it. It is up to each and every one of us to address our own trauma instead of blaming ourselves for the trauma of others who have come before us. Acceptance was liberating for me, and this awareness allowed me to extend grace and forgiveness to others. I accepted that there were going to be things I couldn't change, like my past, my parents, and my pain, but I could change my response to it all. I accepted that Black *could* crack. In fact, Black can break. But things that can break can also be fixed.

I knew that if I didn't take care of my mental health, my physical health would suffer, and that would lead to me falling victim to one of my biggest fears—dying early. When our physical body is harmed, we get treated for it. If we employed that same behavior with our mental health, we would be healthier, happier people.

Yoga is such a great metaphor for experiencing discomfort, addressing it, and letting it go. My yoga practice was just one form of treatment that I happened to stumble upon. Seeking a professional therapist was more intentional and more difficult to accept because I would have to deal with another human. Sometimes, the same reasons you need a therapist will be the same ones that hold you back. My trust and abandonment issues had prevented me from wanting to engage with another person for a long time. Within a few sessions, I had become so accepting of the fact that I needed help that I gladly told anyone who would listen that I was in therapy.

Knowing that my actions are leading to a better version of myself is all the motivation I need now. Acceptance and treatment are liberating.

CHAPTER FOURTEEN

PROCESS OF PERSEVERANCE

The pace at which I move in life has been a direct result of my race with death. When I was younger, I had nightmares that I would die early, so I thought if I wanted to leave an impact on the world, I would have to do it sooner rather than later. For that reason, I often seemed to lack patience in going about life the "normal" way. Besides, to go about life in a normal way, you had to have a normal life, right?

At the same time I was experiencing those nightmares, I was witnessing people in real life fail to make it to their next birthday at extremely young ages. People who I knew had dreams of living long, prosperous lives were no longer with us, so how else could I have responded other than thinking that time was of the essence? Of those people, my grandparents stand out because I realize the impact that genetics has on our longevity. The stress of being a Black man in America, which breaks down our immune systems, shouldn't be overlooked either. My paternal grandfather, Archie, whom I never knew, passed away at forty-four years old, and Popeye passed away at fifty-one years old. Big Mama passed away at fifty-six years old, and my longest-living biological grandparent, Granny, died at the age of sixty-three. In this "normal" life, that would mean that none of them had even reached the traditional age of retirement before dying.

I have chosen a far healthier lifestyle than my grandparents, and I know medical technology is advancing at a pace that may keep us all living far longer than the generations before us. But I can't help but think about my race with death and how the normal pace of life just wasn't meant for me. Was I born to report to a job day in and day out in hopes of earning enough money to sustain a long retirement, only to die before it even started? To the contrary, I want to take risks. I want to not only live life, but I also want to experience life to the fullest. I want to make sure that those who come after me have opportunities that I've never had as a result of my hard work and risk-taking. Everything I do in life is bigger than me. It's bigger than right now. I strive so that those who are able to witness it will realize that nothing is impossible.

———

Pops and I continued to be close, maybe closer than we had ever been. Though he didn't show much emotion, I knew he was hurting. The pain was compounded by the sudden and tragic death of my cousin, Pops's grandson, who was murdered at only twenty years old, later that year. Pops and I attempted to console my aunt, Pops's daughter, who had to bury her son while we were still heavily grieving the loss of Granny. We were all in a state of shock, but we were there for each other, which made things much better. Pops and I started hanging out on a weekly basis, which I loved because it reminded me of the good old days when I would spend every weekend with him. It was a significant silver lining, but that glimmer of light would be short-lived.

Exactly one year after Granny's suicide attempt, Pops called me, out of breath, asking if I could run him to the emergency room. As I opened the door to his apartment, I found him on the ground with his coat over his body and face as he shivered uncontrollably. I checked to see if he was conscious and called for an ambulance. I had never seen him like this, and I was in shock. The 911 operator stayed on the line with me until I heard the ambulance arrive. It only took twelve minutes, but as I was right there watching him shake vigorously, it felt like hours.

As I trailed the ambulance, a numbness came over my body. I stopped hearing the sirens, and all I could do to not break down and cry in my car was to follow the pattern of the lights with my eyes. When I arrived at his bedside, he appeared fine. He talked with me for a short while and started to tell me things like wanting to be buried near Granny. He had told me this countless times before, but it stung a little more than usual hearing it from him in a hospital bed.

He described what was going on to the doctors and was admitted to the intensive care unit (ICU) because it appeared that he had a pretty bad internal bleed. That's when I knew it was serious. In the ICU, one of the first questions the nurse asked him was, "On a scale of one to ten, with one being the lowest and ten being the highest, how peaceful do you feel right now?" Pops's response was ten. I smiled.

That night, he was stable. He insisted that I go home to get some sleep. On my way back to the hospital the following morning, the Top 100 in *Finance Magazine* shared on their social media sites that I had been featured in their 2020 edition, which was a huge accomplishment for me. I couldn't wait to tell him the news. When I arrived, he was in good spirits, and based on the information from the nurse, he had had a good morning of walking around and behaving normally.

While we sat there chatting and making a few jokes, I told him about my good news. He responded, "Oh yeah? You be doin' it! I'm proud of you." I already knew that, but hearing it was a good reminder. Shortly after that, his blood pressure dropped, and he became unresponsive. I was asked to leave the room, and I reflected on how much of a roller coaster life was. In one moment, I had received some of the best news of the year, and in the next, the fragility of life was revealed to me again.

I was eventually let back into the room, and Pops was responsive again. We talked briefly, but he complained about stomach pain, and for the first time in his life, I heard him say that he wasn't feeling good. As the doctors and nurses were out making calls to the specialists, he looked over at me in agony and said, "Go get 'em!" I ran out of the room to call for help, and before I knew it, the room was filled with about twenty people.

I was escorted out by a nurse and asked to wait while they did everything they could to help him. Minutes later, I heard over the intercom, "Code blue in room 343." That was Pops's room number, and I looked up what code blue meant. Just as I did, I fell to the ground and started to cry. I had been texting Katie and my brothers to give them updates, but at the moment, I was all alone. My heart was filled with so much pain, but I tried to remain hopeful that the doctors would be able to make everything better. Hope is a strange concept when you think about it. Nothing about a situation changes when you hope, but it seems so necessary in times of despair. Hope is that tiny light at the end of a dark tunnel that gives you the motivation that you will make it out of whatever you're stuck in. Hope has guided me my entire life. Even as a child, I knew that tomorrow would be better. When you are faced with desperate times, it may be difficult to look at life from a positive point of view, but to persevere and see the other side of your current circumstances, you must have hope.

After several minutes, the hospital's chaplain came out and handed me a bible, which made me weep even harder. My hope was slipping away. He sat with me and told me that the doctors were still working hard. It had been about a half hour since I last saw Pops. Soon thereafter, two doctors came out to tell me that Pops hadn't had a heartbeat for nearly twenty minutes, but they had gotten it back and had him on all sorts of support. They didn't think he would be able to sustain life for much longer. At the same time, Katie had arrived and came running toward me to give me a hug. We were escorted to a private room, where we just sat and waited. After a while, the same two doctors came into the private room to tell us that Pops, at the age of seventy, had died. My heart shattered into a thousand pieces.

Growing up, I had always thought about how I would react to the death of Pops, because our relationship had always been so strong. I used to think that it would break me to a point of no return, and that I would shut down. However, my response was the opposite. Hearing that on his last day he was at peace gave me comfort. While my grandparents are no longer physically here, they are now together again and will forever exist within me. That thought has reenergized me to continue to live out my purpose. And as a promise to Pops, in the context of accomplishing all of my wildest dreams, I will continue to *go get 'em!*

―――――――

People often ask me how I'm able to smile through all I've been through. What keeps me going? What gives me the ability to view life with a positive outlook? It's tough to answer those questions, and I have contemplated them my entire life.

The Center on the Developing Child at Harvard University has done extensive research on resilience in children who have experienced significant adversity. They have found that some children develop resilience, or the ability to overcome serious hardship, while others do not. What they have found is that the single most common factor for children who develop resilience is at least one stable and committed relationship with a supportive parent, caregiver, or other adult. Those relationships help build the skills necessary to persevere through severe dysfunction.

For me, my grandparents had provided that unwavering love and support. From before I can even remember, we had a routine, and it gave me something to look forward to. Whenever the weekend hit, I knew I was going to be able to be at peace with two people who, more than anything, genuinely enjoyed my presence and seeing me happy. As I matured, my community of loyal supporters grew larger despite the dysfunction and conditional support I felt from other members of my family. I shared amazing experiences with coaches and teammates. Teachers and mentors not only guided me through life but also loved me the whole way through. Friends entered my life and became family. Katie became my confidant, and ultimately my actual family. My in-laws showed the love and support for me and Katie that I had always expected from my family. While I may have lacked committed relationships from some people in my life, I found them in others when I needed them most.

From an early age, one of the things that kept me striving to be better was seeing the pitfalls of those around me and wanting to avoid those at all costs. I made a vow to myself that I was going to do better. I refused to fall victim to the same system that had imprisoned those close to me, either literally or metaphorically. I never wanted to become a product of my environment; instead, I wanted to shape the environments around me.

It was a challenging feat to overcome, especially with societal pressures, but my mission never wavered. It took making just one "better" decision at a time. In retrospect, I don't feel that I did anything extraordinarily special. We all have a moral compass and are taught right from wrong, and I simply chose right more times than not. I knew that if I did that, just maybe I would be in a position to impact the world and have control over the things in my life as opposed to the other way around.

Where did that thought process come from? I have no idea. I've contemplated that question a million times throughout my life and have yet to pinpoint a definitive answer. Maybe it is innate, and I was just wired differently from birth. Perhaps it is something I had learned through the experiences I had had before I can even recall. Most likely, it is a combination of the two. But ultimately, when I think about what has made me who I am today, I can't help but think that there was and continues to be divine intervention.

Nothing great has ever been accomplished without faith. Faith is the belief in the truth of something that does not require any evidence and may not be provable by any rational means. It is deeper than hope. While hope is that light at the end of the dark tunnel, faith is that voice in our heads when there is no light at all. That voice guides us even when we have no idea where it is taking us. It grabs hold of us and says, "Follow me."

Many people equate faith with religion, and rightfully so, but I am not here to proselytize. Instead, I want to encourage you to find what you believe to be your faith. Believe in it wholeheartedly. No matter what you believe in, it will be challenged and opposed by others, and that is okay. We are all entitled to our own beliefs. But life will throw you many obstacles, and your faith may be the only thing that gets you through the challenging times when all hope seems to be lost.

After the 2020 murder of Rayshard Brooks in Atlanta, Georgia, I was distraught. The unrelenting disregard for Black lives, even in the wake of a worldwide outcry for justice, continued to persist. A sense of hopelessness came over my body as I started to feel that nothing would ever change. Thinking about the strides that my ancestors had taken for me to be where I am today provided a much-needed reminder that although things weren't moving as fast as I had hoped, progress was being made. I couldn't give up hope, despite how difficult the process was. That is the essence of perseverance through severe dysfunction.

Unable to sleep after learning of Rayshard's death, I scoured the internet, searching for confirmation to make me feel better. Searching for opposition to piss me off. Searching for inspiration to restore my hope. The inspiration came from a drawing that I saw online created by the talented Laurence "Sketch" Cheatham. In the drawing, the focus is on a little Black girl whose head is lowered just slightly, giving her puppy dog eyes, while her facial expression is full of despair. She has barrettes in her hair—pink, blue, and yellow—that display Black fists. Streaming down her face and covering her left arm is blood. Her arms are crossed against her shirt that reads, "YOU KILLED MY DAD." Behind her are the faces of so many victims of racial violence, which float above her like the angels that they have become. On either side of her are protestors standing behind police barricades, wearing surgical masks and holding signs that read, "We pay you to protect us not to kill us"; "Our skin is not a weapon"; "No justice, No peace, No racist police"; "Say her name"; "Stop looting Black lives"; and "Black Lives Matter, Stop Killing Us!!!" They don shirts that carry messages of their relation to those who have been killed: "She was my daughter"; "He was my son"; "He was my uncle"; "She was my mom"; "He was my brother."

The entire image shook me to my core. I immediately began crying as I thought about all the people in my life who could have been floating in those clouds. I thought about myself and how there was no guarantee that I would make it to see old age or my children, my grandchildren, or my great-grandchildren. Then I thought about those children. *What if that were my daughter in the picture?* I was consumed with emotion. The inspiration, like countless times before, led me to write. I wrote a letter to my unborn child:

To My Unborn Child,

I hope you know that Daddy will love you always and forever. Thank you for all the joy you bring to Daddy and Mommy. If Daddy doesn't get around to telling you, I want you to always remember a few things:

This world that you will be entering is a crazy place. In some people's eyes, you matter more now than you will once you are born. They may give you more respect and love when you are in Mommy's belly than they will the moment after you take you first breath, and definitely more than they do Daddy. Don't worry—Daddy is tough, and you will be, too.

The world isn't fair, sweetheart. For no reason other than the color of your skin, you will be treated differently. You'll have to work twice as hard to prove your worth, and even then, it may not be recognized by some. You will rise above it, nonetheless, because you are a king/queen with magical powers—we call that Black boy/girl magic.

You will sometimes be viewed as a scary animal even while you are playing or just walking home. Smile and know that you are a friendly person despite what they think. You may be oversexualized, but that's a story for later. Ask Mommy to tell you about the birds and the bees.

If you see Daddy and Mommy crying, it's not because we are upset with you. We might be crying because all the grown-ups in the world can't get along. We might be upset because we saw someone who looks like Daddy get hurt really bad ... AGAIN. Either way, it's not your fault because you are the best thing that has happened to us, and you will help us forget why we cry.

Sweet unborn child, I love you, but I hope you understand why you may remain unborn. Daddy is strong, but sometimes Daddy fears what you will have to go through. It is a scary place when you look like us, sweetie, and sometimes it feels like things will only get scarier. Daddy will fight all the monsters for you, but there are a bunch of monsters, so Daddy might get tired. Even then, I will rest then get up and keep fighting for you because that's what we do!

But right now, Daddy is tired.

As I wrote, I thought about my mama, and I thought about my dad. Maybe, if she had had the opportunity, my mama would have written a similar letter to me before my birth instead of wishing my existence away after the fact. Perhaps my dad had had the same thoughts that I did but was too tired of fighting all the fights and had let the monsters take control. How many generations had my ancestors had these same thoughts but not enough time, resources, or knowledge to prevent the monsters from wreaking havoc? In spite of the traumas that they passed down to me, but also because of their constant fights to see that things would be better for me, I too must continue to fight.

———

In closing, our time on Earth is as short, in the grand scheme of things, as the dash between our birth and death dates on our tombstone. That dash represents everything that you did in life. Your successes and your failures. Take advantage of every moment in life, and leave a lasting impact. Make the world a better place because you were a part of it.

No matter your background, life will challenge every cell in your body. You will face obstacles, and you will be tested to overcome the most difficult challenges. The difficulties in life won't get any easier the longer you live, but you will get stronger. You may bend, but you won't break.

Your trauma does not define you. While you will always carry the nightmares of your past, you don't have to let them affect your dreams. Everything that you have gone through has helped shape you into the person that you are. Good, bad, or indifferent—it's a part of you. You never completely get over your trauma. You continue to live with it. Even then, it can have one of two effects on you: it can break you, or it can make you stronger. Optimally, you would like to become stronger. The pain of addressing your trauma will be yet another challenge to overcome. No need to run from it. No need to sugarcoat or disguise it. It is what it is, but it won't control you.

It's not the adversity that defines you, either. The defining moment is in how you respond to that adversity. Rather than avoiding it, embrace the struggle and feel the pain because pain is just the first step of the process. As you suffer through the pain, you'll discover your passion. Your passion will force you to fight not only against what had caused you pain but also for what your ultimate purpose is in life. Once you discover your purpose and begin to live in it, it will force you to regain your power. And after you regain your power over yourself and over the outside world, you'll soon be on your way to finding your peace.

Pain to passion. Passion to purpose. Purpose to power. Power to peace. That is the process of perseverance.

To the world I declare, I am Reggie D. Ford, a mental health advocate, a social activist, a published author, and a Black man in America, and I am strengthened through PTSD, perseverance through severe dysfunction.

SUGGESTED READING LIST

- **Books about resilience:**
    - o *How Children Succeed: Grit, Curiosity, and the Hidden Power of Character,* by Paul Tough
    - o *Can't Hurt Me: Master Your Mind and Defy the Odds,* by David Goggins
    - o *Man's Search for Meaning,* by Viktor Frankl
    - o *A Dream Too Big: The Story of an Improbable Journey from Compton to Oxford,* by Caylin Louis Moore

- **Books about race:**
    - o *I'm Still Here: Black Dignity in a World Made for Whiteness,* by Austin Channing Brown
    - o *How to Be an Antiracist,* by Ibram X. Kendi
    - o *So You Want to Talk About Race,* by Ijeoma Oluo
    - o *Forty Million Dollar Slaves: The Rise, Fall, and Redemption of the Black Athlete,* by William C. Rhoden
    - o *The Color of Compromise: The Truth about the American Church's Complicity in Racism,* by Jemar Tisby

- o *Why Are All the Black Kids Sitting Together in the Cafeteria?: And Other Conversations About Race*, by Dr. Beverly Daniel Tatum
- o *Talking to Strangers: What We Should Know about the People We Don't Know*, by Malcolm Gladwell
- o *Me and White Supremacy: Combat Racism, Change the World, and Become a Good Ancestor*, by Layla F. Saad

- **Books about trauma:**
  - o *The Body Keeps the Score: Brain, Mind, and Body in the Healing of Trauma*, by Dr. Bessel van der Kolk
  - o *The Deepest Well: Healing the Long-Term Effects of Childhood Adversity*, by Dr. Nadine Burke Harris
  - o *Post Traumatic Slave Syndrome: America's Legacy of Enduring Injury and Healing*, by Dr. Joy DeGruy
  - o *My Grandmother's Hands: Racialized Trauma and the Pathway to Mending Our Hearts and Bodies*, by Resmaa Menakem
  - o *It Didn't Start With You: How Inheriting Family Trauma Shapes Who We Are and How to End the Cycle*, by Mark Wolynn

- **Books about the criminal justice system:**
  - o *The New Jim Crow: Mass Incarceration in the Age of Colorblindness*, by Michelle Alexander
  - o *Just Mercy: A Story of Justice and Redemption*, by Bryan Stevenson

- **Books about economic inequality:**
  - o *The Black Tax: The Cost of Being Black in America*, by Shawn D. Rochester

o   *The Color of Money: Black Banks and the Racial Wealth Gap*, by Mehrsa Baradaran

- **Books about shifting your mindset:**
    o   *How to Win Friends and Influence People*, by Dale Carnegie
    o   *Think and Grow Rich*, by Napoleon Hill
    o   *The Subtle Art of Not Giving a F*ck: A Counterintuitive Approach to Living a Good Life*, by Mark Manson

ACKNOWLEDGEMENTS

Sharing my story has been one of the most rewarding experiences of my life. As this book details much of my life's journey, I find myself eager to express gratitude to everyone I've ever encountered – you all have made me the man I am today. As it would be nearly impossible to enumerate everyone's impact, know that I am forever grateful if you've been a part of the journey.

To the Higher Power, thank you for blessing me. It was written from the beginning, and You have always made that clear.

To my parents, without you there would be no me. Mama, thank you for your countless sacrifices that allowed me to see brighter days. I could not have done any of this without you. Daddy, I appreciate everything you've done for me. Learning from you has definitely made me a better man.

To my extended family, thank you for providing the love that I needed to persevere during times when it mattered most. To the Baileys, Bateys, Browns, Catos, Davises, Foxxes, Gordons, Hippels, Lees, Rhodens, Sloans, and so many more, thank you for being there for me. Antoinette Avant and Tony Jones, thank you for always holding it down. Evon Batey Lee, you are a saint. I cannot begin to express into words the impact you have had on my life. Thank you for everything.

To my many friends (I wish I could name you all) – Aaron McGee, Adam Barnes, Alyssa Bailey, Austin Carswell, Brad and Andrea Borchers, Brian and Madalene Gruber, Brittany Caldwell, Daniel White, Derek King, DeShaun Clarke, Harrison Sawyer, Hoyt Steel, Hunter Lyle, Jamie Wittman, Jashon Robertson, Javon Marshall, Jessica Quick, Jonathan Krause, Karl Butler, Kayla O'Kelley, Kenny Ladler, Larry Franklin, Libby Byrnes, Morgan and Heather Wills, Morris Eguakun, Nathan Golger, Paul Moore, Pharoah Kirk, Rokeish Wilson, Rod Berger, Rod Spann, Shawn Ryan, Sydney Seabaugh, Taylor Loftly, Tayo Atanda, Tyrone Sanders, Yary Oliveras, and Zac Stacy – I appreciate the over-whelming support in all my endeavors.

I acknowledge and extend deep gratitude to my yoga community. Hot Yoga of East Nashville and Small World Yoga have become homes for me. Thank you to the countless instructors and fellow students for sharing your journeys with me. A special thanks to Ally Dorst, Angela Nixon, Annie Kate Hudson, Caleigh Edler, Carsen McDonald, Cody Mitchell, Emilie Hall, Jaci Conley, Jennie Wu, Laren Hart, McKala Cass, Melinda Ballentine, and Rachell Peace. You all went from strangers to family quicker than any other group in my life. Thank you for providing a safe space for me.

To the many educators, employers, coaches, advisors, and administrators who helped me along my journey, I appreciate your dedication. To my customers and clients, thank you for putting your trust in me. Your support means the absolute world to me.

To the servicemembers, medical professionals, frontline workers, and first responders, thank you for your service. A special thanks to Vanderbilt University Medical Center, Ascension Saint Thomas West Hospital, and Alive Hospice for your remarkable work. To Christy Hinsley, thank you for your patience and care. Teresa Yarbrough, you are an angel. With my back against a wall, you gave me a way out and offered help without truly knowing the impact that our times together had on me.

To the musicians who got me through the toughest times, I appreciate your words. 100ktucc, 2Pac, 6lack, Adele, Alicia Keys, Boosie, Doe B, Ed Sheeran, Future, Gucci Mane, H.E.R., J. Cole, Jay-Z, Kendrick Lamar, Kevin Gates, Lil Baby, Lil Durk, Lil Wayne, Mary J. Blige, Master P, Meek Mill, Moneybagg Yo, NBA YoungBoy, Nipsey Hussle, Polo G, Quez Cantrell, QVL, Rae Sremmurd, Rod Wave, Starlito, T.I., Tee Grizzley, The Weeknd, Webbie, WILX, Young Buck, and Young Jeezy, I thank you from the bottom of my heart. Your art form has saved my life.

Charlamagne tha God, Taraji P. Henson, and every person using your platform to advocate for mental health, thank you for saving lives.

To Malcolm X. and Martin Luther King Jr., thank you for showing the complexity of the Black man in your opposing approaches and for your unrelenting fights for justice for all.

To Barack Obama and Kamala Harris, thank you for inspiring a generation of young Black men and women who now believe that anything is possible.

Lebron James and Serena Williams, thank you for using your platforms as two of the greatest athletes to ever grace this planet to fight for justice and equality.

To Muhammad Ali, thank you for showing me that there were more things important than fame and riches. You took a stand for what you believed and whooped a lot of ass along your journey which inspired me to fight for what is right.

To the many friends and authors who offered advice and inspiration, thank you. Anderson Williams, Andre Hal, Caroline Randall Williams, Caylin Louis Moore, Charles Scott, Chris Hope, Deunta Williams, Richard Batey, Dustin Klein, Ed Tarkington, Jonathan "Wayyback" Wynn, Marcus Whitney, Matthew Clair, Michael Oher, RA Dickey, Rennie Curran, Rita P. Mitchell, I appreciate your support. And the many other authors who provided inspiration without knowing it (far too many to name them all): Alex Haley, Angela Davis, Angie Thomas, Austin Channing Brown, Brene Brown, Cornel West, Daymond John, Don Miguel Ruiz, Ibram X. Kendi, Ijeoma Oluo, James Baldwin, Jason Reynolds, Layla Saad, Malcolm Gladwell, Maya Angelou, Michael Eric Dyson, Michelle Obama, Patrisse Cullors, Paul Ekman, Paulo Coelho, Ta-Nehisi Coates, Toni Morrison, Zora Neale Hurston – I appreciate you immensely.

To the best editor I could've worked with, Kimberly Lim, thank you for the countless hours you spent on turning my rough manuscript into a beautiful book. I could not have done this without your help. Eddie Batey and David Lee, thank you for your dedication and suggestions to make this book even better. Andre Shipp, I am blessed to have shared time during our photoshoot. Thank you for the conversation. Jason Hapney, thank you for your creativity and vision for the book cover design. Danna Mathias, Joel Pierson, and Martyn Beeny, thank you for your important contributions to this book. I am blessed to have you all be a part of my team.

Andrew Maraniss, Emilie Townes, Julie Schoerke Gallagher, Lawrence Jackson and Marissa DeCuir, I owe a tremendous debt to you for your support of my vision with this book. I am forever grateful.

Annie B. Williams, Beattie O'Connell, Daniel McGugin, and Becky Sharpe, I am so grateful to have you all in my life. Thank you for the continuous love and support you have always provided.

Jovan Young and Parez Bailey, I've always loved you like brothers and I thank you for sticking by my side through these many years.

Savage Life, my brothers from other mothers, thank you for continuing to inspire and push me to be my greatest self. Alfonza Knight, EJ Vinsang, Gary Jackson, Jas Rader, Nathan Wade, Preston Bailey, and William Davis thank you for providing feedback and encouragement during this process and life. #TGFA

Demorius Ford, Jarrett Love, Kevin Murphy, and Secret Ford, thank you for being the best siblings I could ever ask for. Thank you for listening to my rants, laughing at my dumb jokes, and for being my motivation to never give up.

Thomas Gordon, thank you for having such a heart of gold and for being the big brother I never had.

Ro Coleman, I am grateful you entered my life and have given me even more motivation to continue striving for greatness.

James Quick, since day one, you've inspired me to be the best version of myself. Thank you for always understanding me in all my complexities.

De'Anté Hughes, blood couldn't make us closer. Thank you for the life you speak into me on a daily basis and for becoming my brother.

To Rosie, thank you for being my emotional support and comic relief when I needed it most. You the real MVP.

To my wife, Katie Ford, thank you for being my rock. I am a better person because of your presence in my life. Your compassion, patience, grace and love are contagious and have served me in ways I never thought imaginable. Thank you for the many reading, editing, and brainstorming sessions on how to make this book a success. But more importantly, thank you for saving my life. I am truly blessed.

And lastly, to my many guardian angels and the spirit of my ancestors, thank you for watching over me. I feel your presence every single day and continue to strive knowing I am never alone. Joe Davis, thank you for helping change my life. Although you never got a chance to read this book, you passed knowing that you left a lasting impact on me. I will make sure your legacy lives on. Big Mama, Granny, Popeye and Pops, I deeply appreciate the foundation you built for me to stand on. I promise to continue to make you proud and to honor you in everything I do. For you, I will always persevere.

ABOUT THE AUTHOR

REGGIE D. FORD is an entrepreneur, philanthropist, mental health advocate, and social activist. A first-generation college graduate of Vanderbilt University, he runs RoseCrete Wealth Management and speaks to audiences about financial empowerment, overall wellness, and the importance of diversity, equity, inclusion and accessibility. Ford lives in Nashville, TN, with his wife Katie and their Rottweiler, Rosie. Website: www.reggiedford.com

CPSIA information can be obtained
at www.ICGtesting.com
Printed in the USA
LVHW031111080821
694567LV00003B/14

9 781736 596326